The Petro-state Masquerade

The Petro-state Masquerade

*Oil, Sovereignty, and Power
in Trinidad and Tobago*

RYAN CECIL JOBSON

THE UNIVERSITY OF CHICAGO PRESS   CHICAGO AND LONDON

The University of Chicago Press, Chicago 60637
The University of Chicago Press, Ltd., London
© 2024 by The University of Chicago
All rights reserved. No part of this book may be used or reproduced in any manner whatsoever without written permission, except in the case of brief quotations in critical articles and reviews. For more information, contact the University of Chicago Press, 1427 E. 60th St., Chicago, IL 60637.
Published 2024
Printed in the United States of America

33 32 31 30 29 28 27 26 25 24   1 2 3 4 5

ISBN-13: 978-0-226-83573-0 (cloth)
ISBN-13: 978-0-226-83727-7 (paper)
ISBN-13: 978-0-226-83726-0 (e-book)
DOI: https://doi.org/10.7208/chicago/9780226837260.001.0001

Library of Congress Cataloging-in-Publication Data

Names: Jobson, Ryan Cecil, author.
Title: The petro-state masquerade : oil, sovereignty, and power in Trinidad and Tobago / Ryan Cecil Jobson.
Description: Chicago : The University of Chicago Press, 2024. | Includes bibliographical references and index.
Identifiers: LCCN 2024017524 | ISBN 9780226835730 (cloth) | ISBN 9780226837277 (paperback) | ISBN 9780226837260 (ebook)
Subjects: LCSH: Petroleum industry and trade—Political aspects—Trinidad and Tobago. | Gas industry—Political aspects—Trinidad and Tobago. | Energy policy—Trinidad and Tobago. | Nation-state. | Decolonization—Trinidad and Tobago. | Petroleum industry and trade—Trinidad and Tobago—History. | Gas industry—Trinidad and Tobago—History.
Classification: LCC HD9574.T7 J54 2024 | DDC 338.4/7665509729364—dc23/eng/20240514
LC record available at https://lccn.loc.gov/2024017524

♾ This paper meets the requirements of ANSI/NISO Z39.48-1992 (Permanence of Paper).

To my grandfathers—Cecil Jobson, a cattle rancher in the agricultural division of Reynolds Jamaica Bauxite, and Richard Atwell, a civil engineering draftsman from Brooklyn, New York—for sharing their love of the Caribbean, the land, and the masquerade

Contents

On Method and Terminology ix

PROLOGUE: A Big Small Place 1

INTRODUCTION: The Petro-state Masquerade 8

CHAPTER 1 Strike Fever 34

CHAPTER 2 Fueling Independence 61

CHAPTER 3 Deepwater Futures 90

CHAPTER 4 State Building 115

CHAPTER 5 Road Work 140

CODA: Play a Mas 165

Acknowledgments 175

Notes 181

Bibliography 219

Index 235

On Method and Terminology

This book takes as its object of study both the hydrocarbon-rich island of Trinidad and the Crown colony turned postcolonial nation-state of Trinidad and Tobago. Throughout, I refer to the island as Trinidad and the archipelagic political unit as either Trinidad and Tobago or T&T.

All participants in my ethnographic research are assigned pseudonyms, with the exception of public figures acting in their official roles or capacities.

On Method and Terminology

PROLOGUE

A Big Small Place

Now Trinidad is 50 miles long by 35 miles broad, a scrap of an island—it is not as scrappy as Barbados which is nothing at all. Now in those islands you could see politics and society in a way that you could not and did not see in Britain.—C. L. R. James, "George Padmore: Black Marxist Revolutionary" (1976)

This book is a study of the relationship between fossil fuels and political power in Trinidad and Tobago. As such, it is also a study of colonial histories and postcolonial predicaments in the Caribbean. The Greater Caribbean is united by the cruel inheritances of settler dispossession, plantation slavery, and monocrop economies. Yet, this history unfolded differently across the region; it did not proceed uniformly. Differences in location, size, topography, and climate impacted the contours of domination and resistance throughout the archipelago and the Caribbean coast. To begin this study, then, I trace the contours of the island known as Trinidad.

The relationship between Trinidad and hydrocarbons is less a historical certainty than a chance outcome of its geological and colonial history. The southernmost island in the Eastern Caribbean chain, Trinidad stands apart in topographical terms from an archipelago composed of volcanic and coral-limestone island formations. Approximately ten thousand years ago, coastal erosion in the Orinoco River Delta separated the landmass now known as Trinidad from the South American mainland.[1] The flooding of the Serpent's Mouth—a strait only nine miles wide at its narrowest point—set the stage for the initial peopling of the island by Ortoiroid arrivants who crossed the channel roughly three millennia later.[2]

This stroke of climatological history, which severed Trinidad from the continental shelf, inspired the Nobel laureate V. S. Naipaul to assume his customary pessimism when he opined, "Trinidad, for instance, was detached from Venezuela. This is a geographical absurdity; it might be looked at again."[3] For the Trinidad-born Naipaul, rising seas and plate tectonics deprived his countrymen of their continental birthright and relegated them to obscurity in a small place. His regrettable colonialist disdain notwithstanding, Naipaul alerts us to the entanglement of history and geology in the Caribbean. The very existence of Trinidad as a hydrocarbon-rich island springs out of rising seas, the mantle convections of the earth, and the seismic shocks of European colonial expansion.

Encountered in 1498 by Christopher Columbus on his third transatlantic voyage, Trinidad resisted extensive colonial settlement for much of the next century. From 1592, Spanish settlement proceeded slowly with the advent of a limited plantation economy fueled by enslaved Africans and Indigenous Arawakan peoples. Under Spanish control, the colony of Trinidad idled as the Spanish Empire fixed its eyes on the South American coast. Meanwhile, Caribbean plantation economies in Jamaica, Barbados, and especially San Domingue (Haiti) expanded with reckless abandon throughout the sixteenth, seventeenth, and eighteenth centuries. Fueled by the myth of terra nullius, the imperial technologies of European powers razed the lands of the Americas and decimated Indigenous peoples for centuries thereafter. Under this incipient capitalist imperative to cultivate land in service of metropolitan accumulation, tropical commodities such as coffee, tobacco, cacao, and, most of all, "king sugar" transformed the consumption habits of the metropole and sparked the rise of modern capitalist industry.[4]

For the historian Bridget Brereton, the scope of plantation slavery in Trinidad prior to the 1780s was "of negligible importance" as Spanish colonization advanced in the mainland colonies of New Granada.[5] After the passage of the *Cédula de población* in 1783, however, French planters flocked to the island with enslaved captives, enticed by land grants from the Spanish Crown. Thereafter, Trinidad resembled a paradigmatic slave society as a plantation mode of production predominated after the island was seized from Spanish control by British forces in 1797. At the turn of the nineteenth century, Trinidad stood ready to replace the "Old Islands" of Jamaica, Barbados, Saint Kitts, and Antigua, where production had dropped precipitously. For newly installed British colonial administrators, Trinidad offered a remedy for a plantation system in decline. In 1824, the governor of Trinidad, Ralph Woodford, appealed for an influx of planters and enslaved labor to exploit the arable land of the southern Caribbean:

> The soil of Trinidad is so fertile that very little labor is sufficient to ensure the cultivator of it the reward of his labor.... When the advantages of these essential objects which the rich virgin lands of Trinidad almost exclusively afford are compared with the drawbacks arising from the sterile and exhausted soil of the Old Islands.... The removal of both Proprietor and Slave would appear to be as advantageous to the interest of the one as it is desirable to that comfort which is fairly due to the other.[6]

In its overlapping histories as a plantation society and petro-state, Trinidad occupies the imagination of the frontier. But Trinidad's short period of intensified plantation slavery came to an end when the Slavery Abolition Act took effect in August 1834 and apprenticeship formally concluded in August 1838. Thereafter, Trinidad served as a chief location of post-emancipation labor experiments in Chinese and Indian indenture as planters and administrators curbed the bargaining power of formerly enslaved African workers.

Indeed, Trinidad's sedimented histories of European colonization and racialized labor conscription are best understood in the words of the anthropologist Lyndon Gill as a "palimpsest ... haunted by the specter of its inescapable pasts."[7] This is evident in the French and Spanish idioms retained in contemporary Trinidadian English from its period of French settlement and long-standing migration circuits to and from the Venezuelan mainland. It presents itself too in the ruins of abandoned sugar estates where enslaved and indentured peoples once toiled and left their own African and South Asian imprints on local speech and practice.[8] And on this landscape, the transition from plantation agriculture to carbon fuels is visible in the arrangement of roads, refineries, and residential schemes constructed to service plantation barracks and oil company towns.[9]

This arrangement becomes especially clear as we pull back from Port of Spain, the capital city and former seat of the Spanish and British colonial governments on Trinidad's northwest coast. In the hills to the east of the capital lay the communities of Belmont, Laventille, and Morvant, founded after emancipation by the formerly enslaved and Africans liberated by

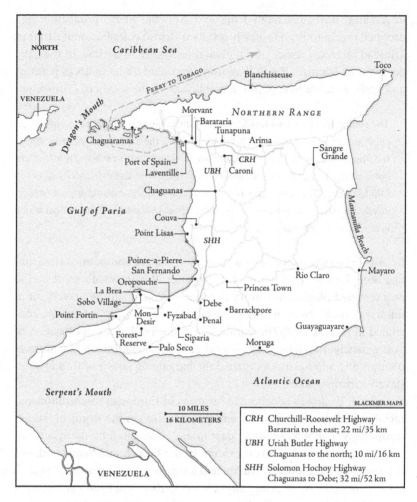

FIGURE P.1. A map of Trinidad.

raids on foreign slave ships who gave the area its former name, Yoruba Town. Stretching further east along the foothills of Trinidad's Northern Range, the dense suburbs of San Juan, Barataria, and Tunapuna give way to former sugar-estate lands in Orange Grove, Lopinot, and Arouca. At the terminus of the Churchill–Roosevelt Highway, built during the US military occupation in World War II, the city of Arima lies where the highway meets more modest roads extending to Toco in the far northeast. (See figure P.1.)

Turning south along the western coast, the central Trinidad metropolis of Chaguanas sits barely ten miles from Port of Spain. On its outskirts are the former sugar lands of Caroni, Couva, and Brechin Castle, the latter now occupied by the imposing Point Lisas Industrial Estate, replete with natural gas–powered steel mills and petrochemical plants. Next, the mothballed oil refinery in Pointe-a-Pierre rises skyward, an icon of Trinidad's petroleum industry for more than a century, from its construction in 1917 until its closure in 2018. Past the refinery lies the region of south Trinidad and its largest city, San Fernando, which sprawls out from the large hill of the same name. Fanning out from the city, the historic centers of Trinidad's oil industry dot the landscape of the southwest peninsula: Fyzabad, Forest Reserve, La Brea, and Point Fortin. Point Fortin, the largest town on the southwest peninsula, now hosts the Atlantic LNG gas liquefaction facility and export terminal. On the southwest peninsula and in the southeastern municipalities of Mayaro and Guayaguayare, agricultural lands brush up against oilfields, pipelines, pumpjacks, and crude-storage infrastructures.

In this way, Trinidad is a microcosm of the energy transitions in the hemisphere at large. In the Americas, fossil fuel economies sprang from the plantation complex of bygone centuries. One cannot help but bear witness to the simultaneity of plantation capital and fossil capital in Trinidad. By virtue of its small size, these histories are ready at hand. This affords a critical perspective through which the global transformations of the past five centuries are inscribed onto the landscape and built environment. In this small place, the enormity of our world comes into view.

Following Jamaica Kincaid, Caribbean intellectuals have come to regard the archipelago as a collection of small places.[10] Trinidad is at once a small place compared to the behemoths of the Greater Antilles—Cuba, Hispaniola, and Jamaica—but a large place in relation to its companion, Tobago, and to its neighbors further north: Grenada, the Grenadines, St. Vincent, and Kincaid's homeland of Antigua. This paradox is captured by Trinidad's favorite son, the luminary critic C. L. R. James, in an address delivered to a North London audience in 1976. James describes his native land as a "scrap of an island," though he is quick to contrast this with his mother's birthplace of Barbados, a smaller, more densely populated island that James insists "is nothing at all."[11] At first glance, it may appear that James looks down on the Caribbean from his adopted perch in London, much as his countryman Naipaul condemned the region as a place where "nothing was ever created."[12] But for James, to be scrappy or "nothing at all" lends the Caribbean a way of seeing that cannot be replicated elsewhere. In the small places of the Caribbean, wisdom is abundant.

James understood this well from his earliest years. Born in Chaguanas in 1901, James began his education at his father's schoolhouse in North

Trace, a small village located in the rural deep south. The isolation of North Trace—a small place within a small place—rested more on appearance than reality. The young James regularly traveled between North Trace and the James family home in Tunapuna, a stone's throw from Port of Spain.[13] The perceived remoteness of small places in the Caribbean is upended by their long integration into a matrix of labor migrations, commodity circuits, and metropolitan markets.

James concurred in another address, where he traced the dimensions of Trinidad again: "You may tell me about the peasant, I say that Trinidad is 50 miles long and 35 miles broad. Where can you find a real peasant? He can jump into a taxi at any time and 50 cents and in an hour he can reach Port-of-Spain."[14] Of course, much has been made by social scientists of a reconstituted peasantry that coalesced as the wave of emancipation that began in Haiti swept through the region.[15] The existence of Caribbean peasants defies the laws of historical materialism. They are peculiar in that they succeed, rather than precede, the "penetration of the Antilles by the West."[16]

In his formative decades, James observed the transformation of south Trinidad from an agricultural region devoted principally to sugar and cocoa cultivation into the largest oil-producing territory in the British Empire. Here, the erection of oil derricks, the digging of roads, and the construction of refineries turned rural expanses into industrial hubs and desired destinations for regional workers. Along with the arrival of pioneering industrialists and oil magnates, the working-class occupants of these areas developed an awareness of their essential role in the empire of oil.[17]

The Caribbean is a place where subsistence livelihoods and industrial capital coexist; it is a place where rural outposts are never as far from centers of metropolitan capital as they appear. In a small "scrap of an island," you cannot help but see that the smallest places have never been disconnected from the world at large. At once central and peripheral to the making of the world, Trinidad, pace Kincaid, is a big small place.

A big small place demands its own anthropology. Here, the classical method of ethnography and its "trinity" that the Haitian *homme de lettres* Michel-Rolph Trouillot described as "one observer, one time, one place" is not up to the task that Trinidad and the Greater Caribbean demand.[18] The fetish of ethnographic presentism—one that presumes that all necessary evidence can be gathered from the immediacy of fieldwork—is particularly misleading in a context where colonial histories are impressed onto the landscape. In other words, to render a big small place as a "small small" place, ostensibly disconnected from the world, is an error that Caribbean scholars can hardly afford.

Small places elsewhere, too, are not as isolated as they are said to be.[19] Their isolation can be preserved only by a distorted colonial imagination and its latter-day anthropological vassals. The gift of a big small place is its capacity to demonstrate the tragic fealty of an ethnographic imagination that presumes the entirety of our social world to be readily observable. It is no accident that Caribbean social scientists have long turned to the archive—colonial repositories, oral histories, and scattered ephemera—to remedy the limits of ethnography. Indeed, for Trouillot, his earliest experiments in anthropological method inspired him to displace this expectation of unadulterated access to an ethnographic subject. In his own inquiry into peasantries in Dominica, Trouillot upends the genre of ethnography by tracing the analytical scales of the "nation" and the "world" in his careful genealogy of the Caribbean plantation economy and European multinational firms before granting his reader access to the iconic peasants in the small village of Wesley.[20] Much of this study is indebted to this methodological charge, one that scholars in and beyond the Caribbean are overdue to revisit. To distill the histories that are ever present in the landscapes and grammars of Caribbean life demands that we understand our archival reveries not as cosmetic accompaniments to ethnographic fieldwork but as part and parcel of anthropology itself.[21]

This book is guided by the way of seeing afforded by this big small place, where politics and society do not conform to the models of governance, order, and rule put down in a Western philosophical tradition. C. L. R. James and his compatriots came to see politics and society in a particular way, by virtue of their location simultaneously on the ground floor and at the colonial peripheries of the oil century.[22] This way of seeing, often attributed to the genius of James himself, sprang first from ordinary people whose labor made Trinidad synonymous with fossil fuels.

INTRODUCTION

The Petro-state Masquerade

In Trinidad in 1937, Uriah Butler wasn't preparing to take power. But he called the people together and they came out in the great strike. It was a general strike in Trinidad and some of you may remember it started in Trinidad but as a fire runs up a forest it went from island to island and it ended in Jamaica. From Trinidad, right up the islands to Jamaica. Please my friends, I don't know where it will start but I want to tell you that in the Caribbean today, there is an impending confrontation: there is an impending fire that will sweep from island to island. — C. L. R. James, "The Seizure of Power" (1975)

The odyssey of the *Deepwater Champion* begins at the Hyundai Heavy Industries Shipyard in Ulsan, South Korea. Commissioned in 2010 by the Texas-founded, Switzerland-based contractor Transocean at a cost of US$740 million, Hyundai fabricators outfitted the sixth-generation ultra-deepwater drillship with two rig stations equipped to drill in up to 12,000 feet of water and to subterranean depths of 40,000 feet. Drillships, prized for their mobility enabled by autonomous propulsion systems, travel expediently from one drill site to the next without the aid of independent towing vessels.

These capabilities allowed the *Deepwater Champion* to make fast work of deepwater hydrocarbon frontiers. Initially leased to ExxonMobil for offshore operations in Turkey, the drillship completed its maiden voyage under a Vanuatuan flag of convenience when it passed through the Bosphorus Strait in Istanbul. After this pilot drilling program, it entered the territorial waters of Romania for another venture in the Black Sea. The

FIGURE I.I. The Transocean drillship *Deepwater Champion*. Photograph by Michael Elleray.

Deepwater Champion then crossed the Atlantic Ocean to the US Gulf of Mexico, where it began a three-year contract in June 2012 before exiting ahead of schedule to spud an exploratory well in Guyana in 2015. Drilling proceeded despite competing territorial claims tendered by the neighboring Bolivarian Republic of Venezuela. The resulting Liza-1 well generated the first major offshore discovery in Guyana with a productive potential of more than 700 million barrels of crude oil equivalent.

The *Deepwater Champion* earned a reputation for its record of commercial success and efficiency during a boom in deepwater oil and natural gas production (figure I.1). Named "Rig of the Year" by Transocean's European and African Unit, the drillship appeared still in the opening act of a lucrative career. The oil bonanza stoked corporate enthusiasm in deepwater futures. For ExxonMobil, the deepwater constituted a chief area of expansion in its portfolio of unconventional oil and gas production. In 2014, ExxonMobil CEO Rex Tillerson forecasted worldwide deepwater production to grow 150 percent by 2040.[1] Alongside the extractive innovations of North American shale and Canadian tar sands, Tillerson's mantra of "going deeper" promised to unlock new reserves in perpetuity.

Unconventional hydrocarbon frontiers ushered in an era of fossil fuel abundance. Advances in extractive technologies and drilling techniques tempered somber forecasts of peak oil.[2] Enjoying the spoils of abundance for the first half decade of its productive life, the operators of *Deepwater Champion* did not concern themselves with whether another frontier would emerge. The commercial viability of the deepwater offered no occasion for pause. Rather than a question of if another deepwater frontier would present itself, it remained a matter of where and when it would deploy to next.

The 2010 *Deepwater Horizon* blowout in the Gulf of Mexico notwithstanding, the commercial prospects of the deepwater continued to attract investors even after the Barack Obama administration issued a moratorium on deepwater drilling in United States territorial waters. As production flourished beyond the Gulf of Mexico in the Brazilian pre-salt and off the West African coast, the future of the *Deepwater Champion* remained bright.

But the deepwater boom did not last. In the final months of 2014, crude prices nosedived when competition between Saudi crude and US shale produced a glut in world oil supplies. The fossil fuel industry long rested on an assumption of market futures marked by regular and predictable cycles of boom and bust. Even when price fluctuations persisted, controlled production cuts by the member states of the Organization of the Petroleum Exporting Countries (OPEC) led by its Saudi vanguard stabilized crude oil markets. The renaissance of US oil driven by the adoption of hydraulic fracturing techniques tilted the balance of geopolitical might and altered perceptions of oil as a diminishing resource. Diagnosed by the *Economist* as a geopolitical skirmish of "sheikhs vs. shale," in which the United States toppled Saudi Arabia as the swing producer capable of setting oil markets, the price of oil dropped below US$27 per barrel in January 2016—its lowest level since May 2003 and a 75 percent drop from its previous peak at nearly US$108 in June 2014.[3]

Compared to their deepwater counterparts, shale ventures involve short production cycles that allow operators to respond swiftly to market shifts by ramping up or winding down active drilling.[4] Moreover, advances in drilling techniques allowed shale production to proceed at a lower break-even price than its deepwater counterparts. In September 2019, US President Donald Trump infamously caricatured the excesses of US shale oil in a Twitter post that simply read: "PLENTY OF OIL!"[5] His social media braggadocio threw cold water on the rumored demise of shale production and staked a dubious claim to the permanence of cheap and abundant oil from fracking reservoirs in West Texas, North Dakota, and Arkansas. While Trump lauded the resurgence of domestic oil production in the United States, the saturated market for crude oil and natural gas conjured anxieties elsewhere in the hemisphere.

For the *Deepwater Champion*, the bear market inaugurated a moment of uncertainty. After the drillship's Guyana venture in 2015, Transocean failed to secure a contract for its juggernaut vessel. Gambling on a long-term market recovery and eventual renaissance in deepwater investments, Transocean opted for a strategy of cold stacking: it powered down its drillship fleet, emptied its crews, and indefinitely stationed its abandoned ships offshore. Unlike a more common practice of warm stacking, where drillships are kept running by a minimal staff in between contracts and drill sites, cold stacking served as a novel cost-saving measure for Transocean to weather the market tides. In the immediate term, the strategy assured shareholders of the company's ability to kill time and curb losses ahead of a market recovery.[6] Even when Transocean removed more drillships from service, the company reported profits of US$77 million in the second quarter of 2016, prompting an 8.5 percent spike in stock value.

While reassuring to shareholders, cold stacking risked the long-term viability of Transocean's deepwater program. For as long as deepwater investments flourished, drillships such as the *Deepwater Champion* had never been shut off. Accustomed to the frenzied itineraries of deepwater operations, one Transocean electrician reasoned that its "drillships were not designed to sit idle."[7] Moreover, it remained unclear what would happen if and when cold-stacked drillships returned to operation. To do so would require engineers to reprogram thousands of drilling presets. The cold-stack gamble was twofold. First, Transocean placed its bets on a long-term recovery of oil and gas markets. Second, it wagered that the capital frozen in cold-stacked drillships could be powered up and returned to active drilling.

The *Deepwater Champion* set off on its final journey in 2016, when it joined Transocean's flotilla of mothballed rigs in the Gulf of Paria off the west coast of Trinidad. A *Bloomberg* news brief relayed the inauspicious scene: "In a far corner of the Caribbean Sea, one of those idyllic spots touched most days by little more than a fisherman chasing blue marlin, billions of dollars of the world's finest oil equipment bobs quietly in the water."[8] Cashing in on its relatively calm waters as maritime storage for inactive rigs, the Government of Trinidad and Tobago leased offshore acreage to Transocean at the minimal cost of US$8,000 per ship, per day.

Plantation Pasts and Fossil Futures

The journey of the *Deepwater Champion* concludes where my study begins, at this far corner of the Caribbean Sea. In Trinidad and Tobago, this is a story of how the market futures of oil and gas and the political futures of a postcolonial Caribbean nation-state became indelibly linked. But this relationship cannot be taken for granted. The tenuous alliance between hydrocarbons and political power enshrined in the hyphenated form of the *petro-state* must be rearticulated at moments where its two sides begin to drift apart. The premature retirement of the *Deepwater Champion* represents one such moment when the extractive futures of the Trinbagonian petro-state could no longer be guaranteed.

Although Trinidad is one of the oldest oil-producing territories—arguably the site of the world's first oil well, drilled by the Merrimac Oil Company in 1857—its commonsense association with oil rests on developments and innovations far beyond its tropical shores. In other words, to tell the story of Trinidad oil requires that we look to Ulsan, Riyadh, and Houston as much as Port of Spain, Fyzabad, and Mayaro.

Oil is inescapable in Trinidad. From the Pitch Lake in La Brea, where bituminous hydrocarbons bubble naturally to the surface, to the common sight of pumpjacks in the south Trinidad countryside, the bright lights of offshore rigs, and, until recently, the luminous gas flares emanating from the shuttered refinery in Pointe-a-Pierre, oil and natural gas permeate the deepest reaches of everyday life. Multinational energy companies sponsor local sports clubs and music, film, and literary festivals, as well as, opportunistically, wildlife sanctuaries and conservation initiatives. Moreover, after more than a century of commercial oil production, Trinidadians enjoy a sterling international reputation for their technical expertise in oil and gas operations. With only the slightest hyperbole, wherever oil or gas is found, you are likely to encounter a Trini.

The importance of oil and gas to the T&T national economy cannot be overstated. Petroleum and petrochemical industries account for approximately 37 percent of its GDP and more than 70 percent of its national exports as a chief avenue of foreign-exchange earnings.[9] Yet, due to advances in extractive technologies and industrial automation, the energy sector today accounts for merely 5 percent of total employment. And despite its vital role in generating state rents and revenues, T&T accounts for only 0.15 percent of global natural gas reserves and 0.04 percent of crude oil reserves. This contradiction sets Trinidad apart from paradigmatic case studies of petroleum-exporting states such as Saudi Arabia, the United States, Venezuela, and Nigeria. In this small place, oil and gas industries loom large in a fashion that obscures its minor standing. Despite its marginal station in the hierarchy of oil and gas producing nations, T&T is regarded as exceptional for its fossil fuel wealth in a region pervaded by agriculture, tourism, and offshore finance and information services. Due principally to petroleum, T&T is deemed by some an "economic miracle" that resists the spiral of indebtedness that plagues many of its Antillean neighbors.[10] In truth, the resilience of Trinidad oil and gas after more than a century of commercial production is less a miracle than a product of its enduring dependence on extractive infrastructures, shipping routes, and multinational firms. In the theater of the Trinbagonian petro-state, however, this dependence masquerades as independence.

The discovery of crude oil in the mid-nineteenth century laid the groundwork for a local oil industry at the turn of the twentieth. Commercial production in Trinidad has persisted uninterrupted since 1908. Oil formed the backbone of the colonial economy and, after independence in 1962, crude oil, natural gas, and petrochemical industries further modified the national energy sector. After a period of upheaval in the early postindependence period, when multinationals fled T&T and radical movements of students, workers, the unemployed, and armed guerrillas threatened to seize power from Eric Williams and his creole nationalist government, the oil boom of 1973 generated unprecedented windfalls and restored confidence in the permanence of Trinidad oil and gas. The construction of steel and petrochemical facilities at Point Lisas, fueled by natural gas as an industrial feedstock, further impressed the permanence of the petro-state on its audience of citizens through a monumental maze of pipes, blast furnaces, and exhaust stacks. Abundant reserves of natural gas permitted Williams and his successors to carve out niche markets for natural gas derivatives such as ammonia, urea, and liquefied natural gas (LNG).

In the decades after political independence, this privileged standing vaulted T&T to the forefront of diplomatic affairs in the Caribbean, with Port of Spain arguably displacing Kingston as the principal location of Caribbean Community (CARICOM) political meetings and summits. Furthermore, some advocates of regional integration championed T&T as a "regional paymaster"—emulating the role of Germany in the European Union compact, much to the chagrin of former T&T prime minister Kamla Persad-Bissessar, who scolded her counterparts at a CARICOM forum in 2010 for treating Trinbagonian petrodollars as an "ATM card" to finance development schemes elsewhere in the region.[11]

The unceremonious arrival of the *Deepwater Champion* to Trinbagonian waters marked a worrying fall from grace for offshore contractors and petroleum-exporting states alike. In T&T, the global slowdown in deepwater drilling unsettled "expectations of permanence" that believed the oil and gas sector would expand in perpetuity.[12] Trinidad has long been understood as a limitless reserve for plantation monocrops and extractive fossil fuels; its transformation into a purgatory for inactive rigs punctuated the closure of the Caribbean frontier. While the *Deepwater Champion* remained out of service in the waters of the Gulf of Paria, the future of the Trinbagonian energy sector hinged on a reversal of fortunes in the deepwater. Like the corporate strategy of cold stacking, in which drilling operations are suspended pending a recovery in market futures, postcolonial futures are suspended by a politics of austerity that includes the privatization of state industrial assets and the winding back of state subsidies on gas and other essential goods.

Though small, T&T historically exploited its strategic position as a petro-state located in the Caribbean Sea with proximity to US port facilities. Perceived as politically stable and compliant in contrast to its neighbor on the South American mainland, Venezuela, Trinbagonian state officials carved out niche markets for LNG and nitrogen fertilizers imported by the US agriculture industry. However, the shale boom lessened US dependence on T&T for gas supplies, and declining production levels of oil and natural gas threatened the viability of downstream and refining facilities. Crude oil production in T&T peaked at 193,000 barrels per day in 2007 before a sharp decline to 57,000 in 2021; natural gas peaked in 2020 at approximately 4.3 billion cubic feet per day and fell to 2.4 billion over the same period.

In this period of uncertainty, petro-states and multinational energy companies nonetheless placed their bets on the lucrative geology of the deepwater. Deepwater plays—generally understood to mean drilling ventures carried out in maritime depths of a thousand feet or greater—are defined by protracted production cycles and low probability of commercial success. Long-cycle plays of this sort often feature lag times of several years between the initial leasing of offshore blocks for exploration and first oil or gas.[13] Even with advances in seismic survey technologies, commercial success rates for deepwater drilling still rest between 15 and 30 percent. Nevertheless, multinational energy giants continue to wager hundreds of millions of dollars on deepwater discoveries that occasionally exceed one billion barrels of oil. None of the first eight deepwater wells drilled in Trinidad between 1999 and 2003 were successful.[14] As I detail later, the commercial viability of successful discoveries is subject to the vagaries of international markets and the whims of multinational investors. But faith in the deepwater persists as a remedy for diminishing production levels and in desires for state windfall profits.

The deepwater frontier, like the fusion of oil and political power under the banner of the petro-state, is the stuff of fantasy. After a landmark survey of deepwater blocks completed by the Australian mining conglomerate BHP Billiton in 2015, the T&T energy minister, Kevin Ramnarine heralded the dawn of a "new energy economy." Even as Ramnarine expressed anxiety over curtailments of gas supplies to downstream industrial and petrochemical facilities, he roused optimism in the prospects of deepwater exploration. Although the deepwater had not yet generated any commercial returns, he invoked its lucrative geology as the spoils to be won through policies of economic liberalization. Lauding the rollback of tax provisions governing deepwater investments under the United National Congress Government of Kamla Persad-Bissessar, Ramnarine pointed to nine deepwater product-sharing contracts signed under his tenure. The signing of the contracts alone did not reverse the decline in natural gas production; still, for Ramnarine, the contract itself masqueraded as an inevitable boom in offshore production.[15]

As Doug Rogers reasons, oil traditionally commanded the attention of anthropologists during boom periods in energy and commodity markets.[16] In turn, social scientific studies of petro-states remain preoccupied with the spectacle of windfall petrodollars and their residual social affects and political effects. The characteristic ills of governance in oil-producing states—euphemized as "Dutch Disease" and "resource curse"—are attributed to deficiencies of policy or planning rather than the material dimensions of fossil fuels or the technologies deployed to harness them.[17]

Hannah Appel tenders a noteworthy exception in her ethnography of offshore oil in Equatorial Guinea. In her inquiry into the "licit life" of multinational capital, Appel disrupts this tendency to treat oil as equivalent with money derived from oil sales.[18] Through intimate accounts of the corporate actors, contractors, subcontractors, technology, and labor that facilitate the production of oil as a market commodity, Appel captures the market boom that facilitated the formative years of the *Deepwater Champion*. As Appel observes, in this moment, state and corporate actors indulged oil as metonymic of money itself even though the extraction of "frictionless profits" paradoxically rested on the unruly frictions of product-sharing contracts, offshore rigs, and racial hierarchies of oilfield labor and management.[19] Despite these limiting factors, the assumption that oil futures would expand in perpetuity is echoed by her interlocutors.

For Appel, this reification of oil as money facilitates the production of a national economy as a stable and measurable object. As a consummately profitable commodity, oil guaranteed the political and economic futures of the Equatoguinean nation-state through assurances of multinational investment and offshore production.[20]

The certainty that defined the moment of her fieldwork in Equatorial Guinea has been undermined by recent negative price shocks. In an extreme case, at the outset of the COVID-19 pandemic in North America in March 2020, spot prices for crude oil turned negative as storage capacity grew scarce amid dwindling consumer demand. At a moment when the permanence of fossil fuels is called into question by depressed markets and competition from renewable energy sources, the hyphenated relation of the petro-state is no longer the immortal confluence of political power and carbon energy that it once appeared to be. As familiar as the term *petro-state* is today, it is a novel political form that came into being only with the subterranean energy transformations of the twentieth century. To expect this fluid political form to persevere through the twenty-first century is perhaps a fatal error on the part of T&T and its fossil fuel–exporting counterparts. But even as the petro-state endures, it defies any stable definition. To wit, Dominic Boyer concludes that the "petrostate enjoys a certain conceptual invisibility. Though the word circulates widely today, it hasn't yet graced the hallowed halls of the Oxford English Dictionary. But a technical definition has coalesced all the same; petrostates are those countries that earn a considerable portion of their revenues from sales of oil and gas. What counts as considerable depends on whom you ask."[21] Indeed, the taxonomic ambiguity of the term is always a matter of perspective: what is or is not a petro-state is less an objective set of characteristics than a semiotic appeal for recognition directed toward audiences of foreign sovereigns and domestic citizens.

Even as the perceived strength of this hyphenated relation wanes, then, appeals to the longevity of the oil and gas sector persist in a *masquerade of permanence*. Troubled by declining production and the risk of deepwater ventures, the Trinbagonian petro-state employs an array of public spectacles to tout its legitimacy to a national public and multinational corporations, creditors, and trading partners. As Gisa Weszkalnys details in her study of the anticipation of first oil in São Tomé and Príncipe, the deferred arrival of an oil boom is tempered by public "gestures" aimed at "materializing an absent potential and promising future gain."[22] This repertoire, perfected in a context where oil production has not yet begun, applies equally to long-standing petro-states such as T&T. Through such avenues of public address, the state adopts the Carnivalesque register of the masquerade. Not unlike Transocean's cold-stack gamble, the uncertain future of the Trinidad oil and gas sector masquerades as certain; the hyphenated relation of the petro-state masquerades as permanent and indivisible. This is the petro-state masquerade.

The State Masquerade

In September 9, 2015, Dr. Keith Rowley was sworn in as the seventh prime minister of Trinidad and Tobago after the People's National Movement (PNM) regained a parliamentary majority from the United National Congress. Rising to power at a moment of declining production, Rowley carried with him the expertise required to navigate the perilous market landscape. A geologist by training, Rowley marked the second geologist to serve as prime minister, following his immediate predecessor as PNM political leader, Patrick Manning. The trend of rule by experts is no accident. Rowley, like Manning before him, inherited the tradition of "doctor politics" perfected by PNM founder and academic historian, Dr. Eric Williams. Just as Williams sutured the government of the nation to his academic credentials, Rowley's vita certified his participation in the petro-state masquerade. As markets contracted, Rowley showcased his expertise to forecast a renaissance of the energy sector.

This masquerade proceeds across multiple scales and theaters. As I detail in chapter 3, Rowley and his interlocutors have expertly staged this masquerade of permanence through press conferences, industry summits, memoranda of understanding, multinational investment bid rounds, seismic surveys, and exploratory drilling programs. Likewise, as David Hughes makes clear in his ethnography of energy technocrats in T&T, this masquerade has also involved narratives of innocence fashioned to avoid reckoning with the effects of carbon-driven climate catastrophe.[23] In January 2022, Rowley addressed the UN Climate Change Conference (COP26) in Glasgow, Scotland, where he reaffirmed his commitment to a transition beyond fossil fuels. Acknowledging the dilemma facing T&T as an economy based principally on oil, gas, and petrochemicals, Rowley nonetheless emphasized the unique challenges it has faced as a vulnerable small-island state. Drawing attention to the "aggressive erosion of our coastline," Rowley called for greater access to climate financing for

Caribbean nations to ease the transition to a sustainable, carbon-neutral economy.[24]

The full contours of his masquerade became clear upon his return to T&T. In a press conference to recap the COP26 summit at Piarco Airport, Rowley reversed course from his urgent clamors in Glasgow for a renewable energy transition. With conviction, he declared: "We are in the business of hydrocarbons and will remain there as long as there is a market in the world."[25] Perhaps in a tacit rejoinder to Hughes, Rowley coolly deflected responsibility for climate change away from Trinbagonian shores. He emphasized that oil giants such as the United States and China are the greatest drivers of climate change in their monstrous exploitation and consumption of carbon energy sources. His move to climate innocence obscured another future, one in which hydrocarbon production persists in new frontier regions, yet quietly leaves Trinidad behind as a graveyard of mothballed rigs. But his masquerade of permanence did not concede this possibility.

While Rowley's masquerade—or *mas*, in Trinbagonian parlance—corresponds neatly to the practice of statecraft in T&T as the home of the grandest and greatest Caribbean Carnival, this is not to suggest that the state masquerade is limited to T&T alone. Rather, the language of masquerade instructively applies to the state form in general. Returning to the foundational thesis of Thomas Hobbes, the doctrine of state sovereignty demands submission to absolute authority as a remedy for the naked violence of human nature. Writing in exile from Paris during the English Civil War, Hobbes conjured the absolutist state as an inoculation to preserve peace and order in seventeenth-century Europe. By definition, the state for Hobbes must be vested in a "Soveraign [sic] Power" that is "incommunicable" and "inseparable."[26] Despite Hobbes's insistence that the state will provide refuge from a brutish state of nature, the histories of modern states fail to conform to the ideal type that he prescribes in *Leviathan* (1651). This distance between the ideal form of the state as total and absolute and its actually existing form as fragmented and incomplete inspired Hobbes's fascist offspring in the twentieth century to resolve this gap by restoring the state in the image of his monstrous imagination. This experiment unfolded to irreparably tragic effect. Nonetheless, the state idea persists in the political imagination of the present century. We might ask, then, how the idea of the state successfully refashions itself against its résumé of failures. To speak of failed states as an aberrant form of statecraft suggests that its North Atlantic experiments in liberal democracy are indeed successful. Instead, against a backdrop of violence and inequality in metropolitan centers, we should inquire further into the narratives the state fabricates to testify to its purported success against its mounting debris of terror and insecurity in the present.

Contrary to Hobbes, political anthropologists instruct us to regard all sovereign power as aspirational and incomplete—an "emergent form of authority grounded in violence."[27] This critique is welcomed by Caribbean intellectuals who have long understood state sovereignty to be a deceptive fiction that prescribes the political aspirations of postcolonial nation-states and putatively nonsovereign territories in the region.[28] At first glance, this tension between sovereignty as absolute and aspirational appears insoluble. How can sovereignty at once be real *and* fictive, total *and* partial, uniform *and* dispersed? This logical impasse demands another approach. Rather than an attempt to balance the scales by bringing the state back in, again, and again, and again—the language of the masquerade demands instead that we ask how the state succeeds in overrepresenting the dispersed *as* uniform, the partial *as* total, and the fictive *as* real.[29]

It should come as little surprise that Philip Abrams, in his foundational essay on the difficulty of studying the state, inhabits the register of the Carnivalesque. "The state," he opines, "is not the reality which stands behind the mask of political practice. It is itself the mask which prevents our seeing political practice as it is."[30] Unlike more conventional invocations of political theater that reduce the practice of state power to an empty spectacle, the language of masquerade captures more precisely the mechanics by which the state lays claim to a monopoly on political practice.[31] In our reverence for Abrams, an insistence that the state is a fiction—a *mask* and a *mas*—too often represents the end, rather than the beginning, of our inquiry into the state.

The Petro-state Masquerade is at once a historical ethnography of the Trinbagonian petro-state and a meditation on the practice of statecraft writ large. Thanks to Abrams and his interlocutors, we understand that the state is not an entity divorced from intimate realms of social reproduction. Still, the impulse remains to reduce the state to an ideal type of power and authority. Nuanced empirical studies of municipal bureaucracies, parliamentary offices, courts of justice, border agents, and police departments productively dismantle an expectation that the state conforms to a set of uniform and generalizable traits. Indeed, we talk of states in the plural and, in turn, inquire into the inner workings and features of disparate state formations. However, this pluralizing gesture (from *the* state to state *forms*) may mistakenly imply that states are indeed tangible objects that can be mapped and distilled through ethnographic exposition.

This is less a deliberate error than a symptom of the difficulty Abrams identifies. As Abrams lets slip in a moment of vulnerability, "this author simply cannot escape from the veil of illusion created by the idea of the state even though he knows it to be a veil of illusion."[32] For this reason, this is not a triumphant story of how a peripheral plantation colony became a successful petro-state. The petro-state is not a permanent arrangement between fossil fuels and political power but a mask that must be refashioned and retrofitted to maintain its coherence.[33] Abrams, in refusing the imperative to unmask the state through thick descriptions of its many forms and arrangements, reminds us to turn our ethnographic eye toward the state's masquerade—the theater of operations that presents this fragile equation between fossil fuels and sovereign power as a mathematical certainty.

Hobbes, of course, famously presents his treatise on sovereignty in the form of a geometric proof. The state must conform to the prescriptions he sets or it is not a state at all. Consequently, he regards deficient state formations as absurdities in the same fashion that a "round quadrangle" would betray the laws of mathematics: "the word *round quadrangle* signifies nothing."[34] The Pan-African social ecologist Modibo Kadalie, though, stands Hobbes the right side up. Kadalie insists that the absurdity of the state lies in its alleged success rather than its failures: "I want to challenge the concept of the nation-state in a way that everyone can understand without belaboring the issue: it is mathematically absurd that approximately five hundred people in Washington, D.C. can make laws for over 350 million people in the United States."[35] That this ratio can be adjusted to the comparatively meager seventy-two parliamentarians for a population of nearly 1.4 million in T&T does not alter the fact of its absurdity. In fact, it is in the small places of the postcolonial Caribbean that the state form appears most absurd.[36]

In this passage, the difficulty that Abrams confronts is laid bare. Unlike the bombastic authority of Washington, which deploys armed deputies to command its authority over a vast settler expanse between the Atlantic and Pacific Oceans and farther-flung territories and military outposts, in Port of Spain—not to mention the capitals of even smaller places in Basseterre, Kingstown, Saint George's, and Saint John's—the necessity of a centralized bureaucratic authority appears all the more odd.

The Jamaican trade unionist and refrigerator mechanic Fundi (a.k.a. Joseph Edwards) says as much in his postmortem for the Grenada revolution and its vanguardist tendencies that precipitated the untimely demise of the New Jewel Movement in 1983. "In the case of Grenada," he reasons, "we are talking about a place 19 miles long and nine miles wide. Y'know you can run around the whole place and still be fresh. You are not talking about a big place. So you don't need stages, you don't need bureaucratic organization of 16 men waiting for the next ten years until the ideas of Lenin are consummated."[37] From the Caribbean, the state is unveiled as a masquerade that secures its authority through projections of national identity and proclamations of economic permanence that, in turn, mask its violent foundations.[38] Here, the mathematical absurdity of the nation-state comes into focus as ordinary people stage masquerades of their own.

Road Work

The origins of the Carnival masquerade in Trinidad are fired in the crucible of emancipation in the British West Indies. On August 1, 1834, the Slavery Abolition Act of 1833 took effect in the British colonies, beginning a six-year period of apprenticeship to prepare enslaved peoples for the nominal freedom of waged work. The fires of protest across the region led to the extension of full emancipation two years ahead of schedule on August 1, 1838. Full emancipation did not alleviate the depraved conditions of colonial rule and plantation labor. But it did set the stage for a new masquerade. The emancipated masses, parodying and refashioning the pre-Lenten Carnival of French Creole settlers in Trinidad, created a tradition entirely their own in what the Trinbagonian theater historian Errol Hill has described as a "complete metamorphosis."[39] Drawing not simply on European Carnival aesthetics but centrally from African traditions of costumery and performance, this masquerade emerged into view in the intermezzo between the passage of the Abolition Act and its formal adoption in the following year. In February 1834, a band of African Creole revelers joined the Carnival masquerade adorned in military dress befitting of a colonial detachment. As Hill details, this began a tradition of military and naval masquerades that sought with "brazen effrontery to debunk the authority that had been paraded before them so often in the display of military force."[40]

The organ of the planter elites in Trinidad, the *Port of Spain Gazette*, rubbished the ingenuity of the masqueraders' road work. The editors did not withhold their disgust toward the debutants in the annual Carnival festival: "The mockery of the best Militia Band that has ever been embodied in the West was in very bad taste, and if intended to ridicule, must have missed its aim."[41] The true genius of the military mas was lost on the editors of the *Gazette*. This "mock detachment" of "sorry figure[s]," rather than a failed effort to emulate the pomp and circumstance of the colonial militia, contained within it a theory of political authority.[42] The military mas unmasked the colonial state and its foot soldiers as the sorry figures that the revelers parodied.[43] It is the state itself, in its performance and pageantry, that adopts the form of the masquerade. The sole difference between the state masquerade and the people's masquerade is that the latter does not shroud its performance under the violent guise of legitimacy and Hobbesian absolutism. It is in the clash between these masquerades that the possibility of direct democratic futures and their limits are drawn.

This clash surfaced again in the confrontation between British authorities and the colonial masses in the "Carnival Disturbances" of 1881. After emancipation, formerly enslaved Africans and their descendants commemorated the August 1 anniversary of Emancipation Day with the ceremonial procession of Kambule. Kambule staged and reenacted scenes of slavery and insurgent resistance against the plantation. The procession traditionally began at midnight lit by flambeaux and accompanied by drumming, singing, and dancing.

In the intervening decades, colonial administrators placed restrictions on the masquerade. First, they restricted the Kambule to the night of Dimanche Gras, the Sunday prior to the pre-Lenten Carnival festival, in a futile effort to detach Kambule from the "rites of August First" and the commemoration of emancipation.[44] Fearing a threat to colonial order, Police Captain Arthur Baker sought an end to the Kambule in 1881. In his dispatch on the Carnival disturbances, Governor Sanford Freeling set the scene: "On the previous night a torch of the masqueraders had been extinguished by the Police and that [as] immediately [as] this was done the Police had been assailed on all sides with bottles and stones."[45] Freeling placed the tally at thirty-eight police who were injured in their "collision with the mob."[46]

The violent clashes on the road confirmed the fears that the torchlit Kambule could at any moment erupt from a benign masquerade to a genuine insurrection against colonial order. While the revelers parodied the colonial state as a mere masquerade, Captain Baker trembled when confronted with the Kambule as a demonstration of popular power. The colonial state could not maintain a monopoly on the terms of order. In turn, the confrontation continued in the ensuing years as Baker and his underlings further suppressed the Kambule with their arsenal of colonial violence. Drumming was banned in 1883, and stick fighting—the *bataille bois* of the African martial art kalinda—was formally restricted in 1884. In 1884, a government edict formally declared the beginning of Carnival to be no earlier than six o'clock on Monday morning and effectively outlawed the midnight Kambule.

But this did not end their masquerade. As Brent Crosson observes in his magisterial study of obeah in Trinidad, the ban of practices regarded as deviant or occult is less predicated on the defense of legitimate religious practice than an effort to extinguish the "experiments with power" devised by ordinary people independent of state sanction.[47] That autocratic Caribbean statesmen from François Duvalier to Eric Gairy indulged the science of vodou and obeah confirms that the ban is an effort not to suppress the occult altogether but rather to confine the legitimate use of its powers to the sovereign alone. Despite the absence of any rumored affinity between Eric Williams and obeah, his "doctor politics" evoked both his degreed credentials as a doctor of history and the role of the doctor as "healers and deliverers of their people" in Caribbean spiritual traditions.[48] Indeed, Williams would *doctor* the history of the Caribbean to his advantage and personal uses. As Richard Burton observes with an oblique dig toward Williams, "Even as [the masses] are told that 'Massa day done,' a new Massa, often black like themselves but wielding Massa's language with a virtuosity Massa never achieved, is spinning his spiderweb of words to entrap them."[49]

For subsequent generations of Caribbean intellectuals, the resolution of these warring forces remained unfinished. In the penultimate decade before his death in 1989, C. L. R. James continued to speak of an "impending confrontation ... between two fundamental elements of the society ... those who have the power, but are not governing the country properly, and the mass of the population who want a change."[50] Likewise, Sylvia Wynter anticipated an "inevitable and inbuilt confrontation between the plantation and the plot ... between those who justify and defend the system; and those who challenge it."[51] For James and Wynter alike, it is moments of insurgency where the people's masquerade spills beyond its formally decreed boundaries that demand our critical attention. For James, this is visible in the Paris Commune, the revolt of Haitian peasants against the plantation economy of Governor General Toussaint Louverture in 1801, the general strike of 1937 in Trinidad, and the twentieth-century uprisings against Soviet state-capitalist bureaucracy in Hungary and Poland. For Wynter, it is the Jamaican uprisings of the Morant Bay Rebellion in 1865 and the militant labor strikes across the island in 1938.[52] However, their revolutionary clarity is troubled by the resilience of the state masquerade. Indeed, the impending confrontation is still yet to reach its climax. In this masquerade, the boundaries between those who defend the system and those who challenge it are blurred considerably. Often, the state masquerade does not manifest merely as violence or repression, but as awe, desire, and delight.

This confrontation is staged annually to diffuse its simmering tension through Carnival masquerades sanctioned by the state. And anyone who has crossed the Savannah Grass on jouvay morning can attest to the power of Carnival.[53] In *High Mas* (2018), the Trinbagonian critic and artist Kevin Browne bears witness to the radical potential and anticlimax of the Carnival masquerade as a ground for freedoms yearned for but still not won:

> From its beginnings among the planter class who came to Trinidad in the eighteenth century, Carnival has been framed as a virtual escape from repressed life—celebrated first among the sunburned aristocracy of thieves, then later among the enslaved.... The vulgarity of this myth of passive adoption and appropriation may be matched only by its pervasiveness as nostalgia.... These days, participants are obliged, through the social conditioning of watchwords and mottos, to return to work or school on Ash Wednesday with resignation and regret for all they have done or tried to do. But to the newly emancipated and falsely free, who wanted more for themselves than what Emancipation and Indentureship had originally promised, the brief luxury of equitable abandon only compounded the idea that freedom existed as a thing to be given by those who possess power, rather than taken by those who do not.[54]

As Browne reminds us, the fears that possessed Captain Baker in 1881 convey the true power of mas.[55] The painstaking, violent suppression of the Kambule confirms the fears that masqueraders would not observe the arbitrary limits of the pre-Lenten calendar. What if the masquerade did not stop by sunrise on Ash Wednesday? What if the masqueraders continued to occupy the road and refused to shed their masks or put down their burning flambeaux? Indeed, following Max Weber, the state claims a monopoly on the legitimate use of force in a given territory.[56] The boundaries of legitimate violence are drawn on the road, where the colonial militia renders one staging of power as natural and permanent (the state's masquerade) and another as temporary and contrived (the people's masquerade). Indeed, this is the substance of Weber's dictum. Competing claims to legitimacy are decided in the confrontation between these dueling forces. That Kambule is understood to be a mere masquerade—while the choreographed processions of militiamen, Royal Marines, and police are not—is a testament to the success of the latter. The triumph of the state masquerade lies in our reluctance to confront it as the mas that it is.

However, the triumph of the state masquerade is not a fait accompli. In the tradition of Carnival performance and creative ingenuity, the kernels of another future rest in wait. The Trinbagonian visual artist Christopher Cozier perceptively names the art historical tradition of Carnival aesthetics as a practice of "roadworks," in which the classical repertoire of artwork imposes itself on the physical infrastructures and geographies of the Caribbean.[57] Cozier pushes back against the impulse to treat the masquerade as a "mere folk or street festival the subject for more renderings of culture by local artists and foreign anthropological studies."[58] Instead, he insists that we must widen the scope of our inquiry beyond the individual auteur to apprehend the art of Carnival as a dynamic practice of popular subversion.

In *The Petro-state Masquerade*, I expand Cozier's frame of roadworks to the repertoires of interruption and occupation of public infrastructures that I call "road work." It is no accident that the expressions of protest in T&T have long assumed the form of marches and blockades along the nation's roadways. Not only does road work interrupt the intended function of streets and highways as avenues of transit and commerce, but it also marks the moments at which the people's masquerade exceeds its mandated routes and the conventions of the Carnival calendar. Road work troubles the narratives of revolution as a singular moment of violent rupture and political transformation. On the road, the "shoulder-to-shoulder" formation of masqueraders stages a suspension of hierarchy and a momentary experiment in democratic power.[59] Indeed, the masquerade is not strictly performative. Real bodies, assembled in shoulder-to-shoulder formation, can at any moment wield their collective power. This is equally true of uniformed police and Carnival revelers armed with flambeaux. But the latter is discouraged from facing the reality of its power. As the literary critic Gerard Aching reminds us, popular revolts are often labeled as "Carnivalesque" or "masquerades" to derisively imply that they are deficient in proper organization and leadership. By this view, revolts are doomed to "fail because they are chaotic, carnivalesque, or improvised."[60]

The history of the Caribbean unveils the bankruptcy of this logic. The petro-state masquerade, like its colonial antecedents, is an incomplete project. While the state represents this relationship between oil and gas market futures and postcolonial political futures as solid and unyielding, the permanence of this masquerade is troubled by acts of road work during and beyond the pre-Lenten Carnival season. At certain moments, this road work has threatened to dissolve the petro-state masquerade entirely and seize power from self-appointed colonial guardians and their successors in the form of postcolonial middle classes and elites. As C. L. R. James implored in a speech delivered to Trinbagonian trade union delegates in 1982, "[Power] was there in the streets in 1937, to be taken up by anybody, but the people who might have been instrumental in bringing down the power then in existence didn't know, or weren't thinking of seizing power. It was there in the streets again in 1970.... You must be prepared to take it."[61] The power he observed takes shape in the people's masquerade: To seize power is not to put an end to the masquerade and reconstruct hierarchical modes of governance and order under more benevolent guardians. To seize power from below is to continue the mas as a permanent refrain of mass politics. In the timeless bellows of the calypsonian Lord Invader: Don't stop the Carnival!

Power/Mas

As a historical ethnography of hydrocarbons and sovereign power in T&T, this book does not rehearse a comprehensive history of twentieth-century Trinidad that is richly documented by several generations of Caribbean scholars.[62] Rather, my aim is to dwell with moments of clash, crisis, and Carnivalesque in which the masquerade of permanence is threatened by external market shocks and grassroots insurgencies. By turning to moments where permanence is imperiled, I am less interested in arbitrating the fact of economic permanence than in interrogating the proclamation of permanence through the construction of public monuments or performances of celebratory excess. This task demands an eclectic methodological toolkit, which in this instance included long-term fieldwork with civil society formations in Trinidad; interviews with state officials, corporate executives, petroleum engineers, and geologists; and archival research in Trinidad and the Colonial Office Records in Kew, United Kingdom. The petro-state masquerade gains its coherence from the production of expert knowledge and staging of public spectacles by government ministers, technologists, and corporate communications officers. But at every stage, the fleeting character of this masquerade is confronted by insurgent workers and collectives that the Guyanese poet Martin Carter conceived as "free communities of valid persons" who interrupt the state's masquerade to fashion alternatives to an export-dependent fossil economy.[63]

In lieu of a chronological treatment of the development and transformation of the Trinbagonian oil and gas industry, each chapter examines the clash between the state masquerade and the people's masquerade at distinct moments and locations. The first moment of confrontation over this masquerade of permanence surfaced in the period of colonial workers' agitation in 1930s Trinidad. As oil expanded through the plantation landscape of south Trinidad, workers and peasants staged a series of hunger marches from the oilfields and agricultural estates of south Trinidad to the colonial government in Port of Spain. Decrying imperial neglect, the hunger marches unveiled the poverty of colonial citizenship in the aftermath of slavery and indenture in the British West Indies. The hunger marches and isolated strike actions by oilfield workers served as a prelude to the general strike of 1937. While workers and the unemployed agitated for living wages, oil magnates debated whether the oil resources of Trinidad were limited or inexhaustible. The latter view won the day as exports of crude oil nearly doubled in the first four months of 1937 before a sit-down strike began spontaneously at the Trinidad Leaseholders' oilfield in Forest Reserve on June 19. Strike fever soon pervaded the entire island.

The general strike of 1937 in Trinidad set off a wave of workers' agitation throughout the British West Indies. Chapter 1, "Strike Fever," examines how the Trinidadian working classes undermined the masquerade of the colonial state and its oil barons through strikes, industrial sabotage, and the occupation of oil company properties and Crown lands. As James would later put it, "It was a general strike in Trinidad and some of you may remember it started in Trinidad but as a fire runs up a forest it went from island to island and it ended in Jamaica."[64] Subsequent generations of historians interpret the labor uprisings of the 1930s as the formative kernel of postcolonial nationalism and preamble to political independence. Differently, however, this chapter turns to the turbulent thirties not simply as a period of workers' agitation or nationalist ferment, but as a general strike against plantation work and the racial order of capital in the post-emancipation Caribbean. During this same period, colonial administrators and technologists debated whether Trinidad's oil was a wasting asset or an unlimited resource. As ordinary workers turned to the oilfields as an alternative to plantation labor, the latter camp insisted that the limitless reserves of oil could expand to uplift the hungry masses. Accordingly, this chapter examines how the political futures of the Trinidadian working class came to depend on the productive futures of extractive fossil fuels—a condition that persists into the postcolonial present.

The road to political independence in T&T captured this workers' insurgency under the middle-class leadership of Afro-Saxon political elites including the historian-cum-statesman Dr. Eric Williams. In 1960, the colonial masses marched behind Williams to the US military base at Chaguaramas, demanding the return of a leased stretch of the northwest peninsula to the people of T&T. At once, this channeled the energies of an embryonic nation against US imperialism sanctioned by British colonial rule. After independence in August 1962, this momentary alliance of the working masses and middle-class political elites fractured. The revolutionary seventies arrived in Trinidad with the Black Power uprising of 1970 and registered a formative challenge to Afro-Saxon political hegemony through several radical offshoots representing Marxist–Leninist, Maoist, and (C. L. R.) Jamesian tendencies. As power descended into the streets again, the prospects for oil production appeared bleak when energy multinationals including Shell and Texaco abandoned Trinidad for frontier regions in Alaska and the Middle East.

The explosion in oil prices in 1973 was fortuitous for an elite governing bureaucracy under sustained assault from factions of the radical Left. Williams assessed the bullish market landscape as "an opportunity to reappraise the local resources which were uneconomic to exploit before the crisis."[65] While the state continued to repress political dissidents in the short term, the Williams administration pursued an ambitious industrialization program to quell insurgent opposition and tighten the People's National Movement party stronghold on national political affairs.

Chapter 2, "Fueling Independence," demonstrates how the boom financed state investments in oil, gas, and petrochemical facilities aimed to uplift a multiracial populace from the legacies of plantation slavery and indenture—from "brown sugar to steel," as Williams put it. Though he understood oil as an unpredictable resource after the energy crisis of 1973, Williams championed steel and heavy industry as bastions of political stability and economic permanence. At the same time, this course of industrial development deepened a national dependence on multinational bodies to exploit new fossil fuel reservoirs and sustain levels of crude production to source downstream industries. While this industrial program intended to stabilize a national economy beleaguered by the aftermath of a monocrop model of the plantation economy, it paradoxically rendered the nation more vulnerable to shifts in international markets once depressed commodity markets plunged T&T into a recession throughout the 1980s.

This masquerade of permanence donned another costume in the 1990s, when Trinidad's hydrocarbon sector strayed further from crude oil toward novel markets for natural gas. In 1992, a boutique LNG importer located in Massachusetts, Cabot LNG, proposed a gas liquefaction project to the Government of Trinidad and Tobago.[66] With an eye toward the New England seasonal market for heating gas, Cabot championed Trinidad's endogenous hydrocarbon resources, familiarity with oil and gas operations, and opportune location in the southern Atlantic. At the proposed LNG processing facility, natural gas supplies could be cooled to temperatures of −260°F (−162°C) and condensed into a liquid approximately 1/600th the volume of its gaseous state. In liquid form, natural gas could be transported by tanker ships across the Atlantic without the aid of pipelines. Despite vocal skeptics, the Atlantic LNG project in Point Fortin, Trinidad, loaded its first shipment to Cabot's receiving terminal in Everett, Massachusetts, in 1999.

The unqualified success of Atlantic LNG as a partnership between Cabot, Amoco, British Gas, and the state-owned National Gas Company of Trinidad and Tobago generated renewed demand for Trinidad's abundant hydrocarbon resources. With the expansion of Atlantic LNG, pressure to discover new reserves of offshore natural gas mounted to keep pace with downstream demand. Chapter 3, "Deepwater Futures," examines the turn to offshore exploration in the deepwater sector beginning in 1998. Characterized by protracted production cycles, deepwater ventures feature prohibitive costs and a comparatively low probability of success. After a series of deepwater-drilling programs failed to yield commercial quantities of oil or gas, the unfulfilled potential of this lucrative offshore geology is still invoked to mitigate uncertainty and secure the long-term viability of the Trinbagonian energy sector.

Drawing on interviews conducted with petroleum geologists, engineers, government bureaucrats, and multinational executives, chapter 3 charts the logics of development that accompany a turn from onshore and conventional drilling to unconventional and deepwater frontiers. In doing so, I trace a shift from a postindependence optimism in the nation-state as an interventionist agent of economic governance to a valorization of speculation and risk. When multinational investment is redirected to frontier areas of unconventional and deepwater production, postcolonial statecraft is oriented toward the production of technoscientific knowledge to unlock deeper and more complex reserves. The result is a condition of governance by speculation in which economic policy and affairs are subcontracted by state actors to multinational corporate entities.

After T&T entered the LNG business in 1999 under the direction of Prime Minister Patrick Manning, gas revenue signaled an end to the economic recession of the long 1980s. Rather than a return to the social democratic vision of investments in public welfare, this period saw state revenues directed toward high-modernist schemes such as skyscrapers, luxury hotels, highways, and stadiums. Chapter 4, "State Building," examines the flurry of state-funded infrastructure investments during the natural gas boom of the early 2000s. Understanding the state as a form of political authority made legible through spectacular infrastructures, this chapter turns to state-funded megaprojects as the principal register of address for the petro-state masquerade in the twenty-first century.

Tracing the transformation of the Port of Spain skyline through archival records and interviews with urban planners and consultants, chapter 4 details how the petro-state masquerade mobilized infrastructural spectacles to preserve its legitimacy with audiences of citizens and its investment and credit rating with external audiences of multinational corporations and financiers. Here, the speculative sovereignty of deepwater exploration and production is at once a sovereignty of the spectacle in which high-modernist architecture and building schemes masquerade as social welfare and postcolonial progress. Awarding attention to the construction of the International Waterfront Centre and Hyatt Regency as the venue for the Fifth Summit of the Americas in 2009—punctuated by the visit of US President Barack Obama to Trinidad—"State Building" considers how the built environment is deployed to translate the largesse of offshore windfalls into onshore sites of diplomatic spectacle and consumerist leisure.

This spectacular sovereignty appears ordinary on the road. From a comfortable distance, the Port of Spain skyline shimmers with its intended gravitas to audiences of diplomats and agents of foreign capital. On the road, however, its aesthetic blemishes and rusted patina are visible in sharp relief. It is in the theater of the road that the masquerade of the petro-state is unsettled and may one day be undone. I trace this "road work" ethnographically through the colloquial venues of rumshops and street corners, the staged performances of the Calypso Monarch, and the street-level protests of everyday people. Rather than emulating the panoramic view from the seaside vistas of the Gulf of Paria, road work dwells with the aesthetic imperfections of the spectacular image crafted by the state itself. In turn, road work unsettles a masquerade of permanence that posits the inexhaustibility of extractive fossil fuels and the immortality of the Trinbagonian petro-state.

Throughout the postindependence period in T&T, roads have permitted state actors to transform oil and gas revenue into bastions of popular and electoral support. As a result, roads operate as sites of confrontation between parliamentary officials and disaffected citizens over issues of public procurement, development, and governance. Chapter 5, "Road Work," draws on long-term fieldwork with the Highway Re-route Movement (HRM), a collective of residents in south Trinidad threatened with displacement by a state-financed highway development. In this chapter, I dwell with the tactics of protest, occupation, and blockade employed by the HRM as avenues of claims-making directed toward a centralized petro-state bureaucracy. Accordingly, I offer road work as a grammar of social criticism through which the production of roads and the state effects they engender are interrupted by insurgent actors. Heeding the dual meaning of *road* in Trinbagonian parlance as a material route of transit and a Carnivalesque space of democratic potential, this chapter defines *road work* as a practice that challenges the extractive logics of the petro-state through a disruption of material infrastructures and bureaucratic formations in postcolonial T&T.

A coda, "Play a Mas," extends the practice of road work to consider how the organic, creative potential of the popular will—expressed in the form of hunger marches, strikes, occupations, and the Carnival road march—holds the potential to stage alternative political futures for the Caribbean in an epoch of carbon-driven climate change. *Play a mas* refers to the participation of ordinary citizens in the annual Carnival masquerade as well as the practice of road work as a tradition that springs from popular desires for novel arrangements of infrastructure and direct democratic governance.

Burn the Flags

Since at least the fifteenth century, island geographies like those of the Caribbean archipelago have functioned as containers for the political ideal of sovereignty: "For European settlers and mainlanders, islands become the early visual tropes of the utopian, insular features of the sovereign state."[67] The equation of islands with the ideals of sovereignty and utopia surfaced in fiction, philosophical treatises, and nonfiction travel writing alike. For Thomas More, the island represented a virgin landscape from which to project a settler-liberal utopia. Karl Marx, taking up *Robinson Crusoe* (1719), invoked Daniel Defoe's fictionalized island modeled after Tobago as a laboratory for the category of use-value in *Das Kapital* (1867). And Richard Ligon's seventeenth-century travel narrative, *A True and Exact History of the Island of Barbados*, is often credited with the first use of the term *Leviathan* in reference to a "well governed Commonwealth" after the publication of Hobbes's manifesto of the same name.[68]

Ligon's description of the emergent plantation economy of Barbados as a "happy Island" is contradicted in his own narrative by an account of a conspiracy by bonded Africans to cut the throats of their enslavers and declare themselves "Masters of the Island."[69] In Ligon's application of Hobbes to the British colonial Caribbean, he makes clear that the state is nothing more than the masquerade of colonial violence as an agent of peace and order. Likewise, though Hobbes penned *Leviathan* in exile from the European mainland, he projected his desire for a well-governed commonwealth onto the North Sea island of Britannia. Whereas he positioned the island as an ideal template for the perfection of the state form, it is islands like Trinidad that provide the clearest evidence for the failed project of the nation-state and its latter-day petroleum-fueled form. As the anthropologist Yarimar Bonilla so perceptively reminds us, sovereignty is itself a fiction: "It is not, *and has never been*, what it claims to be."[70]

In the Caribbean, the perils of sovereignty are so abundant as to be mundane. For its nations that attained independence between 1804 and the present, the celebratory moment of formal decolonization has given way to the existential threats of debt, multinational dependency, climate collapse, and violence.[71] The persistence of insular sovereignties and dependence on foreign capital suggests that the nation-state project in the Caribbean stands at a critical impasse. This disenchantment with the material returns of flag independence leads critics like Bonilla to consider the strategic entanglements of political actors in nonsovereign Caribbean territories.[72] In her "hopeful pessimism" for the future of the Caribbean, Bonilla does not lay waste to the desire for sovereignty and independence so much as to indict its capture by the masquerades of political elites.[73]

This project is indebted to the clarion call to rethink the category of sovereignty from the location of the Caribbean. While Bonilla intricately details the pursuit of "non-sovereign futures" in Guadeloupe and Puerto

Rico, my own writing on the contemporary legacies of independent Caribbean nation-states considers how Caribbean sovereignty is reduced to the flying of "flags of convenience."[74] Not unlike the Vanuatu flag flown by the *Deepwater Champion*, the "'right to run up a national flag' comprises little more than the right to extend a flag of convenience—to offer preferential tax havens and multinational exemptions, ship registrations, economic free zones, and tourism investment subsidies."[75]

The fact that the existential threats facing the Caribbean manifest as a crisis of the state form does not prescribe a clear remedy, as Hobbes presumed. For many, this crisis demands the perfection of the state through the promotion of "good governance," "transparency," and "strong institutions." While none of these platitudes should be dismissed out of hand, too often they circulate as empty signifiers that preserve the fiction that the state and its hierarchical order of rule and discipline can indeed assume a more responsible and democratic character. This is another ruse of the state masquerade, which attributes its many failings to matters of content rather than form. Instead of seeking better masters, the people's masquerade hearkens to the rebellious Africans that Ligon encountered in seventeenth-century Barbados, whose aspirations to autonomy and self-management are reflected in the Jamesian truism "Every cook can govern."[76]

While we most certainly dwell in a world governed by state borders and sovereign authorities, their powers are neither natural nor inevitable. Even as policing and surveillance technologies penetrate the intimate reaches of social life, spontaneous masquerades militate against the petty dictatorship of the state's deputies on the road. *The Petro-state Masquerade* considers how the aspiration to postcolonial sovereignty in T&T came to rest on the exploitation of fossil fuels and their derivatives. The uncertainty that surrounds oil futures and sovereign futures alike need not be remedied. Rather, this book asks what futures can spring from the disarticulation of the hyphenated form of the petro-state. As Fundi reminds us, the small places of the Caribbean and their insurgent tradition of masquerade prompt us to rethink the natural order of the state: "We don't need to go to such forms of organization.... You ought to abandon the notion of the nation-state in the first place. And burn all the flags."[77]

Let the flags burn. Don't stop the masquerade.

CHAPTER ONE
Strike Fever

The burning of the canefields is as plain as ever... the rejection of the whole society based on the plantation system. This militancy is confined not only to workers in sugar. When we look at oilfield workers we enter another world, rejecting in a similar fashion a society based upon the plantation system. The organization of the oilfield workers in Trinidad has formed the strongest barrier in the whole of the Caribbean to the innumerable attempts to crush democracy.
—C. L. R. James, "The Birth of a Nation" (1981)

In the post-emancipation British West Indies, Trinidad captured the imagination of the colonial frontier again. With the conclusion of apprenticeship in 1838, formerly enslaved peoples took flight from local estates to form independent settlements and free towns. Black workers exercised their freedom to bargain with planters for more favorable terms and wages. West Indian planters countered with the conscription of indentured labor from East Asia and, principally, the Indian subcontinent in 1844. Though sugar thrived intermittently for much of the period prior to the termination of the indenture system in 1917, competition from beet sugar on the British market generated negative price shocks beginning in the 1880s, and opportunities for work diminished on sugar estates.

When sugar sputtered, oil clamored to take its place. In the first years of the new century, exploratory drilling remained limited and sporadic. Turn-of-the-century prospectors regarded the oil-bearing regions of south Trinidad as *terra incognita*—an unknown expanse waiting to be surveyed and exploited by colonial officials and financiers.[1] As demand for petroleum gasoline grew with the popularization of the automobile, the local industry pioneers Randolph Rust and Edward Lee Lum courted foreign capital to finance oil exploration in rural southeast Trinidad. Rust and Lum struck black gold with their first wildcat well in May 1902 and drilled eight additional wells by 1907. The natural wealth of the bituminous asphalt Pitch Lake in La Brea encouraged British technologists to mount fantastic projections for the future of Trinidad oil. Rust himself put it bluntly in an appeal to London in 1906: "It is incumbent on everyone who has any power to see that these oil fields are not allowed to lie dormant, but are developed—not for the benefit of the colony only, but for the benefit of our Empire ... To leave them undeveloped will be a crime to the colony and a great loss to the Empire."[2]

The earliest years of the industry involved a painstaking transformation of the colonial landscape. Existing infrastructure concentrated around the ports and sugar estates had been optimized for an economy centered on plantation agriculture. Oil required the clearing of vast acreages of dense forest and brush, the blazing of roads, and the transport of heavy machinery. Because Trinidad was one of the earliest oil frontiers, its industrialists could not turn elsewhere for skilled oilfield labor. This shovel-and-road work fell overwhelmingly to African and Indian workers, who organized themselves in itinerant "Tattoo Gangs" across the oil regions of south Trinidad.[3] As drilling forged ahead, these workers matured in their knowledge of industrial processes and their critical role in the defense of the empire. Arthur Beeby-Thompson, an English geologist and industry pioneer, described these early years of oil exploration in Trinidad with reference to a noteworthy discovery in the summer of 1907:

> News of the oil strike at Guapo attracted considerable attention both locally and in oil circles at home, so that many visitors arrived to view the spectacle gushing from a well. ... As the conditions of the plant precluded any test of the wells I remained behind to endeavor to get the pumps working. In the absence of any technical men or engineers, it was left to me with the aid of a few coloured labourers to clear the machinery of overgrown vegetation, to fix up boilers, pumps and connections, and generally to perform the duties of a fitter-mechanic.[4]

Commercial production of oil in Trinidad commenced in 1908 and boomed after the British Royal Navy converted its fleet from coal to oil power by decree of the First Lord of the Admiralty, Winston Churchill. Locals and migrants from the Windward Islands flocked to the oilfields in search of employment after the decline of West Indian sugar. Despite oil's growing importance to the colonial economy of Trinidad, however, employment opportunities remained scarce.

Though alluring to Caribbean laborers, oil offered an imperfect respite from the perils of agriculture. By 1937, the industry still employed fewer than ten thousand.[5] Workplace accidents were common and sometimes deadly. One crewman succumbed to injuries after an industrial crane landed on his head on the floor of the rig.[6] Another died on the spot after being struck "with terrific force" by a pair of chain tongs.[7] Another still tragically fell to his death after losing his footing atop a ninety-foot rig platform. Undeterred by workplace hazards, workers persisted in their flight from plantation to rig. At a meeting of the Siparia–Erin District Agricultural Society in January 1937, south Trinidad planters decried the shortage of agricultural labor caused by the preference for oilfield work.[8] Sympathetic observers appraised the problem in strict economic terms by attributing the preference for employment in oil to declining wages on planters' estates.[9] The perspectives of the workers themselves struck another chord.

As one onlooker put it, "Whenever oilfields are in proximity to agricultural centres the workers quite naturally abandon the latter."[10] Black workers populated the oilfields and eyed the industry as an avenue of social mobility and dignified work. This exodus continued, however, even as unemployment continued to rise. Oil alone could not stem the tides. As the population of migrants and unemployed squatters swelled, it grew more difficult to secure positions in the oilfields. In January 1937, hundreds of men assembled at an oilfield in Clarke's Road, Penal, but were rebuffed by shouts of "No work" from the rig managers.[11] Crowds of similar numbers returned day after day only to be mocked by the "hooting and booing" of company overseers and sent off empty-handed.[12]

The preference for oilfield work could not be explained by economics alone. While workers sought stability in oil, this did not explain the thousands who opted for unemployment over plantation labor. In Siparia, landholders and overseers disputed reports of depressed agricultural wages. A motion attributed to the manager of the Cyrnos cocoa estate demurred in the pages of the Sunday *Guardian*: "It is alleged that, although oilfields labourers are paid less wages than cocoa estate labourers, yet there are some who feel the lure of the oilfields too strong for them and will not leave the fields."[13] In the towns, hundreds of unemployed women and men roamed the streets in search of work at shops and groceries, congregating in front of government buildings and courthouses.[14] Despite their predicament, they did not return to the estates. When asked why he did not return to work on a nearby cocoa plantation, one former field hand simply replied that "his days for working under cocoa were over."[15]

The turbulent thirties were not simply a period of working-class agitation, but a general refusal of the plantation. Caribbean workers flocked to Trinidad and its oilfields to chart a future beyond the fields of sugar and cocoa in which their ancestors toiled. At this same moment, debates raged over the future of the oil industry. On the one hand, some cautioned that Trinidad's oil held a limited productive life that could soon be exhausted by the frantic pace of crude discoveries. On the other, bullish industrialists contended that the island's oil resources were inexhaustible and therefore capable of absorbing the thousands of Caribbean laborers made redundant by sugar's decline and their refusal of the plantation.

The latter point of view marks the origin of a masquerade of permanence in which the hydrocarbon resources of Trinidad were deemed to be limitless and capable of transforming the entire island into an "oil city."[16] The workers themselves, however, could not afford to wait for this transformation to arrive. Demanding relief in the form of land, work, and wages, British colonial subjects launched masquerades of their own in the form of work stoppages, strikes, and hunger marches. As the colonial state's masquerade of permanence failed to keep pace with the social motion of Caribbean workers and peasants, the inevitable clash between these dueling forces spilled onto the road.

Road March

On a Friday morning in July 1934—days prior to the emancipation centennial in the British West Indies—a crowd gathered at the Caroni sugar estate in central Trinidad. Out of work and deprived of their means of subsistence, Indian laborers demanded a hearing with local authorities after weeks of agitation. One contingent confronted the estate warden in Chaguanas. Another set out to the home of the district representative in the colonial legislature. Finally, a parade of 1,500 strong marched north to deliver their grievances to the governor of the Crown colony in Port of Spain. Marchers clashed with police along their route. When the mob reached the hills of Laventille overlooking the capital, police barricaded the procession at the Toll Gate and allowed passage to just six representatives appointed to negotiate on its behalf.[17]

The police roadblock prevented the Caroni workers from joining demonstrations of the unemployed in Port of Spain.[18] And the threat of colonial violence served a twofold purpose. First, it tempered the spontaneous uprising by enforcing mores of hierarchical order and discipline: the police obliged the mob to split its ranks. Second, it enforced an artificial division between rural and urban labor and, in this instance, between the Indian laborers of Caroni and the majority Black underclass in Port of Spain. This division persisted in the imagination of colonial magistrates as they sought a remedy for the crisis. In their view, "the East Indian [was] as a rule an agriculturalist pure and simple and [was] unsuited for road work."[19] The drama on the road laid bare the symbiosis of race and capital in colonial Trinidad. In Laventille, the British constabulary force exercised its presumptive monopoly on legitimate violence to preserve the racial order of the plantation economy against the threat of revolt.

But the hungry mob did not passively accept this order of things. The mob posed an unexpected challenge to colonial order. The tenuous separation of labor into racially discrete populations caved as the workers moved. The commonsense organization of racialized labor in Trinidad—in which descendants of indentured laborers from the Indian subcontinent occupied rural estates and Black workers and peasants dwelled in peri-urban barrack yards near cities and oil company towns—could be preserved only by the full arsenal of colonial violence. In truth, these boundaries were not as solid as they appeared. In their inquiry into the causes of the labor disturbances, colonial officers conceded that it was "difficult to obtain information as to the organization of the demonstrations."[20] As the unruly multitude marched northward, they spilled into the road and threatened to upend the racial geographies of the post-emancipation Caribbean.

Until the authorities intervened, the hunger marches eschewed vertical organization. This troubled even the editors of the working-class organ the *People*, who urged the hunger marchers to appoint a suitable "class of leaders" to interface with the colonial government.[21] Neither did the labor leaders in Port of Spain greet the crowd unreservedly. Months earlier, on May Day, the venerated champion of the barefoot man Arthur Cipriani called on the working people of Trinidad to join the ranks of his Fabian socialist movement represented by the Trinidad Labour Party (TLP).[22] He underscored the necessity of restraint, adding, "I realise that the wait of the workers, in these Colonies, for relief is at times vexatious, if not heartbreaking; but, if West Indians will realise that their wait, as compared with that of their brothers and sisters in other parts of the world, has been short they would not chafe too much."[23] As the mob pushed ahead, the trade union aristocracy aimed to flag its tempo.

The labor unrest was not limited to Caroni. Troubled by unseasonal drought conditions in the months of June and July, sugar-estate owners targeted field laborers with retrenchment.[24] As crops and exports suffered, money in the colony grew scarce. Creditors responded by refusing loans to beleaguered workers. The prevalence of task work meant that wages were paid only after the completion of their contracts. Employers withheld pay; workers grew indignant.

Unemployment spread through the cane fields of east and central Trinidad. After Caroni, the wave of workers' agitation reached the estates of Woodford Lodge, Perseverance, Orange Grove, Washington, Frederick, Waterloo, Brechin Castle, Sevilla, Rivulet, Esperanza, Phoenix Park, Forres Park, Milton, Esmeralda, and Cottage. In all, more than fifteen thousand laborers of Indian descent took part in the demonstrations across Trinidad in 1934.[25] The drought affected small cultivators and peasants as well. Dry conditions evaporated any remaining hope for relief. Blighted rice plots cultivated by the Indian peasantry cut off an essential source of nutrition.[26] Food insecurity ravaged the sugar estates.

While the trouble in the labor sector received ample commentary in local publications of record, the northward trek of insurgents cut against pleas for patience from Cipriani and his TLP stalwarts. Armed with the slogan "Bread or work," the hunger marchers decried the ills of unemployment, malnutrition, and disease. Plantation labor set out "on the warpath," as the African Trinidadian seaman and communist Jim Headley described it.[27] When erstwhile indentured workers and their descendants erupted in spontaneous strikes, they dismantled the colonial mythos of Indians as docile and compliant. Instead, colonial officials bristled at the "younger generation" of Indian laborers who bucked the authority of estate managers and governing bodies alike.[28] Some Indian laborers joined Black workers on the oilfields. In the 1931 debut issue of what came to be known as the *Negro Worker*, George Padmore observed that "although the vast majority of workers in the oil fields are Negroes, in recent years, however, Hindu workers have been attracted to the industry."[29] Intended by planters and colonial administrators as a buffer to frustrate the demands of Black workers, the new generation born to Indian laborers in

Trinidad provoked anxiety due to its "lack of restraint and absence of sense of responsibility."[30] Refusing to wait for the arrival of welfare provisions from the colonial government, they burgled dry goods stores and absconded with essential supplies.[31] Hunger, rather than sloganeering, ignited their movement.

Predominantly Black oil workers followed the example of Indian sugar workers by staging work stoppages and hunger marches of their own. Workers at Apex Oil declared a strike in 1935. While the strike action quickly lost steam, it received critical support from Tubal Uriah "Buzz" Butler, an African Grenadian migrant and evangelical preacher who headed the Fyzabad branch of the TLP. A veteran of the First World War, Butler earned a reputation as a political organizer for his advocacy in the Grenada Union of Returned Soldiers.[32] In January 1921 he arrived in Trinidad, where he was further radicalized by the work conditions in the oilfields and the obstinacy of colonial rule. Butler gained the trust of the working class in south Trinidad as a charismatic leader who shared their humble origins. He eschewed the bourgeois temperament of labor bureaucrats through his embrace of Christian revivalism and distanced himself from Cipriani, a fellow veteran of the Great War whom he chastised for a service record "hundreds of miles from the firing line."[33]

Cipriani addressed the workers in Fyzabad Junction at the outset of the Apex strike in 1935, pledging the TLP's support in the form of reimbursed wages and food supplies. Exiled from the oilfields due to a workplace injury, Butler challenged Cipriani to match his oratory with the promised material support. The confrontation escalated when Cipriani's supporters forcibly expelled Butler from the meeting hall. Undeterred and buoyed by the vocal support of his National Unemployed Movement compatriot Bertie Percival, Butler returned to deliver a scathing indictment of Cipriani. Either out of bitterness or neglect on the part of Cipriani, the food and financial provisions never arrived. Betrayed by the TLP, the majority of workers hastily accepted a 2 percent increase to hourly wages of seven cents.[34] The remaining strikers were blacklisted by employers, and they followed Butler on a hunger march from Fyzabad to Port of Spain. In doing so, they sought to expose the conditions of oilfield workers to the colonial government and labor party elites in the capital. Despite this betrayal by trade union leaders, the Apex strike demonstrated the willingness of workers to engage in collective action unauthorized by the Labour bureaucracy. The failed strike inspired Butler to part ways with the TLP and establish the British Empire Workers and Citizens Home Rule Party

(BEW & CHP). The first party resolution, dated July 27, 1936, denounced the racist policies that barred "coloured" workers from choice positions as oilfield drillers or inspectors in the local constabulary force.[35]

Indeed, the hunger marches revealed the workers' disenchantment after a century of de jure freedom. Set in motion by the decline of West Indian sugar and negative shocks to cocoa markets in the late 1920s, the unemployment crisis escaped the concerns of Cipriani, who advocated for the completion of civic works and infrastructure improvements such as drains, roads, and bridges instead of heightened wages for the workers themselves.[36] When Cipriani spurned the working class for a post in the colonial legislature, the National Unemployed Movement (NUM) usurped the TLP as the center of working-class organization. Headed by African Caribbean communists including Headley and Elma Francois, the NUM grew its ranks from its headquarters on Prince Street in Port of Spain. On August 1, 1935—Emancipation Day—the NUM led a parade of more than three thousand to the governor's house, where they were confronted by a mounted constabulary force from the nearby barracks in St. James. The hunger marchers enumerated their demands, including a jobs guarantee, food distribution depots for the unemployed, shelter for the homeless, a universal wage for unemployed women and men, the revocation of existing public contracts, and government control of all enterprises and other schemes.[37]

In his account of the 1930s in Trinidad, the historian Harvey Neptune positions the hunger marches as a wellspring of radicalism that sparked the movement for self-government in succeeding decades. "In the aftermath of June 1937," he observes, "the idea of nationalism circulated within the colony (and region) with newly acquired force and legitimacy."[38] Neptune is joined by other historians who identify the Caribbean labor uprisings in the 1930s as the kernel of nationalism that "set Trinidad and Tobago on an irreversible course toward self-government and independence."[39] While the June 1937 general strike in Trinidad and its sister isle of Tobago remains the flashpoint of the era, it risks appropriation as a mere preamble to a romantic narrative of national independence and postcolonial statehood. The significance of the strike fever of the 1930s extends beyond its status as a crucible of state formation. Notably, this insurgency did not articulate a parliamentary state as its principal objective. Rather than a plea for independence under a government drawn from the ranks of local elites, the hunger marches unveiled the poverty of imperial citizenship in the aftermath of slavery and indenture in their demands for living wages and access to land for subsistence cultivation. As a prelude to the uprisings across the Caribbean in the 1930s, the refusal of work by descendants of enslaved and indentured workers bellowed songs of revolt against the extractive levers of colonial rule and the racial order of plantation capital.

Classical political theory ridicules the mob for its characteristic undecipherability. Mobs (and their lexical companion, the crowd) are rendered as politically inert and deficient in organization or leadership.[40] Rather than a crucible of radical democratic politics, mobs appear as vestigial forces—"symptoms of modern savagery" that threaten to engulf or displace an idealized liberal subject.[41] From the perspective of the colonized, however, the disorder of the mob militates against colonial regimes of order. While the mob is derided as a formless and directionless expression of spontaneous revolt, in the cases of Caroni and Fyzabad we might better understand the mob as a deliberate tactic rather than evidence of a dearth of political organization.

The standoff on the road demonstrates how the threat of colonial violence disciplined the mob into permissible avenues of civic redress. When ordinary workers touched the road in the form of a Carnivalesque masquerade, they staged a confrontation with colonial authorities unmediated by vanguard leadership. On the road, the mob played a mas that threatened to explode the artificial racial geographies of the post-emancipation West Indies. At the same time, the colonial state engaged in a masquerade of its own. In other words, while the modern state depends on the dispensation of violence to divide the mob into individual rights-bearing subjects, the state represents this violence as the natural and inevitable order of things. This is the state masquerade.

For C. L. R. James, the origins of the "impending confrontation" between these dual masquerades—the hierarchical state and the leaderless mob—can be traced to the movement of Trinidadian workers in the 1930s.[42] He also observes: "Power was on the streets in Trinidad between 1937 and 1938. The great upheaval had taken place. But nobody was there ready to take advantage of it and do what was necessary to transfer power to the people."[43] Where Jerome Teelucksingh interprets this quote as an indictment of deficiencies in planning and leadership, James dissents.[44] Rather than emanating from the imagination of the intellectual vanguard, organization rises from the streets out of practices of road work that disrupt the masquerade of the state and its seemingly transcendent characteristics.[45] In other words, the task of the intellectual is not to direct the mob toward proper organization but to distill and propagate the political philosophy that the mob represents. In 1937, when Trinidad stood at the precipice of a transition from the somatic energy regime of the plantation to the carbon energy regime of petroleum, power was indeed up for grabs. The permanence of a petro-state directed by middle-class political elites and multinational technocrats, however, had not been settled. The future—including the political futures of Trinidad and Tobago and the market futures of oil—was not certain. This chapter considers how the events of June 1937 staged a confrontation between the dueling masquerades of power by the colonial state and an embryonic Caribbean nation.[46]

The Masquerade of Permanence

After the market crash of 1929, the outlook for the new decade in Trinidad appeared bleak. Export commodities such as cocoa, sugar, and oil traded well below their costs of production. Unemployment spiked further after a rare hurricane struck Trinidad in 1933 and devastated the agricultural lands of the deep south. The price of oil dropped as low as fifty cents per barrel; drilling operations shuttered. But Trinidadians entered the latter half of the 1930s with great expectations fueled by resurgent oil markets. Unlike with sugar and cocoa, demand for oil recovered quickly. As it expanded, oil promised to absorb the reserves of labor who had refused the plantation system. And with it, oil provided relative dignity, industrial knowhow, and social mobility to its masculine workforce.

In January 1936, a motley alliance of colonial legislators, oil magnates, labor leaders, and rank-and-file workers demonstrated at the Princes' Building in Port of Spain in support of an imperial oil preference.[47] Advocating for a guaranteed market in the metropole, proponents of the oil preference underscored its benefits for colonial workers and the necessity of a stable oil supply for Great Britain in the event of war in Europe. The expansion of oil production with a protected market tendered a possible resolution to the standoff between the propertied elites and working masses. A labor advocate captured the scene in clearest terms:

> It was quite true what one speaker said, that the occasion was one that vouched for the complete unanimity of the island on the question that was the purpose of the meeting, namely the granting of oil preference. There can be no doubt about the unanimity of opinion, if this means that all the persons present in that vast assembly wanted something. That every one [sic] had in his mind's eyes

the gratification of a great desire. And it did not matter in the least that these individual desires clashed in some measure or were diametrically opposed to each other. Of the two major interests assembled in that hall on that night the capitalists and the workers each one wanted something.[48]

Oil, indeed, was the object of incongruous desires. Even as the *Trinidad Guardian* reported a "boom in every industry" in its debut issue of 1937 (tempered only by the exception of bananas), oil held the greatest promise for the economic future of the colony.[49] Production of crude oil increased from 2,678,687 barrels in the first quarter of 1935 to 3,143,697 in the same period of 1936 and 3,708,321 in 1937.[50] Apex Oilfields reported profits of £373,781 in 1936 and projected greater production from the discovery of oil deposits in the "deep sands" of its main oilfield in Fyzabad.[51] With the extension of mining leases, new discoveries easily outpaced production. Innovative electric and seismic survey methods yielded large reservoirs in previously abandoned acreage as exploration expanded south to Moruga and Oropouche.[52] In January 1937, the tanker ship *Gulfwing* set sail with a record shipment of 110,000 barrels bound for the United States.[53] Oil flowed aplenty; industrial development proceeded in kind. Trinidad Leaseholders, a mainstay in the local oil industry since 1913, expanded the capacity of its Pointe-a-Pierre refinery to keep pace with the boom in crude production. In the early months of 1937, heavy machinery including heat exchangers and ten-ton industrial cylinders graced flatbed lorries and railways bound for Pointe-a-Pierre.[54] For the moment, more oil meant more opportunities for working people to refuse the indignity of estate labor. Day by day, oil companies "engaged workers by the scores to cope with the increasing activities of the fields."[55]

While oil stirred corporate earnings and popular fantasy, debates raged over the future of the industry. In 1937, Trinidad was the single largest supplier of oil in the British Empire. Workers and industry officials alike underscored the strategic value of Trinidad oil on the brink of war in Europe. Yet they remained keenly aware of its precarious standing in a world where military might and political power increasingly depended on petroleum resources. In the throes of the oil preference debate in 1936, an editorial in the *People* surveyed the uncertain future of oil in Trinidad:

> Every great power to-day is anxious to secure itself against dependence upon foreign sources for its oil needs, not so much in time of peace, but in the event of war. One should not be rash in prophecy, but a consideration that should

be always present is the possibility of the discovery and exploitation of oil in the tropical dependencies of Britain's African Empire. Oil is supposed to exist in Ethiopia. Why not in Kenya or the Anglo-Egyptian Sudan? Being British possessions, they would enjoy the same privileges in the English market as Trinidad.[56]

Just as the innovation of beet sugar ushered the decline of the Caribbean sugar industry in the nineteenth century, the discovery of frontier reserves threatened Trinidad's oil industry in twentieth. Despite this, local stakeholders and technologists offered confident forecasts of future production. They fell firmly into two camps. The first, represented by the Trinidadian barrister and politician Sir Lennox O'Reilly, characterized oil as a "wasting asset" that would disappear in the near term and whose revenue should be reinvested in other industries.[57] One projection in 1928 anticipated a sharp decrease in oil production in ten to fifteen years, only to be revised soon after, when prospectors unearthed additional reserves. The second, endorsed overwhelmingly by geologists and the local press, treated the oil reserves of Trinidad as inexhaustible.[58] Experts agreed that production had barely scratched the surface of the vast onshore deposits and even argued that oil was a renewable asset sustained by "a continual process of subterranean chemical action at some indeterminate point between Trinidad and the Mainland of Venezuela."[59] Expecting that industrial operations would one day cover the entire island, they imagined the entirety of Trinidad transformed into "one large oil city."[60] Fueled by these supposed subterranean transformations, the interminable expansion of oil presented a facile resolution to the labor troubles of the British West Indies.

This latter view won the day. Sir John Cadman, an English petroleum engineer and founder of the Mines Department in Trinidad, insisted that the majority of oil deposits remained untapped. In an address to the Institute of Petroleum Technologists, Cadman singled out Trinidad as a world leader in experimental drilling techniques by virtue of its complex geology. He applauded the innovations since the hardscrabble years of the early twentieth century that, with the introduction of drilling muds and blowout preventers, permitted local outfits to drill to unprecedented depths of the Trinidadian subsoil.[61]

Members of the oil industry reveled in their good fortune. Nourished by windfall profits, company executives and managers gathered in July 1936 at the Hotel Sand in St. Ann's for their second annual gala. Doubling as a retirement party for the general manager of Apex, Colonel Horace Hickling, guests toasted his eighteen years of service and the long-term prosperity of oil in the British Empire. Speeches ranged from congratulatory addresses to comedic juxtapositions of liquid crude to the alcohol imbibed, prompting laughter when a general manager joked "of the mellowing effect of the latter."[62] Rehearsing the opinions of industry experts, he assured the crowd that the peak of oil production remained a distant preoccupation and expressed gratitude to "drink to the prosperity of the Oil Industry and the health of executives and workers within it."[63] When Hickling formally departed from Trinidad to return to England just weeks prior to the June 19 strike in 1937, he received a farewell gift of a solid silver cocktail set and a basket of pink anthurium lilies and roses.[64]

Entranced by profits, the upper crust flouted the plight of workers. The good fortune of the industry did not extend to living conditions in the oilfields. Wages stagnated after the crash and inflation skyrocketed in the intervening years between 1929 and 1937. The divergent trajectories of corporate profits and the poverty of labor became the source of numerous complaints from the oilfields. While company suits drank to a prosperous future from silver cocktail sets, they deprived working men of their due spirits. An oilfield worker in Fyzabad reported weekly wages of $3.18 before cataloging his expenses to support himself, his wife, and six children. In all, basic foodstuffs and cooking supplies such as oil, sugar, flour, rice, beef, and saltfish amounted to $3.26 per week, leaving nothing to cover rent, clothing, or "rum for us to drink as working men."[65]

On the oilfields themselves, workers encountered discrimination and racist abuse. Individual laborers received ignominious grades of A, B, or C based on their performance and were issued service cards upon dismissal from a given company. When applying for work elsewhere, they were required to produce this record or begin once again at the minimum rate of pay.[66] Discharge tickets and the infamous "Red Book" containing disciplinary employment records raised suspicion and discontent among the masses.[67] Oilfields were spaces of racial polarization. Laborers and rigmen were largely Black; management and overseers were almost exclusively white. Trinidad Leaseholders appointed to its managerial ranks several South African whites who earned a reputation for their exceptional vitriol toward Black Trinidadians.[68] The rise of fascism in Europe and the Italian invasion of Ethiopia added fuel to the fiery milieu. Demonstrations in Port of Spain decried the invasion and appealed to Black Trinidadians for solidarity with Abyssinia. But while Trinidad oil provided fuel for the

British campaign against fascism in Europe, Trinidadians faced another fascism in the colonial theater of the Caribbean. As one observer put it, "Italy is not the only place where you would find a Mussolini, for there are many Mussolinis to be found in the Trinidad Government as well as the Trinidad oilfields."[69] The Trinidad oil belt restaged the skirmish of European fascism and anticolonial resistance in the Horn of Africa. In a noteworthy instance, an overseer at the Parry Land oilfield demanded a Black worker shave his beard or be dismissed from work, derisively "telling him he is not Haile Selassie."[70]

The south Trinidad district of Fyzabad epitomized the conditions of the oil belt. Employers constructed shoddy barrack accommodations on the outskirts of oilfields. Each Saturday, traffic piled up on the main road from San Fernando as employees of Apex, Leaseholders, and other companies descended on the oilfields to collect their weekly pay. Living quarters were congested and lacked proper sanitation. Those deprived of work wandered about and were labeled "undesirable" and "hooligan" elements that lurked among men of "comparatively high wages."[71] When suitable housing was made available in the form of semidetached dwellings built by oil companies, they often remained vacant as workers struggled to assemble the posted rental fees.[72] In the absence of a proper food market, vegetables and produce were not sanitized and were exhibited on the bare ground by local vendors.[73] Hookworm, malaria, tuberculosis, and malnutrition plagued the colonial workforce.[74]

As 1936 drew to a close, the center of working-class organization moved south. On December 13, a delegation from the Negro Welfare Social and Cultural Association (NWSCA) in Port of Spain—an organization that counted several NUM veterans in its ranks—ventured south to join a gathering of hundreds of workers in Fyzabad. NWSCA cadres frequented home rule meetings in the months preceding the strike of June 1937.[75] And as Bukka Rennie details, the organic leadership of Butler convinced the NWSCA that "unlike the North, the South had the best objective conditions for the creation of a mass movement to confront colonialism."[76] Rather than the imported rhetoric of a socialist international, Butler embraced Christian revivalism and often compared himself to Moses in a "divine association" between the biblical children of Israel and the colonial workers of Trinidad.[77] This won him a following that included large contingents of women and the elderly who followed him on his travels through the oil belt.[78] The Butler Party, as the BEW & CHP came to be known, held mass meetings throughout the deep south, decrying bloated prices of clothing and foodstuffs, stagnant wages, racial discrimination, and the "Fascist-Capitalist" threat to the working people of the British Empire.[79]

Despite the masses' refusal of estate work, they did not turn their backs on agriculture. Trinidadians cultivated unauthorized plots on Crown lands and along the unruly peripheries of the oilfields. They did not condemn agricultural pursuits as such, but the rigid hierarchy of the plantation. Cane and cocoa fields offered a lifetime of weary and degrading labor. Having endured generations of stagnation after emancipation, the progeny of the Caribbean plantation descended on the oilfields in pursuit of dignity. When they did not find work, they elected for the arduous task of raising their own crops rather than submitting to plantation wages. The peasant life was far from perfect; yet, few of the poor and hungry saw a future on the estates. Many descendants of Indian indentured laborers concurred. As one planter observed, while earlier generations often remained on the plantations after the completion of their indenture contracts, their children opted instead for lives as shopkeepers, bus drivers, and train conductors.[80] A desire for autonomy pervaded among the African and Indian children of the plantation.

Vexed by hunger and inflation, the masses continued to plant crops in unsanctioned plots. The seizure of private and Crown lands for food cultivation, in turn, became a rallying cry of the Butler Party and featured prominently in his public speeches.[81] But the spontaneity of ordinary people outpaced his organization. In the spirit of the hunger marches, the movement exceeded the formal ranks of oilfield workers as unemployed men and women protested the evils of fascism and the meager returns of imperial citizenship. Butler harnessed the independent energies of the peasantry. As an evangelist of the popular will, Butler's rhetoric followed the organic activity of the masses rather than the inverse. As his contemporaries understood it, he was "more or less a preacher" who "had ideas about spirits and God and all this kind of thing and not the realities of the earth."[82]

As the rural peasantry pushed ahead with the illicit cultivation of food, they embraced his narrative of deliverance.[83] In one episode, the Trinidad Lake Asphalt Company (headquartered in Brighton) threatened to displace residents of Sobo Village and destroy their garden plots, intending to convert the lands into oilfields. The indignity of the landless peasant formed the basis of Butler's evangelism. At a home rule meeting in May 1937, he cautioned his followers to heed the example of Sobo:

Just as the good people of the Brighton Company have changed and are today manifesting Fascist principles in their dealings with workers, in like manner the good people of the Apex, Leaseholds and other Oil Companies operating in Fyzabad may change tomorrow, and you might be asked just as the people of Sobo and Vessiny [sic] to leave, vacate your homes and your gardens without payment of a single cent. Yes, Friends and comrades, in their mad scramble for oil the humble village folks of Sobo and Vessiny are faced with a very terrible situation. Some have already as I told you been put off the lands. Yes; with a sword of Damocles hanging over their heads. They are today making frantic appeals to everybody to help them in their fight to secure justice.[84]

Although the people of Sobo were not registered members of the Citizens Home Rule Party, they invited Butler to plead their case to the company and district government. He agreed, securing compensation and the allotment of new lands to relocate their provision grounds.[85] Behind Butler, the frustrated pursuit of autonomy by working people threatened to boil over. This played out on two fronts. On the oilfields, Caribbean workers met entrenched racial hierarchies that blocked them from joining the managerial ranks and deprived them of their rightful share of profits. Meanwhile, landless peasants were faced with dispossession in their independent pursuit of subsistence cultivation and food sovereignty. The Butler movement counted both tendencies among its massive following. Their paths diverged, but their intended destination remained the same. As the Moses of the oil belt, Butler charted a course of deliverance from the degradation and poverty of the plantation to the dignity that eluded them.

Back in Port of Spain, the split in the movement widened between the labor aristocracy of the TLP on the one hand and the nascent alliance of the NWSCA and the home rulers on the other. On successive days, two separate gatherings commemorated International Workers' Day in Port of Spain. The first, convened by the NWSCA on May 1, saw three hundred workers march on Woodford Square, where banners and placards called for independence in Ethiopia and declared, "Long live the memory of Toussaint L'Ouverture."[86]

The following afternoon, more than six thousand attended the TLP convention at Queen's Park Savannah and toasted Cipriani, who had taken leave to the coronation of King George VI in London.[87] Strong in number, party stalwarts championed their station as the vanguard of working people in Trinidad. Acting as president general in Cipriani's absence, Timothy Roodal—perhaps in a subtle jab at the developments to the south—declared that "leaders might go and leaders might come, but ... the Trinidad Labour Party would go on forever."[88] Met with applause, Roodal proclaimed the duty of all in attendance to "pay tribute, respect, and loyalty to their political master."[89] Cipriani submitted a message in absentia from the festivities in London. His dispatch from Buckingham Palace underscored his distance from the desires of working people in Trinidad. Meanwhile, the workers in south continued to move.

Ride with the Mob

Earlier defeats such as the Apex strike in 1935 emboldened rather than demoralized the masses. The hunger marches served as a dress rehearsal for the explosion of 1937. And petroleum—the liquid substrate of modern industry and military might—continued to flow from the Trinidadian subsoil. Exports of crude oil nearly doubled in the first four months of 1937 compared to a year prior, and the total export volume of oil and petroleum products increased by more than 25 million gallons.[90] Meanwhile, local newspapers featured dispatches from Europe and proposed Trinidad as the host of a British air or naval base due to its "position on some of the most important trade routes in the New World."[91] Those tasked with the production of fuel for Royal Air Force planes and warships appreciated their importance in wartime. Unlike with agricultural products, the metropole could not weather a work stoppage in oil by turning to its other colonies. Trinidad, due to its privileged geology, stood alone in the British West Indies.

Workers, too, understood this special status. The oilfield differed markedly from the plantation in this regard. If Trinidad promised to become a vast oil city, it could conceivably satisfy the expectations of modernity for the offspring of Caribbean conscripts of slavery and indenture. And this consciousness extended beyond the oilfields themselves. The transformation of Trinidad by oil reverberated in adjacent industries. As workers tirelessly retrofitted the infrastructure of a plantation economy to meet the requirements of oil, they sought relief from hunger in the form of food and wages. In April 1937, approximately one hundred workers tasked with the digging of slush pits and tank sites put down their tools.[92] To their dismay, they were swiftly replaced by work gangs enticed with flat rates. In May, dozens of road workers on the Coora Road in Siparia descended on the district Public Works Office with axes, shovels, and cutlasses.[93] Appeased with a hearing convened by the director of Works and Transport, they tentatively returned to work.

By June, festering grievances began to boil over. Black and Indian workers alike engaged in work slowdowns and stoppages. While the former predominated in the oil sector, the latter were not unacquainted with oil work or associated industrial action. On June 7, Indian contract laborers who were engaged in "cutlassing work"—clearing dense brush in exploratory acreage—went on strike.[94] Butler sermonized his following with the importance of working-class unity across racial lines.[95] As oil brought a broader array of workers into its productive orbit, strike action offered the course of last resort for hungry workers. Calls for patience from the labor vanguard in Port of Spain wore thin.

On June 9, reports of a strike threat in the oilfields surfaced.[96] Soon after, a detachment of the constabulary force deployed from the barracks in San Fernando. Police stood guard along the roadways to escort buses of replacement workers to the oilfields. They intimidated home rule gatherings armed with bullwhips and threatened the assemblies with violence.[97] As the colonial battalion and company officers dug in their heels, a memo authored by Butler circulated among oilfield and public works employees calling for a general sit-down strike on Tuesday, June 22. He held animated meetings nightly across the south and twice per day on June 17 and 18.[98] Still, the government and labor leadership underestimated his following, holding until the final hours that it "is not expected that many labourers will comply with his circular."[99]

The sit-down strike began spontaneously in the early morning of June 19. At midnight, members of the graveyard shift assumed their posts at Leaseholders' Forest Reserve field. Working by moonlight, they continued until daybreak, when they abandoned their tools and rotary drilling controls.[100] When overseers caught wind of the strike, they summoned white American and European drillers from the field headquarters. Many who previously worked as roughnecks before graduating to management moved hastily to fire boilers and salvage drill pipes prior to freezing in the soil. The West Indian workers looked on in amusement.[101] Unexpectedly drafted into industrial work, senior staff proved clumsy and inept. Hundreds of barrels of oil ran to waste in canals and gutters.[102] By 7 a.m., the striking night shift met the daylight workers at the gate and instructed them to return home. Dancing and singing along the road to Fyzabad Junction, the crowd grew as it passed Trinidad Consolidated Oilfields, where more joined the walkout.

Within hours, police arrived at the oilfields to compel the strikers to resume work. When they refused, the police dispatch threatened to shoot striking workers if they continued to trespass on company lands.[103] By the following afternoon, the strike grew as the remaining employees at Forest Reserve as well as La Brea, Guapo, and Parrylands were forced off the estates.[104] At Fyzabad Junction, the Saturday traffic ballooned with striking workers who joined their comrades at local rumshops. The crowd of nearly five hundred men and women assembled in the yard of a local proprietor where Butler delivered an impassioned address. Police arrived after twenty minutes, marching through a crowd of workers "from every oilfield in the South" to execute an arrest warrant for Butler.[105] Their efforts to read the warrant were drowned out by shouting as the crowd pelted the policemen with sticks, stones, and bottles. Two inspectors drew their revolvers in retreat, leaving the notorious Corporal Charlie King, an African Trinidadian policeman, alone in the melee. He attempted to take Butler into custody but, rebuffed, sought refuge at a nearby shop and hid between two bags of flour. A group comprised mostly of women followed in hot pursuit, located King, and beat him violently.[106] Cornered in a back room, he jumped from an elevated window and a furious mob circled him below. They soaked King in petromax gasoline and ignited the flames with a match.[107]

As King burned, the mob cut telephone lines to San Fernando. When reinforcements did arrive—first from San Fernando and later Port of Spain—police and civilians exchanged barrages of stones and bullets. Another officer, Sub-inspector Bradburn, perished in the gunfire. La Brea Charles, a bystander likely mistaken for Butler due to his noticeable limp, was killed as well. As the crowd began to disband for the evening around 11 p.m., black clouds of smoke billowed over the forest after saboteurs set fire to a pumpjack at the Apex field several miles away.[108] With Fyzabad momentarily under their control, the masses turned to oil as the accelerant of a general strike.

On Monday morning, nearly a thousand workers assigned to the Dubbs cracking units and tank farms at Pointe-a-Pierre reported to the refinery for the start of the daytime shift. Large in number, the refinery workers controlled an essential chokepoint in the supply chain of oil to the British Empire. While a strike at a single oilfield could be compensated for by drilling elsewhere, the shutdown of crude storage and refining operations could bring the entire industry to an effective standstill.[109] Minutes after the open of the 7 a.m. working day, each unit assembled into small meetings. Out of the shop floor conferences, a larger contingent assembled and marched through the facility ordering a stoppage of work. Seamlessly, the crowd grew to nine hundred, fighting off resident overseers as they marched off the refinery estate. An impromptu meeting with the general manager of Trinidad Leaseholders yielded an offer of an additional two cents per hour. The workers refused and marched south to San Fernando. The unemployed joined them and looted goods from shops along the route.[110] In the form of a Carnival procession, strikers ordered the closing of businesses while "masquerading in the streets singing 'We ain't Working no Where.'"[111] Along the route, they compelled the managers of the Usine Ste. Madeleine sugar factory to cease operations. In San Fernando, they promptly shut down the power station and the telephone exchange. Confronted by a volunteer police force from Port of Spain, they levied stones at the officers, who returned a volley of bullets. One striker instantly dropped dead; several others fell to the ground, shot.[112] The crowd dispersed but the strike continued.

On Tuesday, the entire oil belt stretching west to Point Fortin and south to Palo Seco joined the strike.[113] By Wednesday, strike fever gripped the entire island.[114] In short order, the strike spread to harbor scheme workers in Port of Spain, estate laborers in central and east Trinidad, bus drivers, longshoremen, scavengers, lightermen, market vendors, and, as a lighthearted news brief reported, a horse who "suddenly came to a standstill occasioning a slight traffic jam."[115] In Port of Spain, the strikers replicated the Carnivalesque formation of their comrades in south. Carrying a red banner bearing the title of the Negro Cultural and Welfare Association, NWSCA cadres Francois, Jim Barratt, and Caesar Ashby addressed the crowd.[116] The mob, carrying sticks and pieces of iron, marched up and down the commercial thoroughfares of Frederick Street and Charlotte Street, shuttering shops and market vendors along the road.[117] As a constable stationed at the scene later put it, the mob was "not disorderly, the people seemed to treat it as Carnival time."[118]

Hundreds of laborers on the Orange Grove sugar estate followed in turn by setting fire to the cane fields and storming overseers' dwellings.[119] On the Atlantic coast in Mayaro, strikers shuttered cocoa and coconut estates, set bulls loose from loaded carts, and dumped the carts' contents into the sea.[120] The earlier skirmishes between police and workers in San Fernando recurred elsewhere—gunfire killed four strikers and wounded three officers in Rio Claro.[121] Five days after the initial sit-down strike, thirteen had been killed and more than forty others were wounded.[122] Summoned by Governor Murchison Fletcher, the British warships HMS

Ajax and HMS *Exeter* landed in Pointe-a-Pierre and Port of Spain, respectively, with detachments of "bluejacket" marines outfitted in tin helmets and carrying with them Lewis guns and rifles.[123] The Apex oilfields "resembled an armed camp" with armed guards stationed throughout the company grounds.[124]

The marine detachments enjoyed the support of politicians and labor bureaucrats. In addition to statements by Governor Fletcher and the mayor of Port of Spain, the TLP secretary, Vivian Henry, admonished the strikers for their "endeavor to institute mob rule in Trinidad" and reserved sympathy only for those workers who advocated for their just due on legal and constitutional grounds.[125] Labor leaders aligned with their colonial overseers against the popular will of the mob. TLP Vice President Timothy Roodal traveled south to Fyzabad to echo the appeal for peace and order. After he pledged to personally deliver the strikers' case to the proper authorities, the audience of men and women dispersed in protest and promised more violence and looting in the event of Butler's arrest.[126] At sea and preparing to return from the Coronation in London, Cipriani submitted a telegram insisting upon "restraint and self-control" prior to his arrival in Trinidad two days later.[127]

As marines partially contained the strike with the threat of force, colonial authorities maintained their pursuit of Butler. The authorities acknowledged that his arrest posed the risk of renewed violence; nonetheless, they understood his capture as essential to the restoration of order.[128] In a cable addressed to Secretary of State for the Colonies William Ormsby-Gore, Governor Fletcher characterized Butler as "mentally deranged" and a "mischievous agitator."[129] The enigma of Butler complicated desires for a swift resolution between workers and employers. The absence of a formal trade union or a "recognised leader" to negotiate on behalf of labor frustrated the efforts of local administrators.[130]

The power of the general strike was not lost on London. The coordinated uprising presented a chilling reminder to local officials that only a few thousand whites resided on the island with nearly half a million African and Indian Trinidadians. Spooked by the "ever present possibility of a racial clash," the oil lobby called on the British Government to encourage the formation of trade unions and establish clear terms to resolve industrial disputes.[131] Just as the hunger marches were forced to split their ranks nearly three years prior, the restoration of colonial order required that the insurgency represented by Butler be routed into acceptable channels of redress.

Butler remained at large—rumored to be surrounded by a contingent of armed guards in the countryside or the Venezuelan mainland. A consortium of oilfield workers pledged to remain on strike until Butler returned to bargain over wages and living conditions. They demanded no arrest and insisted they "want[ed] no other leader."[132] Only a week removed from the outbreak of the strike, the workers made it clear that no one but Butler would be acceptable as a legitimate representative of their cause. Yet as Butler eluded authorities, the latter sought other channels to remedy the standoff.

Adrian Cola Rienzi, an Indian Trinidadian barrister and associate of Butler, assumed the mantle of leadership and the charge to represent the aggrieved oil and estate workers. On July 26, the Oilfields Workers' Trade Union (OWTU) formed in Butler's absence and in September became the first registered trade union in the British West Indies. Butler reportedly maintained clandestine lines of communication with the union in its formative months. While Rienzi led the union in name, its rank-and-file membership maintained their allegiance to Butler in absentia.

The formal recognition of the OWTU simultaneously marked a victory and a betrayal of the workers who launched the general strike of their own accord. The expansion of collective bargaining rights and union membership created new administrative channels to "mediate between capital and labor in addition to agencies to provide social services."[133] At the same time, MacDonald Stanley, the general secretary of Butler's Citizens Home Rule Party, would later describe this period in no uncertain terms:

> They rushed the legislations through so that the question of protest by workers in organized groups [could] be entertained at a legal level. And so the trade union laws were implemented and the employers of labor and government rapidly got about while Butler was still in prison to see that they forced the workers to formulate themselves into the trade union and bargain and set up the collective bargaining machinery before Butler was released.[134]

On September 27, Butler ended his cover to deliver testimony to the Royal Commission of Enquiry on the labor disturbances. He was subsequently tried for sedition, found guilty, and handed a sentence of two years' imprisonment on Nelson Island in the Gulf of Paria.

All Skin Teeth Eh Laugh

While Butler served his sentence offshore, two tendencies of organized labor began to diverge. Loyalists to the Butler movement, including

McDonald Moses and Stephen Maharaj, continued to rally support in his absence, going from "village to village, estate to estate, oilfield to oilfield" to cultivate the popular base of a mass party.[135] On the other hand, Rienzi and the middle-class leaders of new trade unions gathered public servants and dockworkers under their professional leadership. Rienzi championed Butler's cause during his incarceration and welcomed his release in May 1939 with OWTU rallies in San Fernando, Fyzabad, Siparia, and Port of Spain, the last of which drew crowds of ten thousand to eleven thousand.[136]

In Siparia, Butler broke from the conventional script for increasing trade union membership. Instead, he appealed to the strength of the workers themselves to manage the natural resources of Trinidad and seize power from the colonial elites:

> If you don't realize the real issue, go back to that memorable day, the day of the June rebellion, when those Fascist Imperialist employers, the oppressors of the masses, were on the run before the onslaught might of the combined forces of labour demanding social equality and justice. But is that all? No[,] we are on the onward march to admonish this Crown Colony Govt. lock, stock and barrel; to control the Oil Industry and stop placing millions of dollars in shareholders' pockets; the millions must remain in Trinidad for the children of Trinidad and Tobago. We are out to take control of this beautiful and pleasant land. We want a Government for the people, by the people and with the people.[137]

Butler condemned racial chauvinism and appealed to the crowd to "join forces with [their] Indian brothers," and reserved special praise for the women in attendance for their critical role in the "fight for freedom against economic slavery" that they launched side by side with overwhelmingly male oilfield workers in June 1937. His direct address to the women indicated that his ambitions were not limited to organizing oilfield workers themselves. Instead, the Butler movement sought to cultivate the popular will through his evangelical oratory. Now the workers took their turn to raise a toast to "Comrade Butler's health" with a banquet that included champagne.[138]

The workers' allegiances remained with Butler, but the union bureaucracy declined to offer him Rienzi's post as president general of the OWTU. Instead, they named him general organizer in an effort to retain legitimacy with his thousands of followers. The fragile coalition did not last. On July 26, 1939, mining workers at the Trinidad Lake Asphalt Company in La Brea went on strike without the authorization of Rienzi or the

OWTU after a fellow worker was dismissed without cause. Butler supported the wildcat strike; the OWTU condemned the strikers' refusal to place trust in "more competent persons to interpret the terms and advise [them] rightly."[139]

With the union bureaucracy pitted against the rank and file, the OWTU executive officers blamed Butler for encouraging the unsanctioned strike in a speech at La Brea and expelled him from the union. Regional branch leaders of the OWTU threw their support behind Rienzi. But the workers followed Butler. After his expulsion, Butler established the British Empire Workers, Peasants, and Rate Payers Union, and more than 90 percent of the oil workers left the OWTU for this new organization.[140] Butler continued to hold meetings in south Trinidad, where he sermonized on the corruption of the union aristocracy. Where he had once challenged Cipriani, he now challenged his former comrade in arms, Rienzi:

> Men like Rienzi, Blades, Rojas and Moses are men that you should be afraid of, because they term themselves as members of the Central Executive Committee and go about fooling the people and taking away their money, telling people they have a Union to support them when there are strikes and when they are out of work.[141]

Just as they had in 1934, the ranks of colonial labor split between the rank-and-file workers and the middle-class professional leaders at the helm of the new unions and their regional outposts. Even after the formal recognition of the OWTU, workers continued to organize independently into task gangs and squatter encampments, and to stage hunger marches.[142] While Rienzi preached the necessity of responsible leadership and restraint, Butler mobilized the oil workers and unemployed alike. Once again, the colonial authorities intervened. In November 1939, just six months removed from his previous sentence, Butler was again arrested and jailed under wartime Defense Regulations and remained imprisoned on Nelson Island until the conclusion of the Second World War in 1945. The trade union leaders did not protest. As Nazi U-boats circled the Caribbean Sea — culminating in an attack on the Port of Spain harbor in 1942 — Downing Street insisted it could not risk another disturbance on the scale of 1937. The Royal Navy depended on Trinidad for essential oil supplies to fuel the war effort. And US forces, with a newly leased military base on Trinidad's northwest peninsula in Chaguaramas, began an occupation of Trinidad that would last until the base closed in 1977.[143]

Counter-plantation Futures

In September 1940, members of Butler's Citizens Home Rule Party gathered in Fyzabad to commemorate the party's fourth anniversary. The location of the gathering at the historic center of the oilfield strikes did not escape the attention of the home rulers. The veteran trade unionist and future mayor of Port of Spain, Tito Achong, read from his letter of support:

> From the bowels of the earth in and around Fyzabad gushes forth petroleum. Because of the great quantity of this mineral in this island, Trinidad is now a precious jewel in the imperial diadem. The petroleum industry here has provided huge wealth to the few, and has given rise to a large proletarian class unknown at the beginning of this century.
>
> With the growth of this industry, the perennial blockade against equality of opportunity for the workers has been intensified. Correspondingly, a great part of the best lands on which our ancestors once dwelt has been withdrawn from us. According[ly], poverty is stalking the land. A high level of health is absent among our people because of their inability to provide themselves with an optimum amount of food.[144]

Achong's reflections outlined the contradictions not simply of the turbulent decade prior but the dilemma that would haunt T&T for decades to come. As Trinbagonians marched toward independence in 1962, the successors to the middle-class vanguard of Cipriani and Rienzi like the brash historian-cum-politician Eric Williams stood to inherit the reins of the postcolonial state. In turn, they inherited a tension between two tendencies that promised to supplant the plantation economy of old. The first, embraced by the industrial technocrats and the new class of political elites, understood the "precious jewel" of petroleum as an inexhaustible reserve of wealth that heralded a prosperous future for the nation under the rule of benevolent experts. As the next chapter demonstrates in its treatment of Williams, the dreams of transforming the Trinidadian landscape into "one large oil city" resurfaced as a path to uplift the Black and Indian masses from "brown sugar to steel"—from histories of plantation labor to the comforts of industrial modernity.

Achong, though, exalted another tendency. Shifting his register of address to the workers themselves, the "large proletarian class unknown at the beginning of the century," he alluded to the histories of autonomous settlement by the formerly enslaved and indentured who charted a course beyond the plantation in squatter camps and garden plots that ballasted against the fickleness of wage work. For the Haitian historian Jean Casimir, the practices of cultivation forged by a reconstituted peasantry of African peoples is best understood as a "counter-plantation system" in which the "[peasantries] of the entire Caribbean . . . constituted themselves in opposition to the process of integration and assimilation to the commodity-producing plantation."[145] In other words, the principal aim of nominally free Caribbean peoples—emancipated Africans and Indian "free coolies" no longer bound by their indenture contracts—involved a desire to chart political and economic futures beyond the orbit of the plantation. In Trinidad, this launched the working class on two parallel trajectories. The first, like their peasant counterparts in the Haitian countryside, took the form of squatting and subsistence livelihoods.[146] The thirst for land prevailed over desires for industrial wages and parliamentary representation. On the other hand, Caribbean workers set their sights on the oil industry as a limitless horizon of opportunity. If oil was inexhaustible, it, too, could chart an exit from the plantation past. For the moment, these two tendencies were not at odds.

The calypsonian Atilla the Hun recorded the history of the strike and its aftermath in his griotic compositions on Butler and the grassroots eruption of the general strike. After the Royal Commission of Enquiry and its chairman, John Forster, released its findings to the public in 1938, Atilla countered with the melodic annotation "Commission's Report":

A peculiar thing of this commission
In the ninety-two lines of dissertation
Is there's no talk of exploitation
Of the worker or his tragic condition
Read through the pages, there is no mention
Of capitalistic oppression
Which leads one to entertain a thought
And wonder if it's a one-sided report[147]

In the eyes of the eventual Calypso King, the half had not yet been told. The commission had delivered its report, but the course of counter-plantation futures had not yet been decided for the working people of T&T.

The tension between the emancipatory program of land for the people and a technocratic fantasy of inexhaustible fossil fuels persists into the present. As contemporary statesmen exalt the futures of oil and gas production in Trinidad as limitless in a moment of industrial decline, the origins of this masquerade of permanence can be traced to the critical period of the 1930s when debates raged over the half life of its petroleum reserves. The question of how postcolonial futures in T&T came to be staked to the market futures of oil and gas is where we turn to next.

CHAPTER TWO

Fueling Independence

And people seem to forget the events of 1970. Let me tell you the prosperity in oil now experienced by this country had nothing to do with any policy of the Williams regime. It was a result of the decision by OPEC countries. And when they asked him to join, he refused. And when he wanted to join they refused, because OPEC did not want an agent of the British Government in their fold. In 1970, the whole country moved against him and in 1974, he was all ready to go because the country was bankrupt. The oil saved him. It saved everybody. —C. L. R. James, *Trinidad Express* (April 7, 1981)

During the fifteenth annual convention of the People's National Movement in August 1973, Prime Minister Eric Williams announced his retirement from political life. After a decade of postcolonial rule in Trinidad and Tobago, his address to party stalwarts reeked of exasperation: "When the PNM came on the scene in 1956, we encountered a society in which individualism was rampant," he recalled. "Today, 17 years later, the disease of individualism is more pronounced than ever, and such a national movement as there is does not go beyond increased participation in Carnival and the general desire to migrate."[1]

Twelve years earlier, Williams graced the University of Woodford Square with his defining address, "Massa Day Done." The Trinbagonian working people, after marching with Williams on Chaguaramas to demand an end to the US naval occupation during World War II, rallied behind the PNM as the vanguard of West Indian self-government. For the moment, the promise of sovereignty placed Williams at the frontline of the people's masquerade for self-government. In 1961, with the consummation of the West Indies Federation in his sights, Williams championed the peasants and the smallholders as the beacons of the new society: "Today, with the PNM, the cane farmer, the small farmer growing cane, pitting his puny weight against the large plantation, is receiving a recognition that he never anticipated, and is coming into his own, a man with a stake in his country, with the legal right to refuse his labour if he wishes to and work his own land."[2] Chanting down "Massa" in the form of British rule and US occupying forces, Williams played a mas as the champion of the barefoot man. When Jamaica exited the federation compact, Williams declared that "one from ten leaves nought" and dealt the final blow to the short-lived political union of Caribbean territories. Now tasked with the cultivation of an independent nation-state, Williams preached the virtues of a "people of all races and colours ... with the common bond of a national community" as a counterweight to "Massa's barbarous ideas and practices of racial domination."[3] On August 31, 1962, Trinidad and Tobago gained independence from Great Britain, setting the stage for yet another confrontation between national leaders and the postcolonial masses.

But by 1973, the fellowship forged at Chaguaramas folded as Williams prepared to exit the political arena. The national economy floundered under diminishing investment; armed radicals challenged the sardonically dubbed "Afro-Saxon" orthodoxy of Williams and the PNM. While the oil industry provided the Williams administration with a source of revenue for civic works and welfare programs in the early postindependence era, the exhaustion of proven reserves prompted a decline in crude production and foreign-exchange earnings after 1965. In his retirement address, Williams attributed the state of the economy to the uncertain futures of hydrocarbon extraction: "Anticipating the decline in land production, every effort was made to encourage offshore exploration on the East Coast after the first discoveries at Soldado."[4] The offshore finds lent a temporary reprieve from several years of fiscal instability. Yet, the Soldado discovery did little to resolve an enduring dependence on multinational capital, which supplied the "money required for the actual exploitation of what [had] been discovered so far plus the continued exploration ... in progress."[5] And the specter of "corporate imperialism" remained the foremost obstacle to genuine postcolonial sovereignty.[6] The governing legitimacy of Williams's PNM—staked to its capacity to deliver essential goods and services to a racially heterogeneous and geographically diffuse populace—rested at the whim of metropolitan investment. When he announced his imminent retirement, the price of oil stood at a modest US$3 per barrel.

Over the first ten years of postcolonial independence, Williams had descended from his perch at the vanguard of the anticolonial movement to a place of ignominy among organized labor and its radical offshoots. And yet, just as his masquerade began to falter and grassroots cadres of workers, students, and the unemployed threatened to seize state power, he would be redeemed. The reversal of Williams's fortunes—and his decision to retire—hinged on the oil boom that began mere weeks after his convention address in 1973. When C. L. R. James was asked to comment on the political career of his estranged protégé, he sarcastically quipped, "The oil saved him. It saved everybody."[7] Indeed, to understand this saga requires not simply an inquiry into the personality of Williams as a leader and statesman, but the political and economic transformations set into motion far beyond the borders of T&T.

The Revolutionary Seventies

The Trinidad oil and gas industry sputtered into the 1970s. As proven reserves deteriorated and multinational capital changed course to more-lucrative extractive frontiers in the Alaskan Arctic and the Middle East, the wellspring of hydrocarbon riches threatened to dry up after more than half a century of commercial production in the twin-island nation.[8] The economic crisis triggered a parallel crisis in governing legitimacy. The Carnival festivities in February 1970 took on an overtly political tenor. Black Power suffused the mas. Masqueraders brandished giant portraits of Eldridge Cleaver, Malcolm X, and Trinidad native son Stokely Carmichael, with Prime Minister Williams depicted as a pig in effigy.[9] Days after, on February 26, 1970, demonstrations led by students and disaffected youth erupted in Port of Spain.

Arriving on the heels of protests by radical Caribbean students at Sir George Williams University in Montreal, the February Revolution voiced popular discontent with the PNM and the slothful pace of postcolonial development.[10] As state bureaucrats advanced a Lewisian model of "industrialization by invitation" to attract foreign capital via tax holidays and fiscal incentives, petroleum production continued to decline and rates of unemployment remained high, particularly among the young, Black Trinbagonians who constituted the electoral base of the PNM. An Oilfields Workers' Trade Union editorial published in January 1970 voiced the estrangement of the Trinbagonian working people from the ministers and parliamentarians tasked to represent them:

> It is now quite evident that the strategies of development which the PNM has pursued over the years have failed to eliminate the basic defects of the colonial society which it originally undertook to transform: economic dependence on the metropolitan countries; unequal distribution of the national wealth, with the historically privileged ethnic groups getting a larger slice of the cake; lack of opportunity for popular participation and initiative in the determination of national goals and direction; a cultural system which perpetuates feelings of inferiority and encourages the society to derive its values from the metropolis, thereby frustrating the rise of a genuine national consciousness.[11]

Counting a range of tendencies within its ranks, the Black Power uprising demonstrated the organizational capacity of ordinary citizens and underscored their estrangement from a government aligned with transnational corporations and local business elites. On March 12, 1970, a march of six thousand set off from Woodford Square to the sugar estates in Caroni with its charge of "Indian-African Unity" emblazoned on a banner leading the procession. Reversing the course taken by Indian estate laborers three-and-a-half decades earlier, the marchers trotted through Laventille along Eastern Main Road, where people of all ages "poured out of their homes" to join the demonstration.[12] Turning south on Southern Main Road at Curepe Junction, the marchers received an unexpected welcome from the Indian residents of Caroni.[13] They provided food and refreshment in the form of water and fruit juice to energize the movement. Schoolchildren defiantly raised their fists in solidarity.[14] The racial geographies of the plantation buckled once again.

The greatest challenge to political order arrived on April 21, 1970, when a regiment of Trinbagonian soldiers mutinied after Williams's declaration of a state of emergency. Darcus Howe, a nephew and student of C. L. R. James who had returned from London, fashioned the slogan "Seize power and send for James" amid rumors that the mutinous soldiers harbored Jamesian sympathies.[15] By standing down, the soldiers refused to suppress Black Power protesters in accordance with the directives of their superiors. Williams openly regarded the mutiny as an attempt to overthrow the government, denouncing the "unconstitutional" tactics and "ulterior motives" behind their pledge of solidarity with young Black Power activists.[16] The officers involved would later insist that they had no intention of launching a coup d'état, but merely acted in principled defiance of a corrupt senior corps of officers.[17] Whatever their true intentions, the rebels abandoned their campaign after they were intercepted by a loyalist contingent of the

Coast Guard and barred from entering the capital of Port of Spain. The leaders of the uprising, Lieutenants Raffique Shah and Rex Lassalle, were jailed, as was Geddes Granger of the National Joint Action Committee and several dozen activists from the ranks of Black Power and leftist political organizations. The seizure of power had been prevented for the moment.

Williams shrewdly crafted his response to the Black Power revolt. He introduced a 5 percent tax levy to fund a government jobs program and seemingly acceded to the demands of the young unemployed or otherwise underserved protesters. Though noteworthy, the measure proved ineffective when Williams and the PNM failed to stem the tide of popular mobilization. He momentarily weathered the political storm by declaring a subsequent six-month state of emergency in the latter months of 1971, but his government continued to face insurgent challenges from below as factions such as the National Union of Freedom Fighters (NUFF) conducted raids on foreign banks from outposts in the mountains of the Northern Range and engaged in armed standoffs with local police. Inspired by armed liberation struggles in Africa, Asia, and elsewhere in the Caribbean, NUFF rejected electoral politics as a viable avenue of democratic participation and popular resistance to multinational corporate expropriation.[18] A pamphlet circulated by NUFF reads as follows: "Democracy in its true sense can't be determined by elections in this country. . . . The only alternative is revolutionary democracy. We in NUFF have taken up the task, and as in all revolutions of the world, it is the young who first dare to defy the powers."[19] Although NUFF did not adhere to a strict ideological line, its members remained resolute in their condemnation of party politics and the Westminster parliamentary system.

The years after the uprising of 1970 presented a genuine threat to the terms of political order laid out in the Independence Constitution of 1962. For Williams, the situation was bleak. As the revolutionary seventies soldiered on, the historian-cum-sovereign confronted threats externally from metropolitan interests and internally from armed dissidents. By August 1973, Williams found himself alienated from an aggrieved populace with little viable recourse. Oil production fell. Government revenue evaporated. The agricultural sector, blighted by drought, inflated prices of food and essential goods. Pushed to a breaking point, government spending quickly outpaced state revenue as a balanced national budget in 1969 ballooned to a deficit of TT$124 million in 1972.[20] In the eyes of his detractors, the breaking point was nigh. Williams, at this moment, had no choice but to retire from politics.

In his retirement address, Williams derided guerrilla elements for their misguided approach to the postindependence landscape in which he insisted there was "no foreign or colonial aggressor."[21] To the contrary, he purported to speak on behalf of a general public when he claimed that citizens were not "satisfied that all the avenues of constitutional political opposition have been exhausted" and lambasted the guerillas' lack of a guiding ideology apart from "vague phrases as power to the people."[22] But his dismissal of the guerrillas as a band of quixotic youths masked a more daunting reality. After a diplomatic visit to communist Cuba two months prior, the threat to regime survival posed by an ideologically coherent guerrilla regiment would certainly have been apparent to Williams. His smug dismissal sought to embolden constitutional order and quell conspiring insurgents. But his reliance on a secret-police force to neutralize NUFF and other dissidents—the infamous Flying Squad commanded by Randolph Burroughs—contradicted his confident posture. In all, thirteen young militants were murdered at the hands of the Trinbagonian police and military officials.[23] Yet, in a world pervaded by manifold political tendencies of Marxism–Leninism, Maoism, and the autonomist Marxism of C. L. R. James, the popular purchase of liberal democracy waned as it failed to deliver social protections and economic gains in the aftermath of national independence.

In the eyes of critics, this failure extended beyond commonplace concerns over petty corruption and bureaucratic inefficacy. "Unemployment: Why the PNM Failed Miserably," a report published in a September 1973 issue of *Tapia*, attributed the labor crisis in Trinidad to the privations of foreign direct investment:

> The reasons for our failure to create the required jobs are quite straightforward. Most of our invited industries are of the assembly or screw-driver type, engage in highly capital-intensive finishing-touch activity. The materials used in [the] production process are largely imported and the output is mainly for final consumption. What this means is that there are few links with industries producing raw materials locally, and thus with the rest of the economy. The industries are technically isolated from the rest of the economy.[24]

Tapia, the popular organ of Lloyd Best's Tapia House Movement party, diagnosed the frustrated course of postcolonial development as symptomatic of a more pernicious affliction. Though its chief contributors did not oppose industrialization as such, they disputed the merits of a growth model that encouraged the adoption of liberal trade policies, the promotion of cheap labor as a means of competition, and the production of commodities for metropolitan export. The dependence on foreign capital and markets stood in the way of aspirations for economic stability. Depicting the postcolonial state as a cabal ensnared by transnational circuits of capital, Tapia House joined grassroots leftists in its insistence that independence had failed to displace colonial economic relations.[25] Best said it best in his appraisal of the "plantation economies" of the Caribbean through a potent comparison: "Having landed in the New World, Columbus praised God and enquired urgently after gold. Nowadays the industrialists arrive by jet clipper, thank the Minister of Pioneer industry and enquire after bauxite."[26]

Williams was not unsympathetic to this position. In his public comments, he identified the multinational corporation as one of the principal obstacles facing the Caribbean at large. The dissolution of the West Indies Federation rendered the newly independent states of the anglophone Caribbean—Jamaica, Trinidad and Tobago, Barbados, and Guyana— economically vulnerable and geopolitically atomized. Williams reasoned, in turn, that "small Governments with gross domestic products in most cases below the assets of a multinational corporation, acting independently . . . cannot possibly hope to compete against an international conglomerate with a coordinated policy."[27] Genuine postcolonial sovereignty, he conceded, remained a distant horizon. Yet, his concession offered little solace to the working people or unemployed masses. The talk in the Caribbean was of revolution. The manifesto of the National Movement for the True Independence of Trinidad and Tobago (NAMOTI)—authored under the pseudonym Rafael Fyzabad—evinced this sentiment at the height of radical agitation in the region:

> It is abundantly clear that the people of Trinago [sic] are presently faced with two choices—whether to submit to the unbearable exploitation and oppression of foreign gangsters (mainly U.S. Imperialists) and continue to exist in conditions of neo-slavery; or resist completely this vicious and inhuman burden, wage a national revolutionary struggle to gain true independence, democracy, and peace and national salvation, and enable our glorious fatherland to march forward with the rest of progressive humanity toward socialism and eventually to end completely the exploitation of man by man.[28]

The tenets of this program included a steadfast resistance to corporate imperialism through organized labor and a program of proletarian internationalism. For all its determinist rhetoric surrounding the coming revolution, however, the forecasted socialist transition never arrived.

Capital triumphed in T&T through the opening of extractive frontiers and creation of new peripheries. Even today, social scientific studies of oil exalt its seemingly magical characteristics as a quintessential expression of commodity fetishism that obscures the production of frontiers through the conscription of labor, technology, and expertise.[29] Indeed, the extraction of hydrocarbon fuels is hidden behind injections of petrodollars that sustain fantasies of boundless growth or are blamed for the collapse of adjacent economic sectors as symptoms of "Dutch Disease" or "resource curse." To appraise the mechanics of the petro-state masquerade requires an inquiry into the material infrastructures of oil and natural gas in T&T. And in doing so, we must also resist a logic of predestination that equates oil itself with inevitable political formations and economic afflictions.[30]

Oil fuels the fantasies of abundance inherent to both liberal and state capitalism. To this end, it is when oil markets spike that it appears characteristically transcendent.[31] It is when oil appears to exceed its strictly material properties that it generates state effects and popular attachments to liberal individualism and social democracy alike. But fossil fuels are anything but transcendent. They are material substances whose transition from naturally occurring hydrocarbons to exchangeable commodities is littered with technical nuances and productive contingencies. Scholarship on the phenomenon of resource curse, in this respect, mistakenly regards oil as a uniform and uncomplicated substance.[32] The true source of the phenomenon of resource curse lies in a misguided calculus by which oil comes to be regarded as a simple and inexhaustible resource.[33] This masquerade of permanence, which took shape in the first decades of commercial oil production in colonial Trinidad, resurfaced again as a raison d'être of the postcolonial state. The fantasy of limitless production is called upon at crucial moments to secure political order against clamors for radical democratic futures. For Williams, it proved to be his savior; for Trinbagonian working people, it appeared at first as deliverance, then as damnation.

The state's masquerade of power is never absolute. Its aspiration to permanence "has constantly to be 'worked on,' maintained, renewed, revised."[34] Though they generate impressions of boundless productive potential, fossil fuels and the political projects they underwrite depend on perpetual projects of renewal. Fossil fuels, in other words, cannot fully dispense with their material contingencies. Oil's constitutive "magic," following Fernando Coronil, only extends insofar as it is held together by delicate assemblies of capital and infrastructure.[35]

As T&T's postcolonial bureaucracy consolidated around extractive rents and export revenues, political power interlocked with the productive technologies and market futures of oil and natural gas. Sovereignty, understood as a practice of securing political order through violent coercion and the manufacture of consent, came to rest on the anticipated futures of extractive industries. Under the petro-state masquerade, even when energy resources are depleted, discoveries of new reserves ritually postpone the impending exhaustion of fossil fuels.[36] The fantastic properties of oil lie in their ability to draw the boundaries of the political. While the Trinbagonian 1970s were characterized by a dissident political consciousness that exceeded the strictures of parliamentary order, it was oil that secured this order against radical alternatives.[37] As the history of T&T bears out, it was not multinational capital but revolutionary socialism that once appeared predestined. This chapter is a story of how divinations about petroleum carried the day.

Money Eh No Problem

On October 6, 1973, the fourth Arab–Israeli War began when Egyptian and Syrian forces launched a campaign to reclaim territory lost to Israel during the Six-Day War of 1967. As the skirmish continued, the United States conducted an emergency airlift of arms and supplies to Israel to combat the Soviet-backed troops. In an act of coordinated defiance, the Persian Gulf member states of OPEC deployed the oil weapon by raising the posted price of oil by 70 percent and implementing monthly production cuts of 5 percent until the US-backed Israeli forces retreated from the occupied territory.[38] Furthermore, they imposed a total embargo on crude supplies to the United States due to their continued support of Israel. When the embargo concluded in March 1974, the price of oil had quadrupled from US$2.90 to US$11.65 per barrel.

Oil markets were the pivot on which Trinbagonian fortunes turned. The sudden rise in oil prices, like the military incursion in the Sinai Peninsula and the Golan Heights, arrived unexpectedly. With elections scheduled for December 2 to confirm Williams's successor as political leader of the PNM, the party convention voted overwhelmingly to request that he stand for reelection. Whether he ever intended to step down is unclear, but the market upheaval provided ample cause for him to reconsider. The unexpected bull market for oil offered a welcome respite from the embattled course of economic development in the years prior. After a decade of uncertainty, certainty arrived in a matter of weeks.

It had not always been so. In the years after political independence in August 1962, oil in Trinidad was considered a limited reservoir of government revenue. In October 1965, Williams discussed oil as a rapidly deteriorating fountainhead of national development:

> The production of oil in Trinidad and Tobago, from our soil in Moruga, in Forest Reserve and so on has been steadily declining and is becoming quite serious.... Whilst that decline is taking place in Trinidad, everyday [sic], every week, every year you read of some important new discovery in the outside world; it was Nigeria the other day[,] now it's the North Sea[,] and in the Middle East every year some big new field is found.[39]

Before the coalition of Gulf States triggered the oil weapon, Williams understood his limitations as the political guardian of a small oil exporter overshadowed by the swing producers of the Arabian Peninsula. Though strategically important due to its location in the southern Atlantic, Trinidad could scarcely hope to impact the market price of oil as its counterparts in OPEC later did. This state of dependency was troubling to Williams. "We are so particularly vulnerable," he reasoned, "because so much of what we produce has to be sold outside, our population is so small it cannot provide an adequate domestic market."[40] An undying dependence on oil could not sustain his development ambitions or the expectations of a postcolonial citizenry. Out of necessity, his government pursued diversification into other industries.

Alongside the steady exploitation of oil reserves, Williams advocated for a program of agricultural development and import substitution to mitigate the national food-import bill. PNM pamphlets preached the virtues of local food. In July 1963, the party's Women's League held a "Buy and Eat Local Fiesta" that included a showcase of Creole, Indian, and Chinese cuisines, and the sale of food plants for home cultivation.[41] The government encouraged the production of staple food crops such as carrots, onions, and potatoes and export crops such as corn and soybeans.[42] Public advocacy efforts included television and radio broadcasts, public lectures, youth agricultural camps, and livestock and agriculture exhibitions.[43] As sugar production continued to slide and preferential export markets withdrew in concert with the United Kingdom's entry into the European Economic Community, the sugar industry began its last lap.[44]

Anticipating a decline in oil production, the government convened a commission of enquiry into the oil industry headed by the Iranian national Baghair Mostofi in 1963. The report of the Mostofi Commission, published in 1964, enumerated several dozen recommendations that included the establishment of a Ministry of Petroleum and Mines to coordinate governance of the national energy sector and a shift in focus to "efficient and low-cost refining" in light of competition from Venezuela and the Arabian peninsula.[45] Oil production rebounded considerably between 1965 and 1968 due to onshore drilling in Texaco's Guayaguayare field and offshore production from the North and East Soldado concessions. This did little to mitigate concerns regarding the long-term viability of the energy sector. The persistence of low oil prices, the relatively low volume of Trinidad oilfields, and the high costs associated with the exploitation of their complex geology discouraged potential investors.

To streamline the refining sector, the Mostofi report recommended a reduction in the labor force through phased retirements, layoffs, and the adoption of automated technologies to curb operational expenditure. Moreover, the commission proposed changes to the fiscal and legal terms governing the oil industry to encourage exploration to increase proven reserves, grow refining and downstream facilities, and facilitate the construction of industrial plants through five-year tax holidays for pioneer enterprises that made use of crude oil and natural gas supplies.

Trade union cadres objected to the proposed austerity measures. Relations between the government and organized labor grew more contentious in the years prior to the February Revolution. The Industrial Stabilisation Act of 1965 (ISA) signaled the betrayal of labor interests by the recently inaugurated PNM government, outlawing strikes in essential-service sectors such as electricity, water services, and health and medicine. The ISA undercut radical currents within the union ranks and effectively pitted the erstwhile anticolonial statesman, Williams, against the base of the mass party that had carried him to power after the march on Chaguaramas.[46]

The relationship between organized labor and the state strained as the latter failed to deliver on key development milestones. The *Third Five-Year Plan* hinged on its revised approach to agriculture as an import-substitution mechanism "to make the economy more internally self-reliant" and steady the economy through the expansion of the manufacturing sector.[47] When employment rates stagnated, it exposed the bankruptcy of this growth model. Its spark erupted in the Black Power uprising of 1970.

The Mostofi Commission maintained that the troubling circumstances in Trinidad emerged out of a changing world of oil extraction and refining. While oil and natural gas production had previously been concentrated in the Americas, the expansion of the Arabian oil theater after World War II undercut the strategic import of Trinidadian crudes. Although Trinidad once served as the principal wartime supplier of oil to the British Royal Navy, its diminishing role in an expanded geography of fossil fuels generated little optimism for the future.

If oil production in Trinidad terminated entirely, world markets or petroleum-dependent industries elsewhere would suffer few repercussions. At this moment, Williams and his compatriots held few chips with which to bargain. Shell began a phased retrenchment of four hundred workers in January 1967 as it scaled back its local operations. British Petroleum (BP) followed shortly after by cutting its active workforce in Trinidad as it refocused investment on the more lucrative frontier of Alaska. When BP declared its intent to liquidate its holdings in Trinidad, the government appealed to Shell and Texaco to take over its productive assets. However, both declined as they joined BP in pursuing other extractive frontiers. With BP set to depart, the OWTU saw fit to resuscitate its long-standing call to nationalize the oil industry, outlining its proposal in a memorandum that encouraged the government to tender a buyout to BP.[48]

Williams balked at first, citing fears that Trinidad lacked the technical capacity to take over the BP operations and risked frightening investors by adopting an aggressive stance toward nationalization. Instead, he hedged his bets by entering a joint venture with a minor American company, the Texas-based Tesoro Petroleum Company, and agreed to purchase BP's assets for US$22 million—more than US$7 million above their appraised value.[49] The joint acquisition signaled a turn away from the industrialization-by-invitation model that had defined the early post-independence period and the adoption of a model of state intervention. Rather than an ideological commitment to national ownership, the partial nationalization of BP holdings was a pragmatic response to Trinidad's diminutive station in the world of oil and gas operations. On the one hand, Williams had few options other than nationalization to contain dwindling production and the flight of energy multinationals. On the other, the joint-venture model allowed him to meet the demands of the trade unions without alarming foreign investors.

The state-directed model of industrial development sprang out of economic necessity. But it would take on a new character as trade unionists, youth activists, and guerrillas gained prominence in the decade to come. In the final months of 1973, Williams opened a series of broadcasted speeches on "the energy crisis" to forecast the local impacts of the OPEC embargo.[50] When the Christmas holiday neared in 1973, Williams remained cautiously optimistic as the world adjusted to the renewed tensions in the Levant and their still-uncertain impact on the market futures of oil. His ambitions in the short term remained modest.

In his 1974 New Year's Day address, he warned of the disastrous effects of the oil crisis on food prices and local refineries and manufacturing industries that depended on imported fuel supplies. Williams insisted that any windfall revenue accrued after the embargo should finance food production and industrial facilities to fuel a new national economy. He underscored the latter point: "We must have something concrete and tangible to show when the crisis is all over—a new petrochemical complex, the realisation of Point Lisas...a substantial number of additional jobs in new spheres of economic activity."[51] As oil prices continued to rise, however, his cautionary sentiment gave way to an enthusiastic embrace of national communion and fete.

Efforts to demonstrate tangible returns from the windfall initiated a period of state investment in the energy sector and other productive enterprises. The state-led development of petrochemical and steel production facilities at Point Lisas figured prominently in this phase of national economic planning. The spike in oil revenue, however, permitted the government to pursue a greater stake in the upstream and refining sectors. Following the nationalization of BP in 1969, the Trinbagonian government acquired the operations of Shell in 1974 when the multinational aimed to refocus its efforts on more-lucrative ventures in the North Sea and the United States. Through the buyout, the government assumed ownership of the Shell refinery in Point Fortin and formed the Trinidad and Tobago Oil Company (TRINTOC) to manage its industrial assets.

Encouraged by booming energy markets and his electoral victory in 1976, Williams infamously declared, "Money is no problem" in a ceremony held for the Trinbagonian sprinter Hasely Crawford after his gold-medal performance in the 100-meter dash at the Montreal Olympic Games. His words diverged from his prior emphasis on disciplined austerity. The boom era was in full swing. His boisterous quip captured a renewed faith in the postcolonial state to steward an era of economic prosperity. Yet, it did not prevent his words from being satirized by the calypsonians Bomber, Chalkdust, and Shorty, who enumerated the persistence of social ills against his hopeful declaration.

For example, on "Money Eh No Problem," Shorty cuts through the celebratory rhetoric of the petrodollar boom. His lyrics enumerate a series of grievances in public utilities ("That dirty water we have to drink / WASA [Water and Sewage Authority] say it clean but it smell is stink"); housing ("So much of our people on the streets today / And we can't build a home for them to stay"); civic works ("Our roads are the worst in the Caribbean / We have the most traffic jams you have ever seen"); and corruption ("millions of dollars going down the drain").[52] While oil may have saved Williams, it did not insulate him entirely from the rhythms of popular criticism.

The oil boom ignited a flurry of state investments to harness hydrocarbon resources and generate added value through downstream industries.[53] At the same time, it resuscitated desires for individual affluence. The boom promised to elevate T&T from a condition of foreign dependence to a state-directed program of energy-based industrialization. Crude oil prices ensured that Trinidad oil refineries would operate at capacity, and the abundance of natural gas lent itself to proposals for gas-intensive products such as iron, steel, petrochemicals, and fertilizers. Whereas a decade earlier, Williams considered oil and gas a sector to be exploited before its near-term exhaustion, he now spoke of Trinbagonian industrial futures with an aura of certainty. Money, indeed, was no problem.

This investment profile aligned closely with industrialization efforts across the postcolonial world, in which aspirations to modernity were staked to high-modernist infrastructure projects—chief among them, the Aswan Dam in Gamal Abdel Nasser's Egypt, the Akosombo Dam in Kwame Nkrumah's Ghana, and steel plants in Jawaharlal Nehru's India. For Williams, his masquerade of permanence ran through Point Lisas and its downstream industrial works. When Williams first announced his retirement in 1973, the future of the postcolonial state remained in flux. The arrival of the oil boom renewed a provisional lease on postcolonial modernity through Williams's return to the parliamentary sphere and the preservation of de facto one-party rule under his previously embattled PNM.[54]

The oil boom financed the construction of the Point Lisas Industrial Estate on the former sugar-plantation lands of central Trinidad. By generating opportunities for gainful employment and opening additional streams of government revenue, the boom partially appeased the masses of working people who had troubled Williams. Under pressure from outside and within, the postcolonial state negotiated provisional class compromises between capital and labor by adopting an interventionist role in economic affairs. And so, Williams's desire to construct "something concrete and tangible" from the windfall of the oil boom rested on the promise of Point Lisas.

Go for Steel

In January 1975, the Trinidad and Tobago Ministry of Petroleum and Mines convened a landmark summit to debate the "Best Use of Our Petroleum Resources." In an opening address to the government ministers and corporate officials in attendance, Williams outlined his priorities for the national energy sector. As the prime minister of one of the "oldest but smallest oil-producing countries of the world," he called for the full utilization of existing reserves and new techniques to unlock previously unexploited deposits of oil and natural gas.[55] Moreover, he emphasized the need for greater state participation in the oil industry through product-sharing contracts, government acquisition of drilling operations, and investment in downstream petrochemical, iron, steel, and LNG production facilities. Finally, he insisted that the windfall petrodollars be directed toward the "general economic development of Trinidad and Tobago."[56] Curating a program of economic nationalism, Williams mined the oil boom to restore faith in the political vanguard of the PNM.

The history of the Point Lisas Industrial Estate began in the preindependence period in 1956, when a cohort of Trinidadian businessmen shepherded by Bobby Montano established the South Trinidad Chamber of Industry and Commerce to support the economic and social development of its sugar- and oil-producing regions.[57] His initial proposal centered on the construction of a deepwater port in San Fernando in response to the construction of a harbor facility in Port of Spain that allowed cargo ships to circumvent south Trinidad. This shook the local business sector. To attract government support, Montano paired the port development with a proposal for a sprawling industrial estate. His vision for heavy industry met ridicule as he failed to secure private investors or negotiate a lease for the land concessions at Point Lisas.

Montano was soon vindicated. The discovery of oil and gas by Amoco in three offshore campaigns in 1969, 1971, and 1972 inspired the government to echo his call for industrial facilities to make use of natural gas feedstock. And the arrival of the oil boom allowed the state to assume a new role as entrepreneur. The prophesized rise of Point Lisas came to fruition when the state assumed control over the Point Lisas Industrial Port Development Corporation. More than a dozen proposals for industrial projects were considered between 1974 and 1977, including iron and steel, petrochemical, aluminum, LNG, and polyester textile plants.[58] In all, five such projects were implemented—either through public-private partnerships or state ownership—tallying a total expenditure of TT$3.2 billion. Moreover, the aesthetic features of industrial expansion graced an impatient populace with the appearance of progress. As ground was broken at Point Lisas, Williams luxuriated in the glory of the oil boom and the development it had wrought. "Right on this very dock," he observed, "two of the largest cranes ever installed anywhere in the Caribbean ... are now in the process of being installed. These things are happening, they are there for all to see—the public, the private sector, the Government Ministers, and indeed, even the press and the sceptics."[59]

Tringen, an ammonia production facility, came onstream first in 1977 as a joint venture between the T&T government and the American multinational W. R. Grace. It was followed, in turn, by the state Iron and Steel Company of Trinidad and Tobago (ISCOTT) in 1981; Fertilizer Company of Trinidad and Tobago (Fertrin), a gas-based fertilizer plant built as a joint venture between the state and Amoco in 1981; and state-owned urea and methanol production facilities in 1984.[60] Through state initiatives of this sort, Williams projected visions of a stable and prosperous future. In an address on the problems of industrialization directed toward critics of the costly state enterprises at Point Lisas, he reasoned: the nation must "proceed in an orderly manner to use our oil revenue ... to create an industrial base so that when our energy leaves the shores, it carries with it substantial added value and a better marketability, and provides a more secure existence for the future when the oil boom is over."[61] For Williams, investments in petrochemicals and heavy metals masqueraded as stable markets to insulate the country from the volatility of crude oil prices.

In the eyes of state officials, Point Lisas represented more than the sum of its industrial facilities and port infrastructure. Rather, it indexed a transition from a colonial economy to a vibrant postcolonial modernity of heavy industry. "Here at Point Lisas sugar cane gives way to wire rods," Williams boasted.[62] As he had it, sugar represented the backwardness of a colonial society characterized by racial hierarchy and monocrop dependency.

In wire rods—the signature commodity of the recently opened ISCOTT facility—he envisioned a secure market that would house an emergent Caribbean modernity. Condemning those opposed to the government industrialization program, he derided proponents of a "brown sugar economy" while extolling the virtues of steel as quintessentially more solid and permanent than the cane plots of yesteryear.[63]

If iron and steel were the structure, oil and gas provided their foundation as the feedstock for industrial works. In 1978, Williams surveyed the architecture of modernization in the following terms: "Energy has become a precious commodity in the world and those who need it for survival come to us.... It is a commodity which can trigger off the industrialization programme which cheap labour and fiscal incentives could not hope to achieve."[64] His remarks were a far cry from his restrained tenor in the early postindependence period. Small as Trinidad was, it appeared at the center of a world economy steeped in oil in the eyes of ambitious bureaucrats. When metropolitan countries sought their fix, the smalltime peddler rose to the occasion.[65]

Once construction of the ISCOTT plant began, the scholar-turned-statesman situated Point Lisas in a centuries-long narrative of Caribbean economic history. Williams had argued in his magnum opus *Capitalism and Slavery* (1944) that the labor power of enslaved Africans generated the necessary surplus to finance the rise of capitalism; he cited the use of iron in the civic works of the Industrial Revolution as evidence of iron's enduring value to modern industrial development. Where beet sugar supplanted the sugar plantations of the Caribbean and tumbled the region into economic turmoil, iron and steel were equated with stability and permanence. Williams later disclosed, "I understand what Nasser meant, when he showed me proudly his steel plant, by saying, since you have hydrocarbons, go for steel."[66] To underscore his point, he compared the erratic behavior of raw sugar prices to the price of wire rods, which rose steadily each year from 1972 to 1978.[67]

This juxtaposition of sugar and steel—which conveniently disregarded the circumstances that guided their market behavior in the half decade prior—enforced a developmental telos that relegated sugar and agriculture to a primitive mode of production and elevated steel and heavy industry as the zenith of postcolonial modernization. As Williams reasoned, "A lot of people can grow sugar and perhaps grow it better than we can, but not too many can make steel, and can not [sic] make steel because they have no energy and that is the difference."[68]

Riffing on calypsonian Black Stalin's composition of the same name, Williams titled his party convention speech in 1979 "The Caribbean Man" and placed the industrialization push in a longer arc of Caribbean history. In a turgid address, Williams rehearsed the introduction of enslaved African labor to the Caribbean, the emergence of autonomous maroon settlements throughout the Americas, and the creative and cultural products of dance, music, and religion forged through syncretic traditions. He detailed the genocide of Amerindian peoples in the Caribbean, the imperial ambitions of European explorers, and the "ferocious resistance" to colonization that Indigenous and African peoples waged in scattered uprisings epitomized by the Túpac Amaru rebellion of 1780.[69] Last, he addressed the arrival of Indian, Chinese, and Javanese workers to meet the endless demand for cheap and pliable labor. Williams revised Black Stalin's refrain ("Them is one race / From the same place / That make the same trip / On the same ship") by describing Asian Caribbean peoples as "a next race from the same place to make the same trip on the same ship."[70] In his narrative juxtaposition of the *kala pani* and the Middle Passage, Williams located the inchoate potential of the Caribbean Man in the cumulative labor of African and Asian peoples in the plantation Americas.[71] Trinidad, and its unfolding industrial promise, composed the formative ground of Caribbean modernity.

While the ISCOTT facility had not yet opened, it represented a collective ascendance from backwardness and dependency to civilization and sovereignty. Williams framed the proverbial transition from the plantation economy to industrial modernity in terms of colonial racial divisions and postcolonial transcendence:

> Them is not one race as I have shown. Them is several races juxtaposed, bringing in from outside what they all proceed to modify, but not integrating the various strands. Them is all the races, but if there is a national territory, if there is a flag, if there are the trappings of a national state, what is lacking after the centuries is a Nation, one and indivisible, presenting one united front against all outside forces impeding our development. If it is like baying at the moon to preach this for the Caribbean area whatever that area may be, it is eminently practicable to work for it in Trinidad and Tobago alone.[72]

Williams, who surveyed anthropological theories of Caribbean culture and society in his short monograph, *The Negro in the Caribbean* (1942), borrowed the plural society thesis of the Jamaican sociologist M. G. Smith to forecast a coming moment of industrialization and national unity.[73] While sugar production had relied upon a colonial separation of races into distinct laboring units, the postcolonial nationalist project of steel production and energy industrialization was imagined as a project of creolization. Staking this project to the masculine icon of the Caribbean Man, Williams framed the transition to heavy industry as a pathway for the "consolidation of patriarchal heteronormativity" against the matrifocal family units of the plantation.[74] He peppered his speech with a nationalist charge, spouting the industrial pathway as a means of "bringing in all them races, acknowledging all their contributions, elevating lowly castes, dignifying despised colours, achieving a syncretism here and a new autonomy there, raising up the poor and the lowly and giving them a positive stake in our society."[75]

In sugar, Williams conjured the trappings of a plantation economy and racial dominance. In steel, he forecasted the unending expansion of industrial modernity, bourgeois family values, and multiracial democracy. His confidence rested on the assumption that demand for steel would continue in perpetuity. If the price of steel continued to rise, going for steel would secure the economic future of T&T under the guardianship of the PNM. He concluded his address with the familiar party salutation: "Great is the PNM and it will prevail."[76]

His certainty that iron and steel futures were preordained by the currents of Atlantic history demonstrates the continued purchase of a modernist vision of Caribbean political futures. While theories of modernization depicted the Third World as a site of perpetual backwardness, lagging behind the advances of its metropolitan counterparts, Williams fashioned a counter-narrative in which the spoils of industrial development would integrate Trinbagonian racial polities under a syncretic unity in the figure of the Caribbean Man—a racially transcendent yet explicitly masculine representative of postcolonial nationhood.[77] Steel served as the ballast for his narrative. Williams did not acknowledge the dependence on multinational investment to sustain oil and gas production. Money was no problem. Hydrocarbons appeared limitless, interminable. With an assist from the calypsonian Black Stalin, Williams masqueraded steel as certainty.

Go South

For Williams, the oil boom secured PNM rule through the accumulation of windfall profits and their timely investment in state-led development schemes. For the Trinbagonian masses, it opened pathways for gainful employment. The trade unionist Cecil Paul counted himself among this new class of labor:

> Basically I was an oil worker. I started in the oil industry at a very young age. In those days, to make a fortune, or to make a good life, you had work in the oil industry, you had to get involved in the oil industry. There's a saying, "Go south!" "Go south, you know?" Whether you're a tradesman, whether you're a clerical worker, whatever it is, you go south. They paid better than public servants, better than teachers, better than university professors! ... So that is how I got involved, and quite of few of us! Because I wasn't from the south, I was from the north. But you had to make it, if you wanted to have a good chance you had to go south.[78]

The geography of Trinidad is troubled by undying myths. The capital city of Port of Spain in northwest Trinidad is celebrated as a financial and diplomatic hub due to its cosmopolitan appearance and glistening skyline. By contrast, central and south Trinidad are simultaneously characterized by the industrial hubs of Point Lisas, San Fernando, and Point Fortin and the pastoral landscapes of their surrounding rural settlements. African Trinidadians are commonly understood to be concentrated in the urban municipalities extending eastward from Port of Spain along the Northern Range, while Indian Trinidadians predominantly reside south of Caroni in the erstwhile sugar belt.

Crude generalizations of this variety are contradicted by neglected truths: the impressive architecture of downtown Port of Spain is financed by state coffers supported by refining, petrochemical, and LNG operations located in central and south Trinidad. This racial geography is further unsettled by the prevalence of Indian Trinidadians in north and west Trinidad and African Trinidadians throughout the central Trinidad sugar belt, the "deep south," and the southwest peninsula—not to mention communities of other racial or ethnic backgrounds such as Chinese, Syrian, and white Trinidadians, or the ubiquity of dougla persons of both African and Indian ancestry.[79]

The boom era threw this imagined geography into further disarray. During this period, young Trinidadians and Tobagonians ventured south to pursue the postcolonial good life. Their entry into the productive orbit of energy industries enlarged union membership and invigorated a radical faction of the OWTU that had emerged under the leadership of President

General George Weekes from 1962 onward.[80] If Port of Spain embodied the locus of parliamentary state power, the south captured the power of the Trinbagonian working people much as it had in 1937.

This collective spirit spawned the United Labour Front (ULF)—an alliance of progressive trade unions and leftist political organizations. Initially convened as a coalition of four unions—the OWTU, the All Trinidad Sugar Estates and Factory Workers' Trade Union, the Transport and Industrial Workers Union, and the Island-Wide Cane Farmers Trade Union—the ULF gained traction during the oil boom as the labor of ordinary Trinbagonians yielded dramatic windfalls that the government looked to reinvest in Point Lisas. This led to significant dissatisfaction among the working people of T&T and strike fever spread once again across the nation.

Stalled labor negotiations with management at Texaco, the local industrial equipment and services conglomerate Neal & Massy, and government-run sugar estates inspired a mass demonstration by the ULF on March 18, 1975, that drew a crowd of several thousand union members and sympathizers. Citing the absence of a permit, police forces violently dispersed the march for "peace, bread, and justice" with tear-gas grenades and brute force. In what came to be known as "Bloody Tuesday," thirty-two trade union leaders were arrested as the row between the state and working people intensified.

The events of Bloody Tuesday led to the formalization of the ULF as a political party in January 1976; it sought to displace a popular PNM government hostile to organized labor. Yet, the decision to contest national elections in 1976 did not garner universal support from its membership. Some factions from the radical left wing of the ULF objected to participation in bourgeois elections and the bureaucratization of the ULF through a centralized party leadership. Like the Black Power movement before it, the growing ULF coalition encompassed a diverse set of political factions, including the Marxist–Leninist United National Independence Party, the Maoist-influenced National Movement for the True Independence of Trinidad and Tobago (NAMOTI), and the Left-libertarian New Beginning Movement. As the boom persevered and the bevy of oil and industrial workers grew, the membership and influence of the ULF coalition gained momentum. Heeding populist demands for a "piece of the action," as Black Stalin crooned on his eponymous 1976 calypso, the ULF hoped to assume state power with a platform to nationalize large-scale industries and expand social welfare provisions.

As Ray Kiely argues in his labor history of Trinidad, the scattered character of the ULF membership ensured that "the party never adopted a clear political attitude towards parliament," which left the party open to blatant mischaracterizations as an "Indian party" whose Black members were limited to the card-carrying OWTU rank and file.[81] When Williams and his subordinates cast the ULF as a parochial defender of Indian interests—in contrast to the creole nationalist rhetoric advanced by the PNM—they exploited racial orthodoxy to quell a working-class revolt. In the end, the ULF carried only ten seats in the elections of 1976 to the PNM's twenty-four.

The defeat proved decisive. Despite any initial skepticism toward participation in national elections, the ULF had entered the fray with hopes of mounting a serious challenge to the PNM, if not carrying an unexpected parliamentary majority. The paltry results indicated that the ULF had not made the necessary inroads with the working people who had benefited from the investment policies of the PNM. Moreover, the disappointing returns did little to instill faith in electoral democracy among the insurrectionists of the NAMOTI faction, who insisted that the "revolutionary elements within the ULF must intensify the class struggle within it and help the masses under the influence of the ULF cast off their illusions about elections and the parliamentary road."[82] The disillusionment with the pursuit of electoral politics led to a split in the party and its untimely collapse.

While postmortem analyses of the general elections of 1976 have shed light on issues of sectarianism and racialism that condemned the ULF to a premature end, the party failed most spectacularly in its efforts to construct a compelling counter-narrative to the discourse of creole nationalism and the figure of the Caribbean Man as the proletarian heir to the spoils of the oil boom.[83] Not only did the oil boom secure the borders of a once-volatile political order, but it also drilled the manifold tendencies of a Trinbagonian Left into an ill-fated electoral strategy that reinforced the PNM stronghold on state power.

The oil boom marked a period of contradiction. The rapid influx of petrodollars buoyed the organizational capacity of a Trinbagonian working class deeply enmeshed in the technical operations of the energy sector. While this inspired new challenges to PNM rule, expressions of radical politics increasingly confined themselves to the parliamentary arena. Whereas the preceding decade featured militant labor struggles that culminated in the popular uprisings of 1970, the prospect of boundless profits and limitless development raised by the boom era renewed faith in a Westminster system of government.

The peculiar qualities of fossil fuels as concentrated stores of mineral energy condition an orientation to the future as a "limitless horizon of growth."[84] In the small-island petro-state of T&T, the expansion of fossil fuel production permitted the stewards of a dependent postcolonial economy to lay claim to an independent future for Trinidad and the Greater Caribbean. When oil was perceived as a finite resource, postcolonial orthodoxy appeared in peril. The assurance that oil production would persist against market fluctuations and other production obstacles secured the terms of political order for an elite postcolonial bureaucracy. As an energy and steel economy, T&T would prosper. At its helm, the PNM would prevail. The future was certain.

Fueling Independence

The experiment in steel did not proceed according to plan. Although Williams championed steel as the vanguard commodity of a Trinbagonian ascent to modernity, ISCOTT proved to be the greatest commercial failure of his touted state-owned industrial enterprises.

As the first independent state venture at Point Lisas, ISCOTT opened in 1980 to great fanfare. Accruing costs of more than a billion Trinidad and Tobago dollars, popular assessment of the state-led industrialization strategy hinged on the feasibility of steel production and the presence of ample markets for intermediate or finished products.[85] The design of the ISCOTT plant sought to unlock the full benefits of Trinidad's abundant natural gas resources. The choice of direct reduction technology allowed the government to make use of natural gas as a reducing agent and to limit operating costs in contrast to conventional blast-furnace methods of iron refining. In this metallurgical process, hydrogen (H_2) and carbon monoxide (CO) derived from gas are used to remove oxygen from liquid iron oxide. The resulting direct-reduced iron, also known as *sponge iron*, is commonly used as a feedstock for steel production.

Due to an abundance of natural gas as a source of cheap energy, ISCOTT produced sponge iron and finished steel at competitive rates. Yet, the project encountered unanticipated technical difficulties. Excess sponge iron produced for export—rather than for use in domestic steel production—was commissioned following a deal with a Brazilian supplier of iron ore that agreed to repurchase the refined iron for use in Brazil's steel mills. However, the Brazilian foreign-exchange crisis, sparked by declining commodity prices in the early 1980s, quashed the agreement and left Trinidad with surplus iron and no prospective buyers. Export options were further constrained by a geochemical oddity that rendered iron from the Trinidad plant especially vulnerable to reoxidation, which reverses the industrial process of purification when exposed to air and moisture during maritime transport.[86] Rust spread.

As the geographer Andrew Barry reminds us, metals "are not the inert objects they are sometimes imagined to be, merely shaped by social and economic forces. They are elements of lively dynamic assemblages that may act in unanticipated ways, serving as the catalyst for political events."[87] The commonplace but profoundly mistaken supposition that metals are unflinchingly solid guides the operations of metal production and postcolonial statecraft alike. Just as metals are not pristine objects that exist in isolation from external pressures, neither is the postcolonial state as independent as it appears to be.

Although metals are dynamic substances like their liquid counterparts, we describe metallurgical refining as a unidirectional series of chemical reactions through which purified metals are derived from ores. The direct reduction process of iron refining, for instance, involves the extraction of carbon monoxide and hydrogen from natural gas through a chemical interaction with steam or carbon dioxide. The steam-reforming and carbon dioxide–reforming techniques are expressed in the following equations:

$$CH_4 + H_2O = CO + 3H_2$$

or

$$CH_4 + CO_2 = 2CO + 2H_2.$$

The carbon monoxide and hydrogen byproducts are then used to reduce iron oxide into a purified metallic iron:

$$3CO + 3H_2 + 2Fe_2O_3 = 4Fe + 3CO_2 + 3H_2O.$$

The symbolic representation of these processes presumes a closed system of chemical interactions. But although purified metals may appear stable, they are not insulated from external forces and environmental contingencies. Outside the pristine order of chemical equations, metals are exposed to conditions that generate corrosion or rust.

The troubles extended to steel as well. In 1979, when Williams proclaimed that steel markets would expand in perpetuity, he echoed the findings of consultants from Booz Allen Hamilton, who recommended that steel production be focused on wire rods due to heightened demand from the US and Canada. In a stroke of irony, the destiny of the Caribbean Man rested on the market projections of a US consulting firm.[88]

Booz, Allen, and Hamilton missed the mark. A worldwide glut in steel production led to significantly depressed prices throughout the 1980s, and demand from key markets lagged behind anticipated margins — US imports of wire rods in 1980 amounted to only half the projected total, due to protectionist tariffs successfully lobbied for by American producers. Canada emerged in the 1980s as a net exporter, rather than a buyer, of the same commodity. After steel production began in Trinidad, ISCOTT suffered massive losses of TT$1,132,700,000 between 1983 and 1986. Steel — intended as a buffer to secure political and economic futures against the comparative unpredictability of oil and gas prices — proved to be an albatross.

Iron and steel markets, like the metals they trade in, are not as characteristically solid as they appear. Demand for steel does not expand interminably, as Williams presumed. Moreover, a closer examination of its physical properties unsettles an approach that takes states of matter to be stable and absolute. As the ISCOTT saga demonstrates, the trade of iron and steel products is complicated by factors that may reverse processes of industrial refining and purification. No metal is pure; rather, refined metals are always susceptible to corrosion and reoxidation. In the search for export markets for Trinidad iron pellets, this retrograde process of reoxidation undermined the development ambitions of the postcolonial state. Williams followed the instructive leads of Nasser and Nehru in his bid to "go for steel." In this view, steel would secure the future of the postcolonial state through centralized planning and an elite vertical bureaucracy. He did not anticipate rust.

For a small place like T&T, the beleaguered ISCOTT project proved especially disastrous. As oil markets deflated, the experiment in the postcolonial state–as–entrepreneur was cut short. After reaching a peak price of US$35 per barrel in 1980, prices receded before dropping dramatically from US$27 to under US$10 in 1986. Steel promised to stabilize a national economy against the cycles of energy boom and bust. Instead, the iron and steel complex surrendered to technical challenges and failed to secure markets for its signature products. The Sisyphean task of postcolonial modernity began once again. The future, again, was uncertain.

Party Done

In 1980, Lord Relator received his first and only crown as the Calypso Monarch for his dual compositions "Food Prices" and "Take Ah Rest Mr. Prime Minister." After decrying the everyday perils of inflation in "Food Prices," Relator directed the latter calypso toward Williams himself. Rather than the brash confrontation that characterized the Black Power uprising of a decade prior, Relator suggests modestly that Williams has run out of steam:

> No lights, no telephone and no water
> We in the middle of a big power failure
> I'm sorry but the breakdown is governmental
> And is because of fatigue, physical and mental[89]

Playfully indulging the double meaning of *power failure* as the twilight of the oil boom and the receding horizon of the PNM regime's survival, Relator makes his proposal plain:

> Now this is not an overthrow
> I eh saying that we must kick them out just so
> So please don't jump to any hasty conclusion
> And cause any confusion
> But they exhausted from working too long
> So before they suffer from a nervous breakdown
> As a loving nation we all could suggest
> That Dr. Williams and the PNM take a rest[90]

Relator's proposal that the prime minister to "take ah rest" proved all too timely. Thirteen months later, Williams died in office on March 29, 1981. The triumph of Trinbagonian political futures espoused at the height of the oil boom soon gave way to sobering assessments of the decade to come. His successor as prime minister, George Chambers, surveyed the uncertain terrain in the concluding lines of his January 1982 budget speech to Parliament. With a healthy dose of condescension, Chambers reasoned: "We can no longer permit our vision to be obscured by selfishness and the pursuit of instant affluence."[91] Instead, he extolled the virtues of austerity by closing with a soon-to-be-infamous line: "The fête is over and the country must go back to work."[92]

Though Chambers's tenure in office spanned more than a half decade, his insistence that the festive exuberance of the boom era had reached its dramatic conclusion also extended to the party rule of the PNM. As rates of unemployment peaked in the years that followed, popular support for the PNM dwindled. In the 1986 elections, the PNM retained just three seats in Parliament, with the remaining thirty-three carried by the National Alliance for Reconstruction (NAR) government. While the NAR coalition included several pro-labor factions, it inherited a floundering economy that limited its capacity to install the ambitious reforms proposed by organized labor in preceding decades. After futile attempts to revitalize economic growth through agriculture and tourism, the NAR embarked on a program of structural adjustment in accordance with International Monetary Fund (IMF) directives that included the devaluation of the Trinidad and Tobago dollar from an exchange rate of $3.60 to $4.25 against the US dollar in April 1988, the privatization of state industrial holdings, and salary decreases and job cuts in the public sector.[93]

The descent from the oil boom to IMF-imposed austerity marked the end of state-led industrialization and the arrival of free-market reforms that included cuts in public spending and the retrenchment of public-sector employees. Although Point Lisas failed to yield the expected returns, the NAR could ill afford to allow its industrial facilities to fold for good. Gas-based industries such as iron, steel, ammonia, and methanol required new supplies of gas. To encourage offshore exploration for additional oil and gas reserves, Prime Minister A. N. R. Robinson and his NAR government implemented cuts to the petroleum tax to facilitate multinational investment.

The aspiration to economic permanence proved little more than a pipe (or wire rod) dream. Indeed, the period of prosperity that followed the rapid increase in oil prices appeared to be a predestined outcome of Trinidad's geological wealth. Instead, it was the violent upheaval in the Levant and the machinations of a US corporate lobby that breathed new life into the Trinbagonian energy sector. Pace James, oil itself did not save Williams—the confluence of world events that returned foreign capital to Trinidadian shores did. In the throes of the boom, the petro-state masquerade made windfall profits appear to be the result of the ingenuity of technocratic planning and political leadership.

Oil is not an uncomplicated resource. It is produced by a complex array of technologies, infrastructures, and repertoires of governance that emerge alongside particular extractive geographies.[94] Often, hydrocarbons appear to us nonetheless as an uncomplicated furrow of petrodollar riches. It is this alchemy that allowed Williams to make a claim to fossil fuels as inexhaustible resources to fuel his vision of postcolonial transcendence.

Instructively, Williams staked his masquerade of permanence to steel. In contrast to the liquid character of crude hydrocarbons, the solid properties of steel deceptively appeared to safeguard against the multinational interests that Williams and his radical critics alike aimed to circumvent. Emboldened by the perceived solid character of steel, Williams envisioned an epoch of economic permanence fit to remedy a temporal chasm between the backwardness of colonial societies and the modernity of their metropolitan equivalents. Leftist political formations, guided by the historical determinism of Marxist–Leninist stages of development, equally subscribed to a narrative of the inevitable revolution that would follow the advance of industrial capital in the Caribbean. As David Scott recalls, postindependence radicals maintained that "revolutionary futures were not merely possible but *imminent*."[95] While Scott is particularly attentive to the tragic aftermaths of revolutionary socialist projects such as the New Jewel Movement in Grenada, his formulation is equally pertinent to the modes of state-directed modernization that Williams, Nehru, and Nasser endorsed. The Caribbean Man, as the embodiment of this transition to postcolonial modernity, rested on a mistaken assumption that steel and state power alike are permanent states of matter.

But states and steel are not as solid and permanent as they appear to be. Both are susceptible to their own forms of rust. At select moments and under particular conditions, the hyphenated relation of the nation-state is indeed subject to corrosion, deterioration, breakdown. The form assumed by something we call the state cannot be taken for granted.[96] Rust itself, as a visible byproduct of retrograde processes, provides a "historical record" of metals and their interaction with external forces.[97] The postcolonial state was like steel, but in a decidedly different fashion than Williams anticipated.

As the following chapter details, efforts to resuscitate boom-era fantasies of economic permanence hinged on the exploitation of Trinidad's offshore and deepwater hydrocarbon reserves. However, just as Williams fell short in his mission to "go for steel," his successors would struggle to make good on their ambitious forecasts for Trinidad's deepwater futures. Their masquerade of permanence would not hold. Although the state may appear solid, it bears traces of embattled pasts and suppressed insurgencies. The state masquerade involves a perpetual effort to purge traces of its own corrosive histories.

CHAPTER THREE

Deepwater Futures

I, least of all, expect any miracles. — C. L. R. James, *Party Politics in the West Indies* (1962)

On March 29, 2012, Prime Minister Kamla Persad-Bissessar announced the discovery of 48 million barrels of oil in the waters off the western coast of Trinidad. Brandishing two large jars of unrefined crude to the press corps in attendance, she christened the find as a "jubilee discovery" in anticipation of the fiftieth anniversary of political independence. Moreover, on the eve of a national holiday celebrating the Spiritual Baptist faith community, Persad-Bissessar reasoned that the discovery "did not happen by accident" but instead by divine intervention. She did not give thanks to Olokun, the Baptist orisha of material wealth and guardian of the ocean depths, however. Instead, she rehearsed the familiar adage "God is a Trini."

Carried to victory in May 2010 by a multiracial coalition of opposition parties, trade unions, and civil society organizations touted as the People's Partnership, Persad-Bissessar campaigned on a pledge to wrangle the spoils of the petro-state from the entrenched political elites of the People's National Movement. The prime minister echoed this pledge when she lauded the oil find for its impending windfall to finance development projects such as highways, hospitals, and recreational facilities. At the moment of her electoral victory, the masquerade of permanence had begun to give way. In 2005, crude oil production reached a peak daily average of 155,900 barrels before dwindling to its current output of less than 60,000 barrels per day. Natural gas reserves—which served as feedstock for the post-1973 expansion into iron, steel, and petrochemicals—dwindled as well.

But her message of deliverance landed as intended. As Brent Crosson observes, the saying "God is a Trini" often accompanies moments of collective good fortune as a proclamation of divine blessing and nationalist patrimony.[1] Invoked to punctuate the nation's world-famous Carnival, its location outside the Caribbean hurricane belt, or its tendency to fight above its proverbial weight in international sport and political affairs, in this instance it extolled the blessing of oil to reverse the tides of a flagging energy sector. The jubilee discovery tendered relief for Persad-Bissessar and her People's Partnership government. At a moment in which the hyphenated relation of the petro-state began to drift apart, miraculous resolution arrived in the form of offshore hydrocarbons. God, indeed, was a Trini.

After the discovery in the Southwest Soldado maritime field, though, commercial success remained elusive. Following Persad-Bissessar's announcement, her government contracted a floating production storage and offloading (FPSO) vessel with a little-known Mexican shipping firm, Marítima de Ecología. The public treasury dispensed a commissioning fee of US$1.25 million; the FPSO never arrived. As the offshore reserves laid dormant, benchmark crude markets peaked north of US$100 per barrel in June 2014 before dropping below US$45 per barrel by the following January. The development projects championed by her government were not insulated from negative price shocks. The 2015 national budget—initially pegged to an anticipated crude oil price of US$80 per barrel and natural gas price of US$2.75 per million British thermal units—deflated rapidly as the market spiral compelled a revised budget based on an oil price of US$45 and a gas price of US$2.25. Nevertheless, Persad-Bissessar's performance masked the protracted period between the moment of discovery and the production of first oil.

Conventional wisdom holds that the legitimacy of petro-states positively correlates with upswings in oil prices.[2] Boom markets reinforce the hyphenated equation of hydrocarbons and sovereign power. By conflating the materiality of oil with oil money, state power is consolidated through public expenditures on civic works and social programs.[3] Oil busts, conversely, are associated with fiscal crises and social disintegration. As the spectacle of oil wealth wanes alongside the contraction of markets or the depletion of reserves, the state is no longer taken for granted as a spectacular body that "appears suspended above society."[4]

By this token, Persad-Bissessar's staging of an oil discovery underscores postcolonial sovereignty as a performance directed toward audiences of external observers and internal subjects.[5] The peculiar resilience of the petro-state form in periods of low market prices demands greater scrutiny. In Trinidad and Tobago, the renaissance in North American onshore production curbed long-standing trade circuits with the United States as a primary export market for oil and liquid natural gas exports. As energy multinationals pursued frontiers elsewhere, a decline in crude oil and natural gas supplies imperiled downstream industries. While shallow-water finds provided short-term relief in the form of moderate gas reserves, petrochemical and refining facilities continued to operate below capacity and curtail profit margins for the state and its multinational partners. In this time of insecurity, the immense potential of the deepwater sector tendered a remedy for diminishing state coffers and sputtering onshore industrial works.

Indeed, innovations in extractive technology sparked a revolution in deepwater activity that accounts for more than 10 percent of global oil production. But deepwater ventures feature prohibitive costs and a low probability of success compared to conventional and shale production. Their risks are further exacerbated by long production cycles that typically comprise several years between the initial leasing of offshore blocks and first oil or gas. The immense potential of deepwater discoveries, which in some instances exceed a billion barrels of crude oil, commands multinational interest despite their catalog of risks.

Beginning with an initial bid round for deepwater acreage in 1998, state officials championed the potential of T&T's deepwater geology. In the decades since, a series of exploratory ventures failed to generate commercial quantities of oil. Yet, the masquerade of permanence endures. As Energy Minister Kevin Ramnarine opined in 2012, "The deepwater in Trinidad and Tobago is one of the holy grails of geologists who have long suspected its vast hydrocarbon potential."[6] Alongside a politics of austerity driven by declining production, elite actors in state ministries and private industry boast the geological features of the deepwater to forecast an imminent recovery in oil and gas production and the permanence of the Trinbagonian petro-state.

Sovereignty, as an aspirational political ideal, involves the pursuit of certainty. In the classical definition by Thomas Hobbes, sovereign power aspires to an absolute and unlimited authority over a commonwealth of subjects. Ethnographic inquiries into the margins and edges of contemporary state formations, in turn, have decentered the state as an a priori unit of analysis.[7] Probing those moments at which presumptive sovereign authority falters, anthropologies of the state regard sovereignty as a fiction of absolute rule that breaks down under empirical scrutiny. This critique is welcomed by anthropologists of the Caribbean who have long understood state sovereignty to be a discursive fiction that prescribes the political aspirations of postcolonial nation-states and putatively nonsovereign territories in the region.[8] At first glance, this tension between sovereignty as absolute and aspirational appears irreconcilable. Again, how can sovereignty at once be real *and* fictive, total *and* partial, uniform *and* dispersed?

A resolution to this tension demands an inquiry into the colonial origins of sovereignty. In her study of the early modern Atlantic World, the historian Lauren Benton argues that colonial sovereignty in the Americas did not entail absolute territorial control, but instead rested on the defense of "corridors and enclaves" stationed across contested geographies of Indigenous dispossession and imperial warfare.[9] Nevertheless, European cartographers represented colonial holdings as coherent geographies with definite borders between settler jurisdictions. In this regard, sovereignty is always sustained by masquerades of power in which the speculative map precedes the fortification of territory.[10] Likewise, the political form of the petro-state relies on its own masquerade in which the unrealized returns of extractive futures are called upon to confirm presumptive sovereign authorities. Whether these ventures are eventually successful is less important than the work they perform to preserve the terms of order in the present.

The study of the state requires us to inquire into the peculiar arrangements by which the incomplete political authority forged through corridors and enclaves—or flotillas of offshore rigs—masquerades as absolute. For the state form to function as intended, aspirational maps of colonial possessions and deepwater-exploration blocks must be accepted as the fact of the territory itself. The task of the critic, then, is to demonstrate how the speculative narratives crafted by sovereign actors—in corporate offices, conference facilities, public speeches, parliamentary forums, and technical ephemera—come to be taken for granted. When Persad-Bissessar held up two jars of crude as a harbinger of national progress, she deftly obscured the particulars of fossil fuel extraction and monetization. Instead, the future returns of an offshore discovery appeared certain. Such is the petro-state masquerade.

The Model

As the previous chapter details, state officials in the postindependence period pursued the expansion of extractive-resource and heavy-metal production to unify a racially and religiously heterogeneous populace. After the Black Power uprising of 1970 registered a formative challenge to Afro-Saxon political hegemony, the PNM government of Eric Williams financed a broad industrialization program to quell insurgent opposition and tighten the party stronghold on political affairs.[11] The course of development initiated under Williams cemented the postcolonial state as an elite bureaucracy tasked with the management of transnational capital and the creation of a racially harmonious postcolonial nation. Whereas oil was considered a limited and unpredictable resource, he identified iron and steel industries as bastions of economic permanence. The boom of 1973 breathed new life into a parliamentary state that Black Power insurgents confronted in their demands for radical democratic futures.

The expansion of the natural gas sector ensured the survival of Williams's PNM. As a lower-value product than crude oil, natural gas was of negligible import to the colonial economy in Trinidad. Associated gas occurs as a byproduct of crude oil production, and was historically regarded as an undesirable excess and burned off via flaring. But the creation of new uses for natural gas—plus the discovery of substantial offshore reserves in 1968—inspired state actors to harness and monetize its abundant gas resources. Exercising a claim to flared gas under the terms of existing production licenses, Williams commissioned two compressor platforms to collect associated gas for use in local power generation and a fledgling industrial and petrochemical sector.

The petrodollar boom financed a program of infrastructural expansion optimized to natural gas. In addition to its uses as a commercial fuel, natural gas as a combustion fuel is suited to a range of industrial applications for smelting and feedstock for petrochemical production. As with oil, natural gas development is divided into three phases: upstream, midstream, and downstream. The upstream includes the primary extraction of natural gas in its raw form, which consists principally of methane (CH_4). The midstream involves the processing of methane natural gas through the extraction of natural gas liquids (NGLs)—comprising higher alkanes such as ethane (C_2H_6), propane (C_3H_8), and butane (C_4H_{10})—and the removal of chemical impurities. The downstream sector encompasses the production

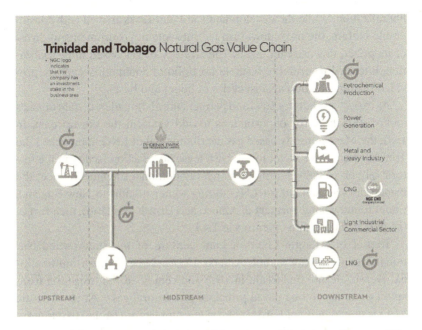

FIGURE 3.1. The value chain for Trinidad and Tobago's natural gas industry. Courtesy of National Gas Company, Trinidad and Tobago.

of finished products including LNG, fertilizers, heavy metals, and petrochemicals. Together, the upstream, midstream, and downstream phases of development constitute a "value chain" in which refined fuels and commercial chemicals are derived from unrefined hydrocarbons (figure 3.1).

Beginning in 1977, the development of iron, steel, and ammonia fertilizer plants laid the foundation for gas-based industrial works. In the decades that followed, the pursuit of added value through downstream industrialization came to be known as the Trinidad and Tobago model of natural resource management. Under this scheme, the government of Trinidad and Tobago sought to diversify its portfolio of investments and lessen its vulnerability to oil price shocks. Here, sowing the gas meant securing markets for downstream products such as iron, steel, chemicals, and nitrogenous fertilizers. Yet, the nationalist veneer of the Trinidad and Tobago model obscured its exposure to negative price shocks and international competition. As commodity markets contracted in the latter half of the 1980s, the Trinbagonian economy fell into a recession. This period of structural adjustment inaugurated a shift toward free-market principles of liberalization. While the developments at Point Lisas arrived with considerable fanfare, the fiscal downturn led subsequent governments to divest of its prized downstream assets. The strategy of gas-based industrialization, intended to promote a stable portfolio of commodity exports, provided scant protection against cycles of boom and bust.

As export markets for steel and petrochemicals floundered, state officials looked elsewhere for opportunities to add value in the downstream. In 1992, the Massachusetts-based gas distributor Cabot LNG approached the Trinbagonian government to establish a gas liquefaction facility in the historic oil hub of Point Fortin. In search of additional suppliers to meet the rising seasonal demand for LNG during winter months in New England, Cabot found willing partners in Amoco and British Gas (BG), then two of the principal upstream operators in T&T.

Train I of Atlantic LNG—a joint venture of the state-owned National Gas Company, Cabot, Amoco, BG, and the Spanish multinational Repsol—came on stream in 1999 and cemented the transition from an oil economy to one based principally in natural gas.[12] At the Atlantic LNG terminal in Point Fortin, natural gas supplies are cooled to temperatures of −260°F (−160°C) and condensed into a liquid approximately 1/600th the volume of its gaseous state. LNG tankers moored on Trinidad's southwest peninsula are then loaded with this frigid cargo and shipped to destinations around the Atlantic rim without the aid of pipelines. At their destination, onshore or floating regasification plants heat the liquid supplies to return the gas to its natural form and deliver to consumers via pipeline.

When gas prices and import demand from the United States rose precipitously, the LNG project appeared especially timely and judicious. Riding the market tides, LNG production increased as trains II, III, and IV of Atlantic LNG came on stream in 2002, 2003, and 2005, respectively. In the throes of advantageous markets, multinational investments maintained levels of upstream production. Offshore drilling campaigns by BP, BG, and the Australian mining firm BHP Billiton yielded commercial natural gas finds to keep pace with the surplus requirements of the subsequent LNG trains.

As LNG windfalls poured in, natural gas utilization for LNG, petrochemicals, manufacturing, and local power generation grew more than fivefold between 1995 and 2007.[13] While the LNG project thrived in the short term, the heightened demand for gas feedstock placed added pressure on the upstream sector. By 2010, downstream demand for natural gas outstripped upstream production and sparked a shortfall in gas supplies that persists into the present.

To maintain production, downstream industries needed more gas. With the four processing trains of Atlantic LNG running at approximately 30 percent below capacity—and in danger of dropping further still—state officials and industry technocrats touted the lucrative but risk-laden deepwater sector as a frontier area to rejuvenate production and supply the downstream sector. Yet, as deepwater production thrived globally with the aid of new technologies to drill to ever greater depths of the offshore, Trinidad endured several failed efforts to return a commercial deepwater discovery. Although Trinidad was an early site of multinational investment in deepwater drilling, the absence of a major find exacerbated the gas shortage. Multinational investors prioritized investments elsewhere, in the thriving deepwater frontiers of Brazil, Equatorial Guinea, and Guyana.

In its ideal form, the Trinidad and Tobago model involves the production of added value through the refining of raw hydrocarbons and the production of finished products for niche markets. But the pursuit of downstream ventures requires a continuous supply of hydrocarbon feedstock. While the flow of chemical processes rendered in the value chain assumes a closed system of production, upstream production must expand in perpetuity to meet downstream demand. And it is the projected returns of the deepwater that elicit fantasies of unlimited supplies of oil and gas.

The Story

When oil and gas prices continued their decline in July 2015, I secured an interview with Kevin De Souza, a Trinbagonian national and executive at a multinational energy corporation in Trinidad. After a short but traffic-heavy commute to Port of Spain, I entered the adjoining car park of a popular cinema multiplex. As the storefronts and cinema began to bustle with commercial patrons, the tightly patrolled entrance to the corporate building in the adjoining lot remained conspicuously quiet. Upon entry, the on-duty security officer furrowed his brow and scrutinized my business-casual attire. When I shared the details of my appointment, he called upstairs to confirm my itinerary before allowing me to proceed up the elevator behind him. Over the course of my fieldwork, I came to anticipate this delicate waltz with private security, exaggerating my American accent to pass muster at multinational corporate offices.[14]

When I exited the elevator several floors above, a receptionist extended a friendly welcome and guided me to De Souza's pristine office overlooking the Caribbean Sea. Following several successful bids for the production rights to deepwater acreage in Trinidad, De Souza's company earned a reputation for its bold investment portfolio in areas of technical risk and at times of market uncertainty. Seated behind a large desk in his corner office, De Souza briefed me on the strategy to invest heavily in Trinidad despite a résumé of unsuccessful ventures in the deepwater.

> If you look at deepwater plays in the Atlantic margin, this is the last unexplored deepwater basin. There are four major deltaic basins that fuel deepwater in the Atlantic margin. One is the Niger Delta, off of West Africa, and of course that story is already told. The second is the Mississippi Delta—the Gulf of Mexico deepwater—and that story is told. Coming off of the Amazon—Brazil deepwater—that story is told. And the deepwater basin that's here as a result of the major river delta in Venezuela. So this is the last one. You look at the three others—very, very prolific deepwater basins. You look at Trinidad and Tobago, it's an established oil and gas province [with] terrific source rock [and the] possibility of very large reservoirs, lots of sand coming from the deltas. You know, it's a place to look. Is it high risk? Yes it is. It's frontier work. But that's sort of the risk that companies like ours take on.

In industry circles, geology is often represented in narrative terms. To tell the story of a geological province is to survey and exploit its commercial potential. As a frontier region, the untapped acreage of the Trinidadian deepwater presented an opportunity to forge a narrative that would follow the models of earlier developments throughout the circum-Atlantic. The unsuccessful ventures in Trinidad to date were paradoxically upheld as evidence of its still boundless potential rather than cautionary reminders of its manifold risks. With the story of Trinidad waiting to enter the annals of industry innovation, the assumption of risk awarded investors the privilege to be the first to the prize that lay in the maritime depths of the Eastern Venezuela Basin.

A compelling story is essential to court investors ahead of competitive bid rounds for the rights to deepwater acreage. A senior geologist who served in the Ministry of Energy under former prime minister Patrick Manning during the first deepwater bid rounds in the 1990s recalled the failed ventures of prior decades and lamented the "exceedingly cautious" drilling programs carried out by Shell, Exxon, and Union Texas. Nevertheless, she regarded a commercial discovery in the deepwater as not simply inevitable, but imminent.

> The day they have a discovery out there—oh, my God. People, companies going to rush for it. A lot of them wait for that, yeah? We have the early adopters coming, and when they come and they find something, you find all the rest just rushing in. It's like in Ghana where you had Tullow and these small companies, and then you had the big ones come in afterwards. It will happen. So I'm assuming that a lot of people are adopting a wait-and-see [approach], although BHP [Billiton] has been very bullish. But the development of the resource will go forward as long as they find something.

In deepwater exploration, a major find often precipitates a series of subsequent discoveries as multinationals race to adjoining offshore blocks. Yet the initial find often proves elusive and requires new strategies to secure capital-intensive commitments from investors. In this instance, the cautious approach to drilling tempered corporate enthusiasm toward ventures in the Trinidad deepwater. As extractive operators channeled investment into thriving productive areas throughout the "Golden Triangle" of the Gulf of Mexico, West Africa, and Brazil, state officials in T&T turned to advanced geological survey technologies such as high-resolution, three-dimensional seismic imaging. Technologies of this sort lend contour to the extractive profile of the deepwater and the corresponding investment profile tendered by Trinbagonian state officials to multinational entities.[15]

Corporate and diplomatic forums provide a staging ground for the production of geological stories to entice corporate partners. At the annual Trinidad and Tobago Energy Conference in January 2015, I joined industry stalwarts, local bureaucrats, and parliamentarians at the Hyatt Regency in downtown Port of Spain for a plenary session entitled, "Gearing Up for the Deepwater Challenge." Perched at the front of an immaculate meeting room, a petroleum engineer and deepwater adviser for Schlumberger in Houston offered his remarks alongside a map of global deepwater activity displayed on the large projection screen. At first, the map registered only three regions as locations of "established" deepwater plays, indicated by oblong areas covering the Gulf of Mexico, the Brazilian coast, and West Africa. As he continued, however, the map lit up with blotches of white and yellow to indicate "emerging" and "frontier" areas of deepwater development. "Deepwater is exploding; everybody's looking for that big elephant," he quipped in a Texan drawl as the map continued to flicker. Despite the litany of failed ventures in the Trinidad deepwater to date, hope sprang eternal in the estimation of energy technocrats.

After cautioning that his professional background was in engineering, he prepared to offer the eager audience a "little Geology 101." He gestured toward a slide displaying a map of the southern Atlantic and said, "Now, take a look at this map right here—what do you see? It looks like a jigsaw puzzle. Don't they kind of fit together?" he asked as he traced the complementary coastlines of western Africa and eastern Brazil. "Now, did you know that what we found here in Brazil we're finding on the opposite side in Angola?" But for Trinidad, he noted, the closest analog was the light-oil deposits in the offshore waters of Ghana. On his keynote slides, the success of the Deepwater Tano Block on Ghana's maritime border with Côte D'Ivoire projected a prosperous future for the Trinbagonian deepwater.

The "Atlantic Mirror" theory hypothesizes the existence of large offshore oil deposits in the Eastern Venezuela and Guyana–Suriname Basins based on the presence of analogous source rocks in the petroleum systems of West Africa. Geological estimates trace the origins of the petroleum systems on either side of the Atlantic to approximately 90 million years before present, when the continental landmasses that eventually constituted Africa and the Americas began to drift apart. Major deepwater finds in French Guiana and Guyana from 2011 onward lent supporting evidence for the mirror thesis. The references to geological analogs choreographed in corporate forums sought to "de-risk" Trinidad deepwater ventures through stories of success. Yet, even as these performances of certainty lured in prospective multinational investors, the Trinidad deepwater did not generate the anticipated oil finds.

As a major oil discovery eludes daring multinationals, the deepwater necessitates the production of narratives to spark investor hype toward risk-laden resource frontiers.[16] Gisa Weszkalnys reminds us in her ethnography of oil exploration in São Tomé and Príncipe that the protracted moment in anticipation of first oil is sustained by "gestures" such as product-sharing contracts and wildcat wells to "provide reassurance and maintain the confidence that prevents investments from turning into outright failure."[17] Likewise, the consolidation of sovereign authority in the petro-state demands the production of stories. Telling the right story ensures that failures do not preclude further investment. Seismic surveys, bid rounds, and drilling campaigns bolster this masquerade of permanence whether or not they result in a commercial success. Still, while the story is essential to generate corporate enthusiasm and capital investment, stories alone do not bring oil and gas to the surface. The story requires a material scaffolding in the form of the play.

The Play

In energy industry parlance, deepwater production generally refers to extractive ventures conducted at water depths of 1,000 feet or greater. A broad consensus holds that deepwater plays—an industry shorthand for drilling campaigns—carry exceptional risks. Compared to onshore and shallow-water ventures, the deepwater is characterized by low-probability plays that involve massive injections of capital. Indeed, the cost of a single well often approaches US$50 million and "is about two orders of magnitude greater than a typical onshore well."[18] The costs of deepwater campaigns are exacerbated by the fact that the majority of deepwater wells are dry holes. Most often, exploratory deepwater wells do not return commercially recoverable quantities of oil or gas. Although no extractive play is assured of success, the deepwater requires that investors cut dramatic losses for several failed wells in their pursuit of an elusive gusher.

The deepwater epitomizes the uncertainty that pervades all extractive plays. Of the eight deepwater wells drilled in T&T between 1999 and 2003, three were abandoned due to insufficient quantities of oil and gas below the total depth of the well. Others were riddled with mechanical troubles or borehole instability that threatened the structural integrity of the well, and adverse ocean currents posed significant problems in three operations conducted by drillships that, in comparison to semisubmersible rigs, lack a secure anchoring system to the seafloor.[19] The careful selection of infrastructure suited to the contours of deepwater-source rocks, therefore, dictates the perceived success or failure of a given well. In the play, deepwater-drilling campaigns wager particular extractive technologies against a geological profile approximated by seismic surveys and expert analysis.

In T&T, the turn to the deepwater marks a turn away from risk mitigation as a hallmark of postcolonial governance—characterized by high-probability extractive plays and state directed industrial development—toward a valorization of risk. The election of Persad-Bissessar in 2010 inaugurated reforms to the fiscal regime governing the offshore. To facilitate investment in risky frontier sectors, special provisions were established to decrease the Petroleum Profits Tax for deepwater production from

50 percent to 35 percent.[20] While the deepwater was yet to generate any returns, its lucrative geology was invoked as the spoils to be won through free markets and economic liberalization. The retreat of the state and its shrinking share of crude supplies and profits permitted multinationals to continue their intrepid pursuit of deepwater hydrocarbons. No longer timely resources to sow judiciously prior to their exhaustion, fossil fuels appeared as limitless resources waiting to be unearthed during an interminable moment at play.

De Souza echoed this sentiment when he traced the steps from initial investment to first oil or gas:

> At the end of the day, Ryan, what we have is data. We've got to convert that into the best information that we can get. We have to have the best people, which we do, interpreting this data and trying to find the best locations for us to drill in an area that is five times the size of Trinidad. So it's not like we're playing in a little place. This is a massive area we're exploring, and it will come down to drilling wells. At the end of the day, we look at all sorts of data and everything else, but we have to drill the well. And when we drill the well, that's when we'll know.

Still, he made no assurances. Instead, he enumerated the risks and expansive cost margins that accompany plays in the deepwater. "These are massive projects," he mused. "These are not small projects. These deepwater things are enormous investments, and in many instances it's difficult for even large private enterprises to do on their own." He lauded the changes to the fiscal regime for facilitating investment and permitting private corporations to venture into areas that national energy companies would avoid due to the litany of risks and prohibitive expenses: "We have no choice because what it available to us requires us to be innovative, to be immense problem solvers, to place capital at risk and to have the balance sheets that allow us to do that. Because this is not a game for the faint of heart. It's just the reality. This stuff doesn't always work."

State functionaries, echoing their partners in the private sector, pinned their hopes to multinational plays on the deepwater frontier. As oil and gas markets continued to contract in the early months of 2015, I turned to a former reservoir engineer at the state oil company, Petrotrin, in search a sober assessment. He assured me that the failed ventures in the deepwater were to be expected.

> That's what exploration is. Before we started to get all these finds in the shallow [water], it was like that. We were exploring. We might get something, we may

not get something. And normally the standard is you might drill seven wells dry hole before you get one good well. That is the standard if you look at the Gulf of Mexico standard. So basically we have drilled about seven or eight in the deepwater, right? We could probably in the next phase really hit something. So I wouldn't say it's due to our work or anything. It's just exploration and that is what it is.

He tempered a disheartening record of unsuccessful developments. After the fiscal reforms installed by the People's Partnership administration, the government accepted bids for several deepwater-exploration blocks from BP Trinidad and Tobago (bpTT), BHP Billiton, and BG, reversing the fortunes of previous unsuccessful bid rounds. Per his industry calculus, Trinidad was due for a significant windfall. Yet his optimism fell unevenly against more than a decade of frustrated drilling.

Again, the deepwater is distinguished from other plays by risk, cost, and time. The break-even price of deepwater production (the price at which its projected revenues equal its operational costs) generally exceeds that of its onshore counterparts. Deepwater ventures are characteristically long plays that occasionally span more than a decade from an initial wildcat discovery to full production. By extension, the temporality of deepwater production precipitates a corresponding temporality of governance. Rather than upholding expectations of stability, deepwater plays operate unabashedly under a speculative register in which subsequent discoveries hold the potential to restore periods of economic prosperity and social welfare.

In contrast to a prior impulse to abate the depletion of reserves through a diversified portfolio of public works, the development of extractive technologies to exploit previously inaccessible reserves fuels an image of permanence.[21] As ethereal substances that appear metonymic of money, modernity, and development, oil and gas fuel bureaucratic and populist ambitions alike.[22] The moment spent at play generates anticipation of an inevitable commercial success and diverts attention from the troubling realities of dry wells, unstable drillships, and disinterested multinational investors. In turn, the protracted temporality of deepwater plays fuels the signature masquerade of the Trinbagonian petro-state.

The language of the play is not incidental. In the classical expression of medieval fairs and religious festivals, the realm of play lies outside the boundaries of social norms and conventions. Recalling the language of the Trinbagonian revelers, to *play a mas* is to perform a masquerade on the road. When ordinary people indulge in play, their creative power calls into question the "ordering of ordinary life."[23] The temporary dissolution of social rules and moral absolutes need not be confined to a Carnivalesque moment of release. Indeed, play permits masqueraders, striking laborers, and other "roadworkers" to reveal the arbitrariness of the worlds they inhabit and, at times, collaborate to fashion them anew.[24]

Sovereignty, likewise, can be understood through the register of play. The appropriation of play by state actors and their multinational partners also adopts the form of the masquerade. During its own masquerades of permanence, the norms and conventions of the postcolonial welfare state are suspended to facilitate the protracted moment of play in the deepwater sector. Per the industry calculus of deepwater exploration, the failure of a given play only rouses greater conviction of an eventual success. Or, following Gregory Bateson, the sober truth of deepwater dry holes can be written off as mere "play" after their failure.[25] Play does not end after a fixed period of time. Instead, the failure of one play simply presupposes the beginning of another. Play only ceases after the anticipated moment of a successful deepwater discovery. Likewise, the sovereign imagination of the deepwater does not oblige a moment at which the guarantees and protections of the social contract are restored. In the time at play, the provisions of the social contract are deferred indefinitely prior to the arrival of certain resolution. Play continues. The petro-state masquerade does not stop.

The Miracle

In September 2015, Dr. Keith Rowley assumed the office of prime minister after the PNM reclaimed a majority of seats in Parliament. As the People's Partnership dissolved amid persistent reports of corruption that Persad-Bissessar had vowed to eradicate, the PNM orthodoxy returned to power when voters returned to conventionally racialized blocs. A geologist by training and longtime parliamentary representative for Diego Martin West, Rowley maintained an ambitious approach to the energy sector. During a visit to an offshore drillship with BHP Billiton corporate officials, Rowley spoke confidently of the hydrocarbon sector as the "lifeblood" of the country and lauded the deepwater as a strategy to stem the adverse fiscal tides.[26] Nevertheless, he was forthright in his assessment of deepwater prospects. Although he underscored the technical capabilities of the drillship—equipped to drill to depths of 40,000 feet—he cautioned that the venture would accrue operational costs in excess of US$1.2 million per day. Rowley placed the costs in perspective, estimating that the campaign would last approximately eighty days in total and conceding that "you can understand why those with deep pockets are the ones who can go into deepwater because after that well ... God forbid that hole is dry."[27]

At first glance, Rowley acknowledged the possibility that the expensive drilling program would mark another commercial failure in the deepwater. But he was not ready to abdicate an exalted Trinbagonian geology. Appealing to the spiritual inclinations of a religiously diverse populace, he added, "So we, as a praying people, will have to keep our fingers crossed that as we face this new province we will be successful in finding oil and gas."[28] Offering a sobering reflection on the troubles of the deepwater, Rowley followed his predecessor in his efforts to stir faith in deepwater futures.

In August 2016, BHP Billiton announced the results of the first well of its deepwater campaign off the east coast of Trinidad. After Prime Minister Rowley visited the *Deepwater Invictus* drillship in June, the LeClerc well was projected as a potential gusher holding in excess of 5 billion barrels of oil. Contrary to expectations, the well did not return an oil find. Although it yielded significant quantities of gas-bearing sands, the more opulent oil discovery failed to materialize when pressure-control difficulties halted drilling at a depth of greater than 22,000 feet. Despite the disappointing returns that did not result in commercial success, LeClerc was hailed as an ample gas discovery at the outset of a longer exploration campaign. "While the focus of our program is a commercial oil discovery, we are encouraged by the results of the first well," BHP Billiton President Steve Pastor surmised. "The results will help BHP Billiton's plans to further appraise the basin, as part of our extensive Trinidad and Tobago exploration program."[29] The lucrative oil gusher continued to elude daring investors as they remained at play in their efforts to explore and unlock complex hydrocarbon reservoirs. The eventual unlocking of the deepwater basin, however, remained certain.

The aftershocks of unsuccessful deepwater ventures reverberated onshore. In March 2016, the Luxembourg-based multinational ArcelorMittal shuttered its steel plant at Point Lisas after persistent concerns over gas supply, sending more than six hundred workers to the breadline. By November 2018, the state-owned Petrotrin oil refinery shut down indefinitely when its debt ballooned following a decline in domestic oil production. According to the Oilfields Workers' Trade Union estimates, 3,500 permanent workers, 2,000 temporary workers, and 3,500 contract laborers were retrenched. Public sentiment apart from the union strongly endorsed the government assessment of the refinery as an outdated enterprise and drain on public moneys. Inside the parliament hall, Finance Minister Colm Imbert underscored this view by declaring the aging refinery "uncompetitive" and "obsolete" in the contemporary market landscape.[30] This view did not signal a diminishing optimism in the energy sector, however. In his address, Imbert highlighted the impending completion of "two additional downstream gas projects in aluminium production" and anticipated a competitive bid round for shallow-water blocks in order to generate additional supplies of gas to service an already imperiled downstream sector.[31]

Imbert dismissed apprehensions over the shortfall in gas supply to the beleaguered train I of Atlantic LNG. Though he acknowledged that two BP wells underperformed in relation to earlier projections, he insisted that gas production would continue to rise, qualifying that when "[BHP Billiton] made it clear that it intended to make a huge financial investment in Trinidad and Tobago, we did not hear one peep out of the naysayers. Clearly they are allergic to good news."[32] Exactly one week later, the completion of the shallow-water bid round did not lend credence to his bombast. While three marine blocks received multinational bids, the ceremonial unveiling of the remaining blocks unexpectedly revealed three empty bid boxes. This did little to temper Imbert's confidence. In his 2020 national budget speech, he assured listeners that train I would return under a new pricing arrangement "once gas [could] be found."[33]

The failure to rouse corporate enthusiasm for the shallow-water bid round compelled the PNM government to look elsewhere to sustain its masquerade of permanence. Even in the conditional tense of "once gas can be found," Imbert presumed that gas would inevitably arrive in time. The massive productive potential of the deepwater again presented a convenient register to remedy the shallow-water letdown. In the summer months of 2020, the oil and gas industry reeled under COVID-19 market shocks. Commodity markets collapsed as the pandemic reduced consumer demand for fuel. Incredibly, spot prices in the shale regions of the Permian Basin briefly turned negative as futures contracts came due and fossil fuel storage infrastructures filled to capacity.

On September 15, Rowley and his energy minister, Franklin Khan, staged a press conference at the Diplomatic Centre in St. Ann's to announce the results of BHP's exploratory Broadside well in the Trinidad and Tobago Deepwater Atlantic Area—specifically, the deepwater block TTDAA-3 (figure 3.2, T3). That August, the *Invictus* had arrived in the

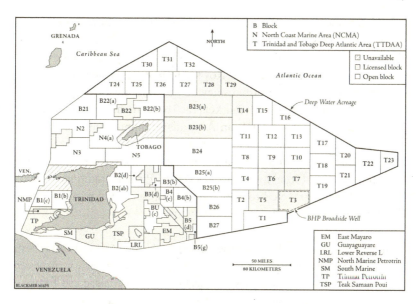

FIGURE 3.2. A map of Trinidad and Tobago's offshore and deepwater acreage.

exploratory block along T&T's maritime border with Guyana to begin a drilling program in partnership with Shell. At the press conference, flanked by banners for the Ministry of Energy and Energy Industries and BHP, Rowley and Khan wore protective masks as they sat behind a long table alongside BHP Trinidad and Tobago President Vincent Pereira. The global vice president of exploration for BHP joined via Zoom from Houston. The staging of this masquerade, carefully curated across borders through digital communications technologies and a cast of industry experts, came to life via livestream.[34]

Khan opened his remarks with cautious optimism: "Today's ceremony is in recognition that the future of the energy sector lies in our deepwater province. No production has yet come on stream from the deepwater blocks. However, there have been exploration successes which have added to the country's natural gas reserves. In the medium and long term, these exploration successes *will manifest* in hydrocarbon production." Khan punctuated the words *will manifest*. Once again, though the drilling of the Broadside well had not yet concluded, he remarked instead on its three geological analogs—the Guyana–Suriname Basin, Ghana's deepwater, and the ultra-deepwater reservoirs in Equatorial Guinea and Nigeria—and the unprecedented depths of the "deepest well ever drilled in Trinidad and Tobago" to confirm his air of certainty. Turning to Pereira, Khan thanked his private-sector colleague for "BHP's continuing exploration efforts and *faith* in the prospectivity of the country's deepwater area."

Khan then ceded the floor to Rowley to toast the commencement of the drilling program. In a rare display of vulnerability, Rowley conceded that the presence of BHP that markets for Trinidadian oil and gas had not always been guaranteed. BHP, an Australian mining multinational, had only expanded in recent decades from its trademark investments in minerals and ores to operations in upstream oil and gas.[35] As BHP weighed its options to divest from hydrocarbons and reaffirm its traditional mining interests, Rowley traveled to Melbourne to preserve the partnership on which the future of the deepwater firmly rested:

> In between the first and second phases of drilling, I visited Australia in May 2018, where I met with the senior executives at BHP in Melbourne. There we discussed in detail BHP's continued investment and presence in Trinidad and Tobago. I impressed upon them the mutual benefits to both Trinidad and Tobago and BHP of this deepwater exploration program. We both agreed and were committed to their success. This visit was important because it was a time when BHP was rolling back its presence internationally and was moving back to its core business.
>
> And we here in Trinidad and Tobago were in some danger of being left out of the new BHP expenditure program. And the competition for investment funds was such that there was no guarantee that this exploration pioneering work in Trinidad and Tobago would have continued in the way it is continuing now.
>
> *However, as a geologist I genuinely believe what the Minister [of Energy] has just said.* Maybe we geologists are overoptimistic, but it's our profession looking into the earth that we remain an area of significant hydrocarbon potential. And the provenance which Trinidad and Tobago lay claim to is an area which is still exciting for geological exploration. I'm pleased that those discussions in Melbourne resulted in the decisions to continue to invest significantly in these pioneering works in Trinidad and Tobago.
>
> Today we are one of the few areas in the world where such exploration is taking place in the deepwater, especially in the new deepwater zones. The government gave BP the commitment—BHP, sorry—that we would do all that is necessary to facilitate the success of the program by amending the various production-sharing contracts where appropriate to ensure exploration success.

Rowley validated his conviction with his professional expertise. As a geologist, he testified to the promising qualities of T&T's deepwater prospects.

His optimism in his domestic geology, however, buckled as he feared the withdrawal of BHP's corporate presence—as his PNM forebear, Eric Williams, faced the flight of Shell and Texaco before him. As the geologist-cum-sovereign, Rowley tacitly acknowledged that the capacity to declare the state of exception and suspend political order lay not only in his state residence at White Hall in Port of Spain, but equally in Houston, Melbourne, and London. His desperate plea to BHP in Melbourne preserved his authority for the time being. His masquerade did not stop.

The press conference occupies a distinct position in the state masquerade. When successful, the declarations of state actors are taken at face value. In this instance, the press conference laid claim to the success of the drilling program before it concluded. Even as Rowley hedged his remarks in the conditional tense, issuing the caveats "if [gas is] found to be economic" and "if the finds of the Broadside well are promising," he proceeded as though the outcome were already predestined. If successful, he reasoned, the Broadside find would inform the exploitation of adjoining maritime blocks by continuing, in his words, to "de-risk" the deepwater through a proven résumé of commercial success. To do so, Rowley again flouted his geological credentials:

> There's this thrilling possibility that the Broadside exploration well, once it successfully encounters its first target at a measured depth of 20,537 feet, may then be deepened to test two further targets. If this is executed, the Broadside exploration well will be the deepest well ever drilled in Trinidad and Tobago, exceeding 20,000 feet of TVD [true vertical depth] below the mudline. And as you heard, this is taking place in water over six and a half thousand feet deep. The Broadside well is not only significant because of its depth, or location; the well will test the oil play within BHP's southern deepwater blocks, which includes TTDAA-3, which is right up on the Barbados border, and TTDAA-5 and 6, which are the adjoining blocks. If the finds of the Broadside well are promising, it can inform the drilling of further exploration wells in nearby open blocks.

Uncertainty followed. Mere days after Rowley's hopeful appraisal, the crew stationed on *Invictus* detected a stuck pipe that brought drilling to a halt. When drilling resumed, greater tragedy struck when the well failed to return commercial quantities of hydrocarbons. Broadside-1 returned another dry hole. This confirmed fears that the period of industrial decline and labor retrenchment would continue unabated. Moreover, the hype of a commercial discovery once again proved elusive. In the subsequent deepwater bid round, which opened in December 2021, only four blocks received competitive bids out of seventeen placed up for auction.

While the local press and international business media published reports on the dry Broadside-1 well, the Diplomatic Centre did not play host to a press conference of the same fanfare. By commemorating the launch of a deepwater campaign, Rowley and Khan played a mas. As Khan surmised, "There is a saying in the exploration circles that the only way to find oil and gas is to drill." By hailing the unprecedented depths of the exploration program, the moment of drilling masqueraded as a commercial success. After another failed venture, faith in the miracle of deepwater hydrocarbons did not subside. In search of the elusive gusher, Khan chided the multinationals for their "reluctance to undertake deep drilling to go after oil." As he had it, success was inevitable if only they dared to go deeper.

Mus Eat Ah Food

The miracle is the foundation of state sovereignty.[36] In this secularization of theological concepts that we know as the modern state, the miracle is that which masquerades the fictive *as* real, the partial *as* total, and the dispersed *as* uniform. Carl Schmitt opines in his treatise on political theology: "Exception in jurisprudence is analogous to the miracle in theology."[37] The miracle draws its power from the faith of religious adherents in the same fashion that sovereigns derive power from the faith of their subjects. Just as the status of the prophet can be determined only ex post facto by the success of the miracle, the status of the sovereign as "he who decides on the exception" can be determined only after the successful suspension of the law.[38] The figure of the sovereign draws its legitimacy from the theological category of the miracle. Or as Marshall Sahlins and David Graeber make plain: "Kings are imitations of gods rather than gods of kings."[39]

The deepwater is well suited to the production of miracles. For Hobbes, a miracle is an event such that "we cannot imagine ... to have been done by naturall means, but onely by the immediate hand of God."[40] While deepwater hydrocarbons can be unlocked only by meticulous assemblies of capital and technology—via the "naturall means" of human ingenuity—they are comparatively detached from the pressures of labor dissent and popular claims-making. Unlike the onshore, conventional fossil fuels that formed the basis of labor uprisings throughout the twentieth century, deepwater production is characteristically opaque and suffused with the incongruous expectations of multinationals, statesmen, and publics.[41]

Some have interpreted Hobbes's commentary as a cautionary posture toward miracles as a threat to political stability. A careful reading of *Leviathan* conversely validates miracles as an essential feature of sovereign power. Hobbes turns to the biblical narrative of Exodus to distinguish between the deceptive enchantments of the magicians in the pharaoh's court and the divinely ordained miracles performed by Moses.[42] Rather than necessitating the abolition of miracles, Hobbes's ideal sovereign defines the limits of the miraculous in order to establish the terms of political order. Tracing the foundation of sovereign absolutism to Hobbes's apostolic incantation in the thirty-sixth chapter of *Leviathan*, "Jesus is the Christ," Schmitt reminds us that the practice of sovereignty is held together only by the acceptance of the miracle as its foundation. The miracle is that which renders the uncertain returns of the play as a preordained success. Not unlike the colonial cartographer who demands that the aspirational technology of the map be accepted as a perfect representation of settler possession, Schmitt insists that sovereignty is a theological exercise in which the authority of the sovereign "determines what subjects of the state have to believe to be a miracle."[43]

At the same moment that Hobbes forged his thesis on sovereignty, the plantation zone of the Caribbean emerged as a geography in which sovereignty remained unthinkable in the imagination of European planters and settlers.[44] Rather, the fictive ideal of Westphalian autonomy and noninterference masked an enduring reliance on "colonial markets, outsourced labor, and nonsovereign enclaves."[45] Hobbes's status as an early investor in the Virginia and Somers Isles (Bermuda) Companies underscores the colonial Americas as a foundational, albeit uncredited, grounds for the consolidation of sovereign absolutism in the metropole.[46] At its conceptual origins, sovereignty relied on the production of plantation frontiers—a speculative enterprise later extended to mines, oilfields, and offshore rigs. In T&T, the deepwater frontier constitutes the miracle that promises an exit from a permanent state of war or the perils of postcolonial disenchantment.

In their treatise *On Kings* (2017), Marshall Sahlins and David Graeber hypothesize that we may discover that the state "was, at best, a fortuitous confluence of elements . . . that came together in certain times and places, but that, nowadays, are very much drifting apart."[47] At present, the border-eclipsing crises endemic to industrial society can no longer be defused by the nation-states tasked to contain them. Nevertheless, when a wholesale retreat from the perils of ecological crisis is impossible, the idea of national sovereignty presents itself as ever more compelling. At the same time, it grows more practically unsustainable. As Hughes concludes in his ethnography on the production of "moral innocence" by energy technocrats in Trinidad, "geologists, economists, and other experts on oil and gas still propagate a myth of liquidity and inevitability" that insists hydrocarbons not only can but *must* be extracted from subterranean source rocks.[48] This myth of inevitability is at once the founding myth of sovereignty. In its insistence that state power is made manifest through the exploitation of deeper and more complex hydrocarbon reservoirs, the speculative sovereignty of deepwater extraction extends a perpetual lease on the political unit of the petro-state and discourages conscientious alternatives to carbon-fueled industrialization.

If the state constitutes merely a passing moment, it behooves us to resist sycophantic testimonies to its fictiveness or incoherence. Rather, we must attend more thoroughly to the persistence of the idea of sovereignty and its capacity to enchant would-be sovereigns and disaffected publics. Following Deborah Thomas, the miracle permits a reified view of the state that "masks the centrality of violence as an organizing principle of state formation."[49] In T&T, market downturns are accompanied by the mobilization of national security forces and the militarized policing of crime "hot spots" that disproportionately target Black, poor, and unemployed residents in its urban centers.[50]

From the militarized peripheries of Port of Spain's urban sprawl, young artists have applied the protest repertoire of calypso to fusion genres of soca, rapso, and hip-hop that matured during the decades of exploratory deepwater play. Artists like the Diego Martin–born Make It Hapn engaged in their own wordplay to articulate the gap between the masquerades of industrial permanence and the ordinary reality of hunger. On the 2010 hip-hop medley "Mus Eat Ah Food," Make It Hapn cleverly pulls back the double meaning of another common Trini idiom. *Eat ah food* refers to practices of corruption in which petty officers elicit bribes or government officials demand a "taste" of state contracts in the form of illegal kickbacks. In this dialectic, the indulgence in deepwater play permits the state and its deputies to eat ah food even when exploratory ventures fail and production stagnates. At the same time, ordinary people grow more desperate in their efforts to fill their hungry bellies. Make It Hapn echoed his calypsonian predecessors in decrying the food and energy prices of twenty-first-century Trinidad:

> It have a war with the rich and the poor
> Check the prices of food in the store
> Then check how much a man does work for
> Then check rent
> Lights, clothes, and water
> If yuh have youths in the school
> Yuh have to pay transporter
> If yuh have a car, yuh need gas
> Yuh have no car, yuh need cash
> To move around
> Twenty dollars it cost you to move in town
> That's 20 percent of yuh day paid down
> And we ain't even count lunch yet
> Hence the reason for bounce check[51]

The depravity of hunger fueled the critical grammar of ordinary citizens once again. Where it once took the form of hunger marches and calypso standards, it now surfaced in the digital production and distribution of Trinidad's independent hip-hop circuit.

Make It Hapn's mathematics placed the petro-state in its sights as well. Where the masquerade of permanence continued to supply provisions to the statehouse and parliament halls, scarce crumbs trickled down to the road:

> Justice for sale
> But we can't afford it
> While we fighting over these crumbs
> Oil getting exported
> So it's time these crooked rich
> Start getting extorted
> Cause the people wrothed
> Tired of being shorted
> The fact is the economics off balance[52]

From the road, the speculative sovereignty of the deepwater appeared nearer to the brutish conditions immortalized by Hobbes than the order of peace, food, and justice. Yet, in the hermetic spaces of corporate offices and governmental ministries, the deepwater is held up as a miracle divorced from the vexed realities of the road. In this iteration of the petro-state masquerade, the deepwater is "itself the mask which prevents our seeing political practice as it is."[53] If fossil fuels are not inexhaustible, then we might ask what might become of Trinbagonian sovereignty when the taken-for-granted equation of the petro-state begins to drift apart.

Even as the Caribbean is derided as a political geography of weak states and incomplete sovereignties, the state form persists as a political ideal against insurgent clamors for radical democratic futures.[54] Michel-Rolph Trouillot points out that it is in Caribbean states where the hyphenated relation of the nation-state is most clearly thrown out of joint.[55] In T&T, the hyphenated form of the petro-state is likewise sustained by a masquerade of permanence that declares the speculative futures of oil and gas production predestined by virtue of its divine geology. The Caribbean is defined not by its failure to adhere to the prescriptions of state sovereignty, but by its testimony to the enduring reliance on the production of miracles to resolve a widening gap between the purported omnipotence of sovereign actors and their fragile hold on political power. It is where the miracle is laid bare as the foundation of sovereignty itself.

The future of the deepwater must be certain. Sovereignty must be absolute. God *must* be a Trini.

CHAPTER FOUR
State Building

Mr. Nehru talks about India's new steel mills, President Nasser talked about his dam which caused a war, President Nkrumah talked about and preached about his Volta Dam for ten years before he got it. A West Indian politician talks about how much money he will get from the British Government or from the United States. —C. L. R. James, *Party Politics in the West Indies* (1962)

On November 26, 2014, I sped eastbound on the Churchill–Roosevelt Highway toward Piarco International Airport. Ahead of a brief visit to New York for the holiday season, I hitched a ride with an offshore paramedic, Scotchie. His older brother, Curtis, rented me the Nissan Tiida sedan that I relied on for the duration of my fieldwork. Curtis brokered our introduction on WhatsApp since Scotchie was headed to Piarco as well. His generous offer spared me the hassle of afternoon traffic and the cost of overnight parking during my week in the States. Rather than taking a commercial flight, though, Scotchie set off for the helipad to begin a two-week shift on an offshore rig.

Scotchie knew of my interest in oil and gas from his brother, another oilman by trade. As we rolled down the highway from Curepe, he seized the moment to vent to my sympathetic ears.

SCOTCHIE: I was supposed to be offshore since the twentieth, you know?
ME: Eh? Which platform?

SCOTCHIE: Repsol.

ME: That is the one out east?

SCOTCHIE: Yeah, that is the one, boy. Worst place to work offshore. Platform is already thirty-five years old.

ME: No retrofits or anything?

CCOTCHIE: None.

ME: So, it's BP building most of the new offshore rigs, nah?

SCOTCHIE: BP thiefing Trinidad, boy. Don't do anything at all for we country.

ME: All of them thief, ent? And then the government build plenty skyscrapers.

SCOTCHIE: Skyscrapers? You call twenty-two stories a skyscraper? All of them. BP ain't do anything. Amoco ain't do anything. Now BHP ain't do anything. Repsol ain't do anything either. I work in [emergency medical services]. They don't even have a dedicated unit. Just a helicopter with a stretcher in the back. Look at the southeast and the southwest, where all the oil and gas come from. You telling me they make all that money and can't give Mayaro or Point [Fortin] a decent hospital? Trinidad don't even have a dedicated burn unit. If somebody come back with burns, they does fly them to Florida—Jackson Memorial [Hospital].

My exchange with Scotchie recurred in conversations with friends and passing encounters with countless others at rumshops and backyard limes. At first, his cynical barbs appeared laden with contradictions. Scotchie relied on the oil industry for his livelihood and his brother's entrepreneurial success. Yet, he condemned the industry itself—particularly the multinational giants of BP, BG, BHP Billiton, and Repsol—as a cabal of thieves set on plundering Trinidad of its hydrocarbon resources.

This bargain with multinational capital is widely accepted as a condition of doing business or, for the chosen few, of entry into the withering ranks of the middle class. I detected an air of resignation in his voice as he gathered himself for yet another shift of offshore work. After all, how much could he offer as an emergency paramedic when Trinidad lacked a dedicated burn unit anywhere within its borders? The airlifts of injured workers to Jackson Memorial Hospital appears all the more absurd when we consider that Trinidad lies in the southern Caribbean Sea, merely seven miles from the South American mainland at its nearest point, but more than 1,500 miles from Miami.

Colloquial mockery of the state is often punctuated with the observation that "Trinidad not a real place" or "Trinidad not a real country." Exclamations of this sort index a vernacular disdain for postcolonial society. This disdain is directed in equal parts toward unsatisfying encounters with fellow citizens and frustrations with ruling classes and political elites. In the latter instance, to declare that Trinidad is not a real country underscores the distance between the narratives the state crafts for itself and its failure to make good on its lofty goals and projections. For Scotchie, the farce of the petro-state was unmasked by the unequal distribution of gas windfalls under Patrick Manning in his two tenures as prime minister, from 1991 to 1995 and from 2001 to 2010. Today, regions of the historic oil belt in the southwest and southeast—Point Fortin and Mayaro, specifically—are held in persistent poverty while vanity projects such as the International Waterfront Centre and the National Academy for the Performing Arts (NAPA) reshaped the Port of Spain cityscape. That the NAPA building on Queen's Park Savannah shamelessly evokes the iconic design of the Sydney Opera House provided even more fodder to mock Manning as a "mimic man" in the tradition of V. S. Naipaul's eponymous fiction—one who molds Trinidad in the image of developed countries such as Australia and the United States. To declare this mimicry insufficient, in which Trinidad and Tobago is "not a real country," provides a grammar through which the masquerade of the state is laid bare in rumshops, on street corners, and on chance encounters en route to Piarco Airport.

Like Eric Williams before him, Manning parlayed the country's hydrocarbon largesse into infrastructural monuments to cement his legacy as a three-term statesman. Manning, a former petroleum geologist for Texaco, rose through the party ranks of the People's National Movement as a member of Parliament, minister of energy and natural resources, and finally, political leader and prime minister. Where Williams turned to downstream heavy industries and steel wire rods in his pursuit of economic permanence, though, Manning's turn to "go for steel" instead involved the construction of skyscrapers to transform the Port of Spain coastline. Feted as the largest construction project in the history of Trinidad and Tobago, the International Waterfront Centre promised to deliver a bustling commercial hub replete with a convention center and a Hyatt Regency hotel (figure 4.1). Once completed, the complex transformed the historic port into a glistening skyline positioned against the tropical sun and surf of the Gulf of Paria. Tallying more than US$300 million in expenses, the Waterfront Centre extended the comforts of luxury hospitality to distinguished visitors and cemented Port of Spain's status as the principal hub of diplomatic and economic affairs in the anglophone Caribbean.

FIGURE 4.1. A view of the International Waterfront Centre and Hyatt Regency Trinidad from the Gulf of Paria. Port of Spain, Trinidad and Tobago. Photograph by CaraMaria/iStock.

Scotchie mocked the waterfront scheme by demoting the size of its twenty-six-story towers to a more modest twenty-two floors. Many of his fellow Trinbagonians shared his wry disdain for the skyscrapers as a waste of public funds. Similar sentiments resurfaced elsewhere. When I spoke with Bobby and Ancil, two veteran trade unionists who served in the OWTU during the tenure of President General George Weekes, this critique reached its climax. Our chat began innocently, with talk of the fanciful projections for national oil and gas production that persisted alongside depressed energy markets in early 2015.

ANCIL: All their projections are premised on that they'll find some oil somewhere.
ME: They always make a token gesture toward diversification, just like you said. Everyone talk about diversification, but then they bring it back and say fundamentally you need to explore new regions, and you need to give the fiscal incentives to allow that to happen. That's the only way in their eyes that you get any investment.
ANCIL: Check the irony, though—the folly. If you have to diversify your economy, will you try to diversify the economy in times when your finances are at its lowest or at its highest?
ME: At its highest, no?

ANCIL: It makes no sense when things are down. That's the equivalent of when you out in the ocean and you see a hole in the boat and you say, "Where the bucket?" Yuh understand me? Can't make sense!

BOBBY: That is the Keynesian thing, you know. When things going good in the economy, you strain the economy. When things were good here, we just spend a lot of money and build all kind of stuff. You strain the economy and try to control how things going. And when things inevitably collapse, you have some buffers where you could stimulate back the economy. A counter-cyclical thing there. When the cycle is up, you try to pull it back. When the cycle is going south, you try to pull it up. But here, I mean like Keynesian—normal capitalist Keynesian style. But here, once somebody running on it, they say let we spend it. Let we spend this money, boy, on big tall buildings! Manning say—somewhere, you know he was going somewhere—and he see the skyline coming in from the sea.

ANCIL: Miami.

BOBBY: Somewhere in the States, boy ...

ANCIL: Miami. Miami. Miami.

BOBBY: He see these buildings coming in from the sea—

ANCIL: And he orgasm!

(*Collective laughter*)

BOBBY: And he say he had to build a set of skyscrapers down there. What a madman, boy!

(*More laughter*)

ANCIL: Now it have them down by the waterfront there. One set of tall buildings, right? It cost billions of dollars, not bringing in one blasted cent in the country. And that is the tragedy, you see.

We should not dismiss the reference to Manning's masturbatory jouissance as merely an instance of the crude humor that remains characteristic of Trinbagonian masculine sociality.[1] Although, undoubtedly, it is. To wit, Jacques Lacan's encapsulation of *jouissance* as that excess of desire that "begins with a tickle and *ends in a blaze of petrol*" warrants another look.[2] The resonance of this image with the transformation of gas windfalls into shining phallic edifices should not be taken as a straightforward confirmation of Lacanian psychoanalytic theses. Rather, it demonstrates how the language of psychoanalysis empowers Trinbagonians to make sense of the peculiar drives that ignite the petro-state masquerade. A blaze of petrol, like the flaring of excess natural gas, provides a safety valve to burn off caustic excesses in industrial and refining operations. The joke, of course, is that Manning's climactic moment arrived prematurely. His steel icons of development did not ignite a leap to economic permanence or burn off innocently. The safety valve of the gas boom would not last. What placed Manning in the cynical crosshairs of "ole talk" was the failure of his semiotic vehicle to reach its intended destination.[3] Port of Spain did not successfully masquerade as Miami, despite Manning's best efforts to the contrary.[4]

Miami Mas

To understand the onshore transformations that accompanied the boom and bust of the LNG sector requires us to step back to the moment of Manning's two terms as prime minister. During this period, efforts to make the oil and gas largesse visible to audiences of everyday citizens, multinational financiers, and foreign dignitaries rested less on the expansion of heavy industry than on the production of infrastructural spectacles as icons of Caribbean modernity. After all, Manning had not always been the principal object of cynical barbs and petty mockery. For a time, his desire to grant Port of Spain a makeover in the tropical modernist image of Miami garnered international plaudits and the adoration of his party's rank-and-file membership. Manning hitched his masquerade of permanence to the built environment. He prepared to play host to the hemisphere's political leaders at the Fifth Summit of the Americas—the first Caribbean meeting of the Organization of American States (OAS) in April 2009. By directing his mas toward fellow statesmen, Manning privileged the vibrant patina of the capital city over the industrial regions due south. As the state masquerade shifted its location and form, this generated newfound opportunities for masquerades of ordinary citizens to interrupt and subvert his semiotic messages of modernity and permanence.

The linguistic anthropologist Michael Silverstein perceptively defines political messaging as "communicative extravaganzas made up of events in long, long chains punctuated by elections."[5] During this electoral interregnum, Manning's message traveled principally along the trails blazed by architectural behemoths along the Port of Spain coastline. For Manning, the Waterfront Centre reflected his aspiration to "build a developed nation"—a goal enumerated in the *Vision 2020 Draft National Strategic Plan*, published by his government in 2005. Fueled by offshore discoveries and the expansion of natural gas liquefaction capacity, the LNG boom sparked plans for brick-and-mortar structures to entertain multinational technocrats and foreign dignitaries. The twin towers of the Waterfront Centre and the Hyatt Regency joined a flurry of commercial building projects that graced Port of Spain in the first years of the new millennium. New corporate headquarters for bpTT, BG, and BHP Billiton sprang up along Queen's Park Savannah, St. Clair Avenue, and at the Movietowne Complex on the Audrey Jeffers Highway, respectively. In the cultural hub of Woodbrook, the historic Phase II steelpan yard found its boundary encroached on by the construction of One Woodbrook Place, a mixed-use building featuring 419 luxury condominium units across its three high-rise towers and upscale retail establishments (figure 4.2). Phase II stood firm in its long-standing home as construction proceeded. As the residential towers pushed toward the sky, the panyard retreated into their long shadows along Hamilton Street. In its former vista, the commercial units of One Woodbrook Place welcomed fine-dining restaurants, a supermarket, and the first IMAX Cinema to operate in the Caribbean. In contrast to the homegrown sounds of steelpan, the cinema boasted a lineup of blockbuster Hollywood films including sequels to the Mission Impossible and Pirates of the Caribbean franchises. When the IMAX theater prepared to open, one of its chief architects, Giant Screen Entertainment CEO Ingrid Jaha, assured the audience at a newly opened cocktail bar that "everything in the IMAX theatre is designed to immerse the audience in the movie."[6]

Fittingly, traversing the city resembled an immersive cinematic experience akin to the mega-screen cineplex. Whereas filmic representation is a medium in which unrealized desires are "displaced into the imaginary diegetic worlds of the cinema," the production of images and icons of sovereignty unfolded on a concrete backdrop of Port of Spain rather than the silver screen.[7] The developments of the prior decade, sprawling out from the historic downtown stretching north and west from the City Gate bus terminal along the commercial corridor of Charlotte Street and Independence Square, peppered the outskirts of town. Apart from a nostalgia for the classical architecture epitomized by the Magnificent Seven (a row of colonial mansions located opposite the western edge of Queen's Park Savannah) the transformation of Port of Spain proved disorienting to the commonsense organization of urban life for residents and visitors alike. For the Trinbagonian property surveyor Afra Raymond, the first years of the new millennium marked a shift in emphasis for state planners and private financiers: "It is clear that the downtown area has lost its appeal and that the 'centre of gravity' of the city has indeed shifted away from

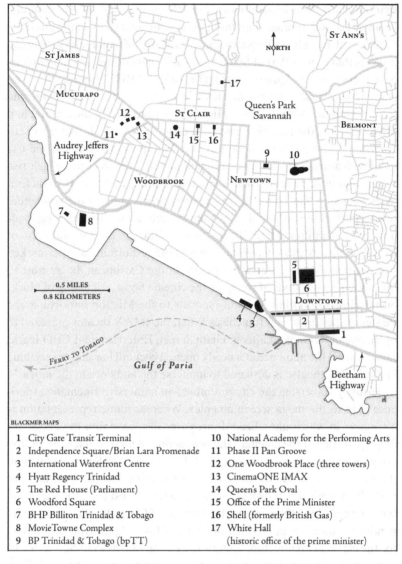

FIGURE 4.2. A map of major landmarks and developments in downtown Port of Spain and Woodbrook.

its traditional core. Of course, the dispersed pattern of the new developments would seem to challenge the very idea that our capital city even has a single such centre any more [*sic*]."[8]

The architecture of these developments buoyed the cinematic reinvention of the Port of Spain cityscape. While open-air panyards remained accessible to pedestrians, allowing their percussive melodies to descend out onto the road, the built environment associated with the next phase of leisure industries privileged bourgeois vehicle traffic. Without the aid of a pedestrian overpass, reaching Movietowne by foot required a brave dash across the six-lane Audrey Jeffers Highway. The One Woodbrook Place development included an underground parking garage for residents and visitors, but conspicuously lacked a pedestrian entry along the adjoining stretch of Damian Street. Instead, it greeted passersby with tall, unpassable gates looming above the sidewalk.

Elsewhere—behind the Waterfront Centre, located at the terminus of the Beetham Highway where it empties into Wrightson Road—the entrance to the Hyatt Regency sat in a cul-de-sac cloistered away from the sidewalk stretching west from the Tobago ferry terminal. Instead, the multilevel parking garage located at the end of Dock Road serviced travelers and well-to-do locals as the Hyatt earned a reputation as a choice liming destination for young professionals and elites. The aesthetic displacement of cultural heritage sites by modular icons of development countered the slot occupied by the Caribbean in the cinematic imagination as a tropical hinterland "where the local people are unable to govern themselves."[9] Manning, in his bid for sovereignty, exchanged the Caribbean cinematic slot of an exotic, primal landscape for the modernist spectacle of the skyscraper.

In her literary history of the skyscraper in the prewar United States, Adrienne Brown recalls that urban planners first envisaged skyscrapers as "economic and spatial solutions helping to order and contain the new masses crowding into downtown sectors" in the midst of population expansion driven by international and rural migrants to North American cities.[10] Brown, too, alerts us to the sensorium of steel behemoths formed in Manhattan and Chicago in this period as a "shock architecture" that at once inspired awe and unease among city dwellers.[11] The location of the Waterfront Centre, tucked away from pedestrian thoroughfares beyond the coastal highway, betrayed Manning's true intentions. Cynically jeered by the domestic public, his skyscrapers were not conceived as a remedy for migration circuits and demographic shifts as they were in the United

States over a century before. Emulating the architectural modernism of another American metropolis, Miami, Manning announced his bid for developed country status through shock architecture alone.[12] Rather than courting the desires of ordinary Trinbagonians, the towers projected outward into the Gulf of Paria toward an audience beyond Trinidad's shores. In Manning's efforts to court multinational capital and curry diplomatic favor, the steel spectacle of the Waterfront Centre and the leisure facilities of the Hyatt Regency portrayed the nation as a safe and reliable zone of multinational investment.

The outward-facing character of Manning's statecraft marked the beginning of another phase of the petro-state masquerade. While the practice of state building is most often associated with the construction of civic and municipal infrastructures aimed at the delivery of public goods and services, the new millennium fused this practice with the spectacle of the building itself. The contours of this masquerade culminated in April 2009, when the freshly minted International Waterfront Centre hosted the Fifth Summit of the Americas.

Yes, We Can?

The Fifth Summit of the Americas served as a testing ground for the development ambitions of Manning's Vision 2020 compact. As the first Caribbean country to host the periodic gatherings of the OAS, T&T followed the lead of Manning's model city, Miami, which played host to the First Summit of the Americas in December 1994. Fewer than fifteen years later, the natural gas boom permitted Manning to close the visual gap between his capital city and south Florida's tropical metropolis.

The visual contours of the summit mattered most for Manning's mas. The three-day summit represented an opportunity to showcase the new Port of Spain to a distinguished cast of foreign dignitaries and heads of state that included the Venezuelan premier Hugo Chavez and the recently elected president of the United States, Barack Obama. Though it was not Chavez—the president of Trinidad's closest geographic neighbor—that commanded the attention of the local press. Instead, Obama fever gripped Trinidad as its residents prepared for the arrival of the first African American to hold the Oval Office in Washington. Obama, the charismatic prophet of hope, had campaigned on a slogan of "Yes, we can!" that resonated with communities of African descent across the Americas. The

Summit of the Americas in Trinidad played host to Obama's own political masquerade of postracial hemispheric détente—a mas sutured to his "mythic autobiography, in which he emerges from black and white, foreign and domestic, Third and First Worlds, poverty and privilege, prejudice and opportunity, ignorance and education."[13]

The failure of this mythos to bear the fruits of Pax Americana over the course of Obama's eight-year tenure in White House should not distract us from the potency of his message when he made his debut to the Americas in 2009. Many, including the Bolivarian socialist Chavez, viewed Obama's election as a moment to shift the tides of US diplomatic and economic relations with the rest of the Americas. When the two men encountered each other in Trinidad, Chavez offered Obama a Spanish-language copy of Eduardo Galeano's *Las venas abiertas de América Latina* (1971; *Open Veins of Latin America*) as a symbolic olive branch. This, indeed, was a precious moment when the sanguine rhetoric of Obama's campaign resounded elsewhere in the hemisphere. For Manning, Trinidad's own Black sovereign, the entry of Obama into the OAS circuit represented an opportunity to appropriate Obama's charismatic message for the first Caribbean summit. As a Reuters news dispatch observed, rather than the protests that met George W. Bush in Argentina four years earlier, Obama was welcomed with "smiles, the cheery clang of Caribbean steel drums and prime ministers and presidents seeking out his autograph."[14]

The Trinidad summit was not without protests, however. The Trinbagonian activist Verna St. Rose Greaves took to the road on the eve of the summit, donning a white dress splashed dramatically with red paint. Indicting the neglect of children, women, the poor, the differently abled, and the unhoused in favor of the outlandish, Carnivalesque summit, St. Rose Greaves faced condemnation from those swept up by the optimism of Obama's Americas. Still, she remained firm: "Millions of dollars are being spent but what can it do for us? ... The public does not need the summit."[15]

In preparation for Obama's arrival, Manning embarked on a "spring cleaning" exercise ahead of the summit's opening on April 17. Ignoring the clamors of local activists and civil society groups, Manning hurried to clear the streets of the unseemly trash and unhoused vagrants who St. Rose Greaves advocated for in her protest mas. On Monday, April 13, the formal removal of "vagrants" began in the area surrounding the Waterfront Centre and the adjacent Brian Lara Promenade. By Tuesday, thirteen individuals had been removed from the road and detained for assessment at the St. Ann's Mental Hospital. Minister of Social Development

Avery Browne, though, assured a civil society forum that any deemed "free of mental illness" would be forwarded to the Centre for Socially Displaced Persons, where they would receive counseling from rehabilitation aides and social work professionals.[16]

Security measures included the imposition of a restricted "Red Zone" that stretched beyond the Waterfront Centre grounds northbound to Park Street, eastbound to Abercromby Street, westbound to Colville Street, and southbound to the port facilities on the coast. A special extension of the Red Zone included the Hilton hotel at the junction of Lady Young Road in St. Ann's. Trinbagonian officials required all entrants to the Red Zone—including hotel staff, security guards, and janitorial workers—to carry specially issued accreditation badges. Surrounding the Red Zone, two further restricted areas—Yellow and Blue Zones—were also restricted by security checks of "less onerous types."[17] The Red Zone lockdown ensured that Manning's Port of Spain could successfully play a mas as Miami for the three-day summit. That Miami is itself not immune to poverty or an unhoused crisis did not figure into his masquerade. Rather, for his audience of fellow sovereigns, "developed country" status meant hiding these blemishes from plain sight to preserve the pristine silhouette of his skyline.

Manning's pièce de résistance involved the installation of a five-foot-tall concrete barricade along the highway in the low-income neighborhood of Beetham Gardens.[18] As the only thoroughfare outfitted to carry diplomatic guests directly west from the international airport in Piarco to the Hyatt and Waterfront Centre in downtown Port of Spain, the Beetham Highway represented an unfortunate eyesore for Manning. After neglecting this community in pursuit of his glistening skyscrapers, he hurried to hide the poor, Black communities from the view of the first Black president of the United States. To complete his mas, Manning built the wall.

Manning's opening remarks at the Hyatt Regency bellowed the hopeful tenor of the new era with a message to Obama himself: "His presidency brings with it a tremendous amount of hope and we here in Trinidad and Tobago share the positive anticipation of so many others all around the world that his administration will indeed be heralding the dawn of a new day."[19] Later, during the opening ceremony, Obama ambled to the pulpit to sermonize his message of hope to the Americas at large. Citing the "energy, the dynamism, the diversity" of the Caribbean as his inspiration, he roused his audience with a message of cooperation: "So together, we have to stand up against any force that separates any of our people from that story of liberty—whether it's crushing poverty or corrosive corruption;

social exclusion or persistent racism or discrimination."[20] The people of Beetham, hidden from view, did not receive any special recognition. Manning's mas was complete.

Uff the Wagon

In the run up to the Fifth Summit of the Americas, Manning's construction schemes drew criticism from popular sectors and political opponents. Suspicion rose within the ranks of his own government. The upstart PNM parliamentarian Keith Rowley objected to the procurement structure under which construction projects received approval and public funding without proper oversight from him or his fellow cabinet ministers. For his troubles, Rowley was sacked from his post as minister of trade and industry. Many understood this conflict—Rowley's rabble rousing and Manning's reprobation—as a proxy for their rival campaigns for political leadership in the party. In their fraternal dispute, Manning labeled Rowley a *wajang*—a Trinidad creole term for a badly behaved person—citing his uncontrolled outburst as cause for his dismissal. Of course, Rowley would eventually take his own turn at the helm of the state masquerade; but for the moment, he had pierced a hole in this masquerade from within Manning's own party ranks.

Opposition parliamentarians rallied in turn. On May 23, 2008, allegations of corruption formally entered into the Hansard record of parliamentary debate, when the lower house of the bicameral legislature approved the appointment of a joint select committee to investigate the administration and procurement procedures of the Urban Development Corporation of Trinidad and Tobago (UDeCOTT). UDeCOTT, a state enterprise headed by a Canadian-born naturalized citizen of T&T, Calder "Cobo" Hart, served as the principal body for the procurement and oversight of construction megaprojects under Manning's government.

Ramesh Maharaj, a United National Congress (UNC) representative from the central Trinidad district of Tabaquite, opened with a summary of the Brian Lara Cricket Stadium in Tarouba, one of the flagship projects of UDeCOTT intended as a host site for the Cricket World Cup in March 2007. The budget for the stadium, set at TT$240 million, ballooned with cost overruns that more than doubled the initial contract terms. In May 2008, Maharaj complained that the project remained incomplete, concluding: "[The] Tarouba Stadium is a national disgrace; in respect of the contract, the award of the contract and the overruns."[21] When Maharaj entered this into the Hansard, it captured an embarrassment felt broadly after the One Day International Tournament hosted at eight venues across the West Indies that conspicuously excluded the Lara complex. Director of venue development for the World Cup, Don Lockerbie, shirked responsibility ahead of the cricketing spectacle before adding, "Construction as you know is very, very difficult in this part of the world sometimes."[22]

Maharaj lent credence to the difficulties of construction in the Caribbean—of contract tenders, cost overruns, and grand larceny—when he laid his accusation at the feet of the foreign-born Hart. Maharaj then turned his attention from the Tarouba Stadium to the Ministry of Legal Affairs Building (another tower set opposite Wrightson Road from the Waterfront Centre) and implicated Hart directly:

> The UDeCott on May 05 awarded this contract to CH Development and Construction Limited. That company was incorporated in Trinidad and Tobago, and it was given a contract to build the 22-storey Ministry of Legal Affairs Tower, that is the Richmond Street Complex. The contract was for $368,902,000. Six companies had tendered for the contract, but the contract was given not to the lowest bidder Karamath, and not to the second lowest bidder, Johnson International, but it was given to CH Development and Construction Limited.
>
> [...]
>
> The same day that the contract was awarded, steps were taken to change the name of the company. The persons who were directors and shareholders when the company was formed—the name was Lee Hup Ming—and our investigation shows that Lee Hup Ming is the brother-in-law of Calder Hart. [*Desk thumping*] It is his wife's brother, and Ming Chin Fu is Mrs. Hart's sister's husband. You can check the records at the registry because I have done it myself.
>
> [...]
>
> I want to say in this House that our investigation shows that at the time of the award of the contract, CH Development and Company Limited had no track record; they were only in existence for two or three weeks; and they could not prequalify. [*Interruption*] Well, Calder Hart and Company gave them the contract. That is the point. The point is that without [the] proper prequalification process—I am told that "CH" refers to Calder Hart.[23]

The allegations tossed at Hart compelled his guardian, Manning, to appoint a commission of enquiry into the construction sector. In March 2010, the commission, chaired by the lawyer and civil engineer John Uff, released its final, 512-page report to the public. Among its findings, the report concluded decisively that "corruption is a problem of serious proportions in Trinidad & Tobago ... to which the construction industry is particularly prone."[24] The report condemned UDeCOTT specifically for an inconsistent application of its own rules and procedures, which allowed the agency to dodge regulatory oversight and eschew transparency in its procurement of contracts. Uff implicated Hart too. Following the trail of evidence first put forward by Maharaj in the Parliament House, the Uff Commission found that "the appearance of Mr Calder Hart's fax number on the notepaper, which was no doubt hurriedly printed by CH Development, remains unexplained.... The fax number remaining on the CH Development notepaper between October 2004 and April or May 2005 with no attempt to have it removed or corrected suggests strongly that Mr Calder Hart cannot have been unaware that his number had been so used."[25]

The findings of the Uff Commission confirmed what many already knew. Even prior to Maharaj's challenge to Hart and his associates, rumors of preferential contracts and kickbacks for politicians circulated with reckless abandon. In the characteristically rowdy arena of parliamentary debate, opposition MPs did not hesitate to insert these rumors into the public record. Junior Sammy, an infamous local contractor with longstanding ties to the PNM, became the target of one of Maharaj's UNC compatriots, Couva South MP Kelvin Ramnath.

HON. C. IMBERT: Each one of these noise makers has an axe to grind. Each one of them wants the status quo to remain. [*Interruption*] Each one of them is uncomfortable with the situation that currently occurs where the Government is moving to make contractors responsible and accountable for projects, so that the people of this country will get value for money, because at the root of all of this is value for money. At the root of all of this is the timely delivery of projects; at the root of all of this is access for everyone, for every citizen in Trinidad and Tobago, to the economy; at the root of this is access for everyone to the economy, and not some little group, some little cartel, some little cabal, some little monopolistic grouping.

MR. RAMNATH: *You are not talking about Junior Sammy there?*[26]

In 2008, Ramnath had jabbed back at Manning's minister of works and transport, Colm Imbert, with a snide allusion to Junior Sammy as a beneficiary of PNM kickbacks. However, it was "Cobo" Hart, not Sammy, who bore the brunt of the Uff Commission exposé. Opposition MPs seized the

FIGURE 4.3. Nicholas Laughlin holds a placard depicting Calder Hart for the 2010 Cat in Bag Productions masquerade, "Cobo Town." Photograph by Georgia Popplewell.

opening to condemn the PNM government with an eye toward Hart's dealings. In an address to his Tabaquite constituents mere days before the Fifth Summit of the Americas in April 2009, Maharaj suggested that the nation at large had been deceived by another masquerade: "I say tonight that Patrick Manning is not the real Prime Minister of Trinidad and Tobago. The real Prime Minister is Calder Hart."[27] Rhetorical contests of this sort are a fixture of Trinbagonian politics. Yet, Maharaj had issued more than a harmless rebuke. Crowning the foreign-born Hart as the real sovereign interrupted Manning's masquerade of national development.

As Trinbagonian citizens anticipated the release of the Uff Commission Report in 2010, they took to the road for Jouvay Morning on February 15. The scandal of Cobo Hart did not escape the satirical jabs of Carnival revelers themselves. Nicholas Laughlin, a Trinbagonian writer and co-curator of the collaborative art space Alice Yard, played a mas with the small band, "Cobo Town." Satirizing the scrutiny placed on Hart by Uff and his deputies, Laughlin joined the march on Carnival Monday with a placard that read COBO SINGS THE BLUES (figure 4.3). The placard featured a facsimile $100 bill, the largest currency denomination circulated by the

Central Bank of Trinidad and Tobago. On the blue banknote, Laughlin replaced the national coat of arms with the grinning face of Cobo Hart. Furthermore, a King Cobo (Corbeau) vulture took the place of the bird of paradise, diving ominously toward its prey. For Cobo to sing the blues, of course, holds a clear double meaning: Hart sang the blues of the Uff Commission enquiry and joyously crooned to the sound of money-counting machines as they assembled stacks of blue $100 bills courtesy of UDeCOTT.[28]

Nineteen days after the streets of Port of Spain played host to Laughlin's masquerade, Cobo Hart abruptly fled Trinidad on a Caribbean Airlines flight bound for Fort Lauderdale, Florida. Later that afternoon, UDeCOTT submitted a press release that announced Hart's formal resignation. Implicated by a series of documents from the Uff enquiry leaked to *Newsday*, Hart's sudden departure from Trinidad marked a decisive split from his long-standing defender Manning.[29] Later, reports confirmed that Manning personally issued the request for Hart to step down. But this belated effort to distance himself from the melee fell tragically short. The semiotic conflation of Manning with Hart—articulated in different registers by Rowley, Maharaj, and Laughlin—had already taken hold. The simmering confrontation between the state's masquerade and the people's masquerade had come to a head once again.

Design and Build

One of the lasting innovations of Hart's tenure at UDeCOTT is the proliferation of design-build contracts. In broadest terms, design-build is a system of project tender and delivery that allocates all phases of a construction project to a single entity—the design-build contractor. By contrast, design-tender (a.k.a. design-bid-build) agreements award contracts to individual outfits for each phase of the scheme. Often, this involves multiple subcontractors for the purposes of design and construction, respectively.

The advantages of design-build (over design-tender) for construction megaprojects were clear for state enterprises like UDeCOTT. Most important, as government ministers argued, design-build models clearly defined a single point of responsibility for the "difficult" matter of construction in the Caribbean. Efforts to avoid a blame game between contractor and consultant remained paramount for Colm Imbert, which he detailed in his written submission to the Uff Commission.[30] The single-tender process, preferred for the timely completion of infrastructural marvels in the new Port of Spain, was viewed by skeptics as a means of circumventing regulatory oversight. Moreover, design-build often favored large foreign firms capable of undertaking complex projects without external assistance. And despite the claims of government ministers, the Uff report cautioned that "most design-build projects in Trinidad and Tobago had not finished on time or within budget."[31]

My own concern over the proliferation of design-build projects compelled me to visit the offices of a real estate surveying firm in downtown Port of Spain. Its managing director, Afra Raymond, also served as president of the independent council and watchdog for the construction industry in T&T. Raymond's anticorruption advocacy through newspaper columns, legal challenges, and freedom of information requests earned him a national reputation. In our conversation, he concurred with the Uff Commission's distrust of design-build as a "one size fits all" model for state-funded megaprojects.

> Is a very involved discussion. Design-build really works best, Ryan, when you have a well-developed design brief. And well-developed design briefs are very rare in this part of the world. And in fact, you need to put a lot of effort in before you tender a project. You have to conduct a thorough means assessment, talk to all the stakeholders, look at previous projects you did that were like that, draw the lessons from that, and create a design brief that actually captures as best as possible what are the desired outcomes or the required outcomes of the project. A good design brief gives you a high possibility of having a design-build that really works. Design-build is best done, in my experience, on large projects that are what we would call generic. So, if you are building [*pauses*] schools, [then] design-build.

Under Hart, UDeCOTT did not heed this caution. Rather, Manning's government saw the extension of design-build models to a range of projects that could hardly be deemed generic. This included the Waterfront Centre, the prime minister's residence, and NAPA. In these instances, the design-build model largely avoided cost overruns and construction delays by accepting bids from international contractors.

The success of design-build projects, though, remained in the eyes of the beholder. For Manning, the completion of the performing arts hub, NAPA, successfully mimicked the vaulted concrete shells of its counterpart in Sydney (figure 4.4). As cars and route taxis rounded the southeast boundary

STATE BUILDING   133

FIGURE 4.4. A view of downtown Port of Spain with the National Academy for the Performing Arts in the foreground, the International Waterfront Centre in the far-right background. Photograph by Nandani Bridglal/iStock.

of Queen's Park Savannah, their passengers would be enraptured by its familiar outline. Awarded as a design-build contract to the China-based Shanghai Construction Group, NAPA opened in November 2009. At the gala to mark the project's completion, Hart gifted a scale-model replica of the building to Minister of Community Development, Culture, and Gender Affairs Marlene McDonald. The ceremonial exchange between two members of the government communicated that the building itself, rather than its contents, masqueraded as the measure of its success.

The spectacle of the building's silhouette broke down under closer inspection. From inside, the errors of design and construction became visible to local stakeholders. Only in January 2010 did artists, theater professionals, and dance practitioners receive an invitation to tour the NAPA grounds for the first time. The disastrous tour triggered a complaint in the form of a pamphlet entitled *The Tragedy and Hidden History of NAPA*. Compiled by the Artists' Coalition of Trinidad and Tobago (ACTT), the document includes a first-person account of the infamous tour by the artist and community activist Rubadiri Victor: "During the tour one could hear the muttering of disbelief, the exclamations of horror, and sometimes peals of laughter on the unveiling of each room."[32] The ACTT estimated an additional $80 million to retrofit the facility for use by the very arts communities for whom the construction of NAPA was intended. The list of complaints cited design errors including the complete absence of a loading dock for the main stage (to transport set materials, large Carnival costumes, or large bass steelpans), no outdoor stage or amphitheater for the performance traditions of Mas, Hosay, and Ramleela, no costume rooms, no set construction rooms, and an orchestra pit that inexplicably sat a full story below the stage with no sight lines in between.

For the ACTT, the Shanghai Construction design-build contract exemplified the hasty methods of state building. Rather than a consultative process that incorporated a range of artistic stakeholders and consultants, the foreign firm received minimal input or oversight from the initial design to the supposed completion of the NAPA complex. The authors of the pamphlet shared the further indignity that the technical boards and stage controls were labeled only in Mandarin Chinese and therefore unintelligible to the vast majority of locals. They did not pass up the opportunity to poke fun at Manning's Vision 2020 development fantasy: "No-one can say what switch is for what on hundreds of switches. So you then have to manually go through each one to find the corresponding switch. And then label it with masking tape ... very 2020!"[33]

These structural defects were exacerbated by the authors' own frustration at the masquerade of Manning and his UDeCOTT functionaries. Cobo Hart convened the spectacle of gala openings and state-funded extravaganzas to charm unwitting audiences with his glass-and-steel behemoths. For the ACTT, this "charm offensive" revealed the true objective of NAPA and its sister megaprojects: "The building was obviously constructed for show and not for purpose."[34] By privileging NAPA's exterior silhouette over its interior features, Manning reduced his practice of state building to the steel outline of the building itself. Whether the buildings actually worked as intended mattered none. The stately outline of the building was complete.

They Too Bright!

In other instances, even the outline of design-build structures did not hold. In 2002, UDeCOTT acquired land in a former quarry adjacent to the Lady

Young Road in Morvant with the intention of constructing a residential complex to serve the low-income PNM stronghold in the East Port of Spain hills. In December 2003, UDeCOTT awarded the Las Alturas Towers project to another China-based outfit, China Jiangsu, in a design-build agreement. During the construction process, China Jiangsu contractors encountered soil problems that could threaten the structural integrity of the towers. Under the terms of the agreement, the single point of responsibility for soil analysis, design, and construction remained with the contractor. No changes were made to the existing architectural plans. Construction proceeded on the precarious soil in blocks H and I between 2008 and 2010. Severe cracking surfaced almost immediately after their completion. Visible blemishes tarnished the facade on each of the twenty-four-unit buildings. By May 2012, the structures were condemned and demolition scheduled. Costs of construction and demolition for the two structures approached TT$29 million.

Unlike NAPA, these structures did not survive the wave of public scrutiny. As cracks appeared in the facade of Las Alturas, so did the cracks in Manning's governing mandate widen. Intending to cash in on his masquerade of state building over the decade prior, Manning called a snap election for May 2010—two years ahead of the constitutionally mandated deadline. Even with the embarrassment of Las Alturas largely hidden from view, the corrupt dealings of Hart and the disappointments harbored by artists and workers alike reached a fever pitch again. While Laughlin marched into the road with his mas, calypsonians joined the fray with biting compositions of their own.

On Dimanche Gras—the night of Carnival Sunday—Kurt Allen delivered his Calypso Monarch–winning performance on the outdoor stage at Queen's Park Savannah. While calypso had long played second fiddle to the more popular road-march anthems of soca mainstays Machel Montano, Bunji Garlin, Iwer George, and Patrice Roberts, Allen adapted the classical form with expert precision. His composition for Carnival 2010, "Too Bright," holds Manning's feet to the fire. Allen masterfully curated a set that included facsimiles of the Red House and the gazebo at Woodford Square, where Eric Williams rallied the masses with anticolonial speeches and forums on the eve of national independence. Rather than Williams, though, it was Manning who took center stage, in the form of a tall African Trinbagonian man in a dark suit and red tie who emerged with a briefcase emblazoned with *PM*. Playing a mas as Manning himself, the actor performed a skit in which he is confronted by a fictional reporter:

"REPORTER": One question! Do you think that your Vision 2020 is failing?
"MANNING": Well, well my friend, when I went to Cuba, I had excellent laser eye—eye repairs. So, my vision is excellent. It's fine.

Ignorant to the queries of the reporter and the details of his own signature development plan, "Manning" dismisses the reporter and continues on his way. He then disappears stage right through a door in the false-fronted "Red House." As the calypso melody of "Too Bright" begins, Allen takes the stage dressed as one of the quintessential vagrants known to roam Woodford Square and its surrounding environs. Onstage, Allen wears a soiled jersey and yellow boxer shorts to occupy the position of the masses abandoned by the state-building model of Vision 2020. At this moment, the real Manning had not yet called the snap election that would herald a premature end to his final stint as prime minister. But Allen already crooned with his hopes for the next election, whenever it did fall:

> What is happening to sweet T&T?
> Ask them boys in Parliament for me
> Education is indeed a golden rule
> But not to make you become a power-hungry fool
> Next election I telling yuh flat
> I want a candidate who dunce like a bat
> I will campaign 'til the very end
> For somebody who can't count from one to ten
> Because them fellas they bright
> They too bright
> And that is why they nah run this country right

Allen expertly traces the degeneration of Afro-Saxon political leadership from an anticolonial vanguard—in which they stood at the helm of the people's masquerade—to a caste of detached technocrats at the helm of the petro-state's masquerade of permanence. The inability of the faux Manning to hear the question properly—or to see the realities of his Vision 2020 from the road rather than the distant, distorted views of the architectural renderings and planning documents—indicated that these technocrats were too bright for their own good. Allen assumed the role of the road dweller, the unhoused vagrant, to fashion a critique of Manning's political masquerade. The rule of experts, in the form of the historian Williams and the geologist Manning, climaxed not with the arrival of Caribbean modernity but with its simulation in the form of unusable performance halls and uninhabitable residential units.[35] To preserve this image, Manning pushed the vagrant masses out of the field of view. In his calypso, Allen mused:

> They seeing bright with they 20/20 vision
> But don't see people live in 1920 conditions
> (They so bright)
> Look at vagrants in the city
> They could easily overthrow the Chinese army
> (They so bright)
> I see they built a Great Beetham Wall to ensure
> That Obama don't see the squalor at all
> So for me, there is no other answer
> Is best we elect a stupid prime minister

Whether Allen intended to slyly implicate the China-based contractors embroiled in Manning's construction deals with allusions to the Chinese army and the "Great Wall" along the Beetham Highway, his song rang true to the dedicated audience at the Savannah. More important, he captured a sentiment that had already taken on a life of its own prior to his defining calypso. Allen concluded his stage performance by evicting the Manning stand-in, who leaves the Red House to take the place of the vagrant by sleeping on a park bench in Woodford Square. His real-life counterpart would soon lose his lease in the statehouse as well. If Manning had tuned out those left behind by his Vision 2020, he now faced the music again.

The Las Alturas fiasco in Morvant epitomized the experience of communities beyond Manning's narrow field of view. Unlike with the Waterfront Centre and NAPA, cosmopolitan visitors and motorists rarely stopped at the junction along the Lady Young Road in Morvant where its residential towers unceremoniously crumbled. Manning called a snap election on April 7, 2010. Once again, Manning's gamble was premature. Thirty-eight days after Manning called an early parliamentary election, Kamla Persad-Bissessar's People's Partnership prevailed by assembling an unorthodox coalition of minor political parties with her United National Congress. Aided by the notorious consulting firm Cambridge Analytica and the embattled Trinbagonian FIFA executive Jack Warner, Persad-Bissessar's campaign embraced the multicultural patina of Obama's 2008 presidential run in the United States and encouraged disaffected Black youth (including those in Morvant) to withdraw from the electoral process. While Cambridge Analytica conspired to sour this demographic on party politics, the simmering resentment needed only the smallest nudge to boil over.

While the rise of Persad-Bissessar appeared to mark the end of the old politics of Manning and Hart, her turn as bandleader merely shifted the location of the petro-state masquerade. Even as she promised to leave the corruption of the PNM behind with a multiracial vanguard taking the reins in her band, the new prime minister turned once again to the embattled China Jiangsu outfit, awarding them a design-build contract for one of her signature megaprojects—the south Trinidad law campus of the University of the West Indies in Debe. Rather than staying in Port of Spain, she elected to "go south" to Caroni and Debe in pursuit of her own state-building schemes. As Raymond had it, Persad-Bissessar's reliance on the same contractor responsible for the condemned Las Alturas site unveiled a persistent crisis of state building:

> Two buildings are demolished plus twenty-nine million dollars. And the cost of demolishing them was four and a half million dollars! So, it is a big thing, you know? So there are real questions at work about how responsibility is exactly borne. So the whole argument about a single point of responsibility—China Jiangsu is trying to pass it on to the engineers and the engineers trying to pass it on to that guy and that guy is saying he not coming and China (CJIC) say they not coming either. So they've tried to stymie the whole enquiry. But what is interesting to go to the next point about this moment in national development is that, in fact, China Jiangsu have not been disbarred. The UWI–Debe project is their project. And they are still in line to get work. And the [Joint Consultative Council's] opinion on that since May of 2012, before the building collapse at Morvant, was that in fact, based on technical considerations alone, China Jiangsu should never get any more work in the country. The amount of shit that those fellas build. And there are six-hundred-million-dollar contracts to build a university on one hundred acres of land in Debe. What are they doing here?

By the time I sat down with Raymond, Manning had long since faded from his stately perch. In hindsight, Manning's masquerade halted prematurely when he conceded the snap election to his upstart opponent only thirteen months after his skyscrapers debuted to a distinguished cast of hemispheric statesmen. Of course, this change in government marked merely a shift in the costume, not the form, of the state's masquerade. Persad-

Bissessar emulated Manning in more ways than one. On the one hand, she entered into contracts with the same ignoble firm, China Jiangsu, to complete her signature development projects, such as the UWI–Debe campus. But more so, Manning's design-build approach to postcolonial state building survived beyond his tenure when Persad-Bissessar embraced it as a feature of her masquerade of permanence.

The UWI–Debe campus suffered the same fate as Tarouba Stadium before it. More than a decade after China Jiangsu received the contract for its construction, the campus facilities remained empty. Despite assurances from the university principal that the south Trinidad campus would open in time for the 2019/20 academic year, additional delays forced administrators to abandon their plans to begin housing students and offer a law curriculum in Debe. To add injury to insult, the vacant dormitories were utilized for the for the first time in March 2020, when they were converted into emergency quarantine facilities to house returning Trinbagonian nationals affected by the COVID-19 pandemic.[36]

Throughout her tenure, Persad-Bissessar's government launched a number of design-build schemes, including the Sir Solomon Hochoy Highway extension and Couva Children's Hospital and Training Center, located in pivotal electoral constituencies. For all state-sponsored development schemes and civic improvements, the appearance of billboards often preceded the breaking of ground on civic improvements and building works. Even as many trifled at the language of this campaign and ridiculed Persad-Bissessar as an alcoholic—the very dunce that Allen had pledged support for in his signature calypso—she proved as bright and cunning as her predecessor. Featuring the tagline "Your government working for you," the billboards embraced the design-build model in an effort to conflate the signing of contracts with the completion of infrastructure.

Like the buildings at Las Alturas, the cracks in the foundation of the petro-state masquerade remained. But, for the first time, its frontline costume adorned an Indo-Trinbagonian woman. In her masquerade, she guaranteed the completion of her signature development projects even once energy markets contracted and production fell. And as her masquerade faltered, another mas erupted on the road.

CHAPTER FIVE

Road Work

Here is another of the innumerable facts of Carnival. An enormous amount of work, of sheer hard labour, goes into the preparation and organisation of these Carnival shows and particularly of the Carnival bands.... The thing to note ... is the amount of work that is done. — C. L. R. James, "Carnival," *Nation* (February 21, 1959)

It was Carnival time in Trinidad. In the first weeks of 2014, Machel Montano released the power soca anthem "M.O.R." in which he crowns himself the "Minister of Road," the perennial champion of the road march.[1] His boast was vindicated when "M.O.R." claimed the road-march title as the most-played song during the annual procession of Carnival bands. Punctuated by the infectious refrain, "Give we more / We want more," the track extols the excesses of music, dance, and fete that accompany masqueraders on the roads of Trinidad and Tobago each year.

The music video for "M.O.R." extends this performative excess to the bureaucratic metaphor of Montano as lead administrator of the mas.[2] The video opens with a fictional newscast of a reporter flanked by protesters chanting the chorus, "We want more!" The reporter approaches a strident protester who enumerates his demands: "Listen. We are challenging the Minister of the Road to come down here now! ... Because we want more! We want more road!"

Montano obliges by arriving at the helm of a motorcade of Range Rovers, tractors, and trucks. Indulging the clamors for more road, Montano performs the track atop a truck owned by the infamous local contractor Junior Sammy. Industrial vehicles conduct road works: bulldozing the route, laying asphalt, and sweeping the finished pavement. After, Montano joins the construction workers, dancers, and erstwhile protesters to survey the new road; heavy machinery is carried off to the approval of all.

"M.O.R." embraces the characteristic hyperbole of the music video genre. Montano swings suggestively from an industrial crane while his dancers perform choreographed routines on a flatbed truck. Moreover, by setting the revelry of Carnival against a backdrop of construction vehicles and machinery, he invokes the double meaning of *road* in Trinbagonian parlance as a public space of democratic potential and a route of transit and commerce. In doing so, he inhabits the spectacle generated by musical performers and state representatives alike. As Minister of Road, Montano accrues legitimacy from his ability to satisfy the desire for more road—to mean the energy, sweat, and bacchanal of the Carnival masquerade.

During Carnival, it is performances of this sort that conjure a communitarian ethos embodied in the nationalist aphorism "All o' we is one." On the road, this celebratory excess appeals to a shared temporality that momentarily appears to resolve ethnoracial, class, and regional divisions. At the same time, "M.O.R." caricatures the bureaucrats and parliamentarians who derive legitimacy from fantastic demonstrations of state resources such as the construction of roads and highways. Extending the Carnivalesque rendering of the road as a "ritual inversion" of societal norms and hierarchies to the material construction of infrastructures, "M.O.R." demonstrates that the seemingly inert qualities of the road can be subverted by Carnival revelers and aggrieved publics alike.[3]

In T&T, politics are practiced on the road. In the postindependence period, roads serve as a state-directed mode of address to translate the largesse of oil and gas revenue into bastions of electoral support. The construction or repair of roads, box drains, and standpipes often coincides with national elections to court prospective voters. On the other hand, informal blockades of burning debris are assembled to disrupt traffic in appeals for employment, fiscal redress, or civic improvements. The road is where the state is made manifest through performances of fiscal and administrative capacity. It is also a site of inversion, where the hegemony of the state is called into question. The road is where the state is made and unmade.

Revealingly, "M.O.R." debuted amid a public row over the largest proposed highway development in the English-speaking Caribbean. The long-anticipated highway from San Fernando to Point Fortin promised to ease the passage of traffic and goods from commercial centers to the oil company towns of Trinidad's southwest peninsula. It also pledged to bring unprecedented development to neglected regions of south Trinidad. A newly proposed section of the highway, referred to in planning documents as the "Debe–Mon Desir segment," promised to deliver the spoils of development to municipalities that formed the electoral base of the ruling People's Partnership (PP).

Although construction stalled under the PP coalition government, the highway was invoked by state functionaries as evidence of their commitment to historically underserved constituencies. With construction confined largely to the less-controversial thoroughfare from San Fernando to Point Fortin, Prime Minister Kamla Persad-Bissessar nonetheless spoke of the disputed segment with an air of inevitability: "We are working to bring the highway down from Golconda, down to Debe and no one will stop us.... The people of the south deserve as much development as the people of the north."[4] Reinforcing a dubiously racialized regional politics—in which descendants of enslaved Africans are deemed to be concentrated in the urban settlements of the east–west corridor and descendants of indentured Indians in the "sugar belt" south of Caroni—Persad-Bissessar championed the highway as an overdue remedy for the deferred development ambitions of rural Indo-Trinbagonians.

While the highway enjoyed popular support during a period of economic growth sparked by an upswing in energy markets, residents threatened with displacement tendered an alternative proposal to reroute the highway, preserve historic settlements, and protect vulnerable wetlands. In 2011, these residents formed the Highway Re-route Movement (HRM) as a vehicle for legal challenges against the highway segment. The fictional protest in "M.O.R." deliberately evokes the HRM and the protest tactics employed by Trinbagonians to appeal to government bodies and functionaries. Yet, in "M.O.R.," the fetish of the road is rendered in its purest form. The location of the protesters is never disclosed. The finished road does not originate from or lead to a specified location. Rather, the calls for "more road" privilege the spectacle of building works above the technical attributes of the roadway. In the music video, it is assumed that the road works as intended. But what are we to make of instances when roads and infrastructures do not work, in which they succumb instead to failures of design, procurement, and structural integrity? Perhaps we may regard instances of this sort as errors of planning that underscore patterns of corruption. Another possible view takes failures of this sort as significant in their own right, generating new avenues of political participation and staging alternative democratic futures.

Mobilizing the Trinbagonian vernacular concept of the road, this chapter proposes *road work* as an insurgent political practice and theoretical framework in political anthropology. This is not merely to suggest that there are lessons to be drawn from roads as ethnographic objects, as many convincingly argue.[5] Rather, while political anthropologists have illuminated the ways in which state power is fortified by quotidian documentary practices and bureaucratic procedures, road work attunes us to the political acts that coincide with moments of infrastructural breakdown and bureaucratic neglect.[6]

The state as such is not a thing. Like the spectacular imagery of the music video, it is a fiction endowed with magical faculties that obscure its dependence on ancillary actors and infrastructures.[7] Here, the study of the state demands an inquiry not only into its bureaucratic and parliamentary divisions, but the spectacle of material edifices, design-and-build models, and deepwater extractive technologies. Periodically, though, this magic wanes and fails to "bridge over the dangerous gaps" that roads, pipelines, and other infrastructures are intended to mitigate.[8] Rather than dismissing moments of this sort as a pathological symptom of failed or weak states, this chapter is concerned with how insurgent collectives exploit such moments to unsettle hegemonic terms of political order.[9] Through acts of protest and refusal, road work contests the dominant meanings and functions of infrastructures as vehicles of sovereign power. Put simply, the practice of road work disrupts the magic that awards the state with its seemingly transcendent qualities. As the state professes its capacity to deliver essential goods and services, it is on the road that its boastful claims are weighed against the sobering realities of faulty or unfinished infrastructures.[10] To study the state from the road, therefore, is to take account of the narratives the state crafts for itself and to question the authoritative perch on which they rest.

More Road

During the early colonial period in the seventeenth and eighteenth centuries, roads in Trinidad were sparse and notoriously treacherous, prohibiting ease of movement throughout the island. After 1797, British colonial administrators surveyed the oppressive terrain and pursued innovative channels of transit and commerce. When asked to enumerate the three requirements of a successful colony, the governor of Trinidad, Sir Arthur Gordon, replied, "Roads, Roads, and again Roads."[11] The obstinate soil and lack of building materials, though, forced Gordon and his associates to pursue alternatives to vehicular roadways.[12] Construction of a railway network to serve the island's sugar plantations began in the early 1870s, eventually extending east from Port of Spain to Arima and south of the capital to Princes Town.[13]

Transit infrastructures in colonial Trinidad principally served the needs of plantation agriculture and colonial management. The Churchill–Roosevelt Highway, for instance, was constructed during the military occupation of Trinidad by American troops during World War II. Initially restricted to US military convoys, the highway opened to the public in 1949, shifting conceptions of the road from a symbol of foreign occupation to a fixture of Trinbagonian social life.

When T&T attained political independence in 1962, the postcolonial state inherited colonial infrastructures oriented toward the demands of North Atlantic capital and military prowess. Oil wells, refineries, roads, and railways buttressed the "infrastructural power" of the fledgling postcolonial state by expanding its "capacity . . . to actually penetrate civil society, and to implement logistically political decisions."[14] Long viewed as alien technologies of colonial administration, infrastructures acquired new meanings as vehicles of state expansion and popular address.

Roads and highways featured prominently in subsequent five-year development plans and national budgets. In its commitment to infrastructural expansion, fledgling state representatives sought to strengthen their hold over a centralized political bureaucracy. The narrative of state development in T&T is a story of infrastructure. Fueled by the oil boom of 1973, Eric Williams's People's National Movement government embarked on an industrialization program that included investments and partnerships in manufacturing and petrochemicals. Tasked with the management of foreign capital and windfall petrodollars, the state turned to infrastructure as a semiotic register to articulate the gap between an elite bureaucracy and plural civil society.[15]

The preoccupation with roads heralded the closure of rail operations; the oil boom itself precipitated the expansion of highways, a rise in automobile ownership, and an upswing in traffic. Transportation was increasingly concentrated on roads—particularly, the two highway thoroughfares running from north to south and east to west. A highway extension to

Point Fortin was first proposed in the early postindependence period as a fix for traffic congestion. But the project idled under the leadership of Williams and the PNM and was discontinued when declining commodity prices triggered a nationwide recession in the 1980s.

As Williams's successor, George Chambers, surmised in the aftermath of the oil boom: "Notwithstanding all these achievements and the continuing programmes and projects already underway, the problem of moving commuters into and out of our urban centres in an orderly fashion appears to defy solution."[16] Efforts to construct more road were thwarted by declining energy prices, and the highway halted abruptly at the Tarouba turnoff north of San Fernando. The unseemly discharge of traffic onto the adjoining San Fernando Bypass Road signaled a failure of governance and fiscal management. The state, unable to implement its technical objectives, sought other means to retain legitimacy with a citizenry attuned to its administrative failings.

The short-lived Jamaat al Muslimeen coup in July 1990 arguably marked the nadir of state legitimacy, after a small but regimented segment of Trinbagonian civil society seized control of the parliament building and the national television network.[17] Although the National Alliance for Reconstruction government was reinstated after six days, public confidence wavered when the government brokered an unpopular loan agreement with the International Monetary Fund. Oil prices remained tepid throughout the 1990s, eclipsing $40 per barrel for only a short period during the Persian Gulf War, and road works were confined to minor improvements and occasional maintenance.

Thereafter, periodic extensions of the Point Fortin Highway coincided with upswings in oil and gas prices. The four-kilometer (two-and-a-half-mile) stretch from Tarouba to Golconda, for instance, opened in 2003. At first glance, modest advances of this sort appear as an insufficient remedy for cyclical crises in state legitimacy. However, road works were inevitably accompanied by promises of more road. As Prime Minister Patrick Manning assured onlookers at the opening of the Golconda extension, construction works would continue south to Point Fortin once his government embarked upon "the most expansive road transportation taking place in the English-speaking Caribbean."[18] While existing infrastructures sustained networks of government patronage, it was the promise of more development that kindled state effects. To this end, the state represented itself as an autonomous repository of windfall petrodollars that would persist into the future. The promise of more road masqueraded as the road itself.

Ride with the Mob, Again

When oil and gas markets spiked in the new millennium, the Manning government tendered a more ambitious scheme for the Point Fortin Highway. The proposal for an additional stretch of highway between Debe and Mon Desir in 2005 sparked the formation of the Debe–San Francique Action Committee, a precursor to what later became the Highway Re-route Movement. In contrast to earlier designs that enjoyed support across the political spectrum, the additional segment threatened to displace established settlements in the rural towns of Siparia, Fyzabad, San Francique, and Debe. In search of tactical guidance, area residents approached Wayne Kublalsingh—a university lecturer and veteran of earlier confrontations over government-sponsored development projects—to serve as an adviser to their campaign.

The local press exalted "eight years of victories for Kublalsingh," during which he halted the construction of proposed industrial smelter plants in Cedros in 2005, Claxton Bay in 2009, and La Brea in 2010.[19] Kublalsingh's involvement with the HRM brought with him a cult of local celebrity and ignominy. In the eyes of supporters, Kublalsingh boasted a pristine history of protracted campaigns against the petro-state and its toxic investments in the downstream industrial works. For detractors, Kublalsingh embodied the roadblocks to economic growth glossed as a misguided commitment to environmental conservation over national development.

While no construction contract had been signed prior to the 2010 elections, the disputed highway segment fueled opposition rhetoric throughout the campaign. Persad-Bissessar, then leader of the opposition and member of Parliament for Siparia, infamously promised there would be "no highway, no byway, no way," redoubling her commitment to underserved constituencies and denouncing persistent corruption and wasteful public expenditure. Her campaign was handed a boost by the signing of the Fyzabad Declaration in April 2010, marking the official formation of the People's Partnership that included Persad-Bissessar's United National Congress, the Congress of the People, Tobago Organization of the People, the National Joint Action Committee, and the Movement for Social Justice. United under the banner of "new politics," this multiracial and cross-regional coalition marked a departure from the bureaucratic machine of the PNM. Instead, the PP advanced a platform of decentralization that promised to break from postcolonial orthodoxy. Although the

PP electoral victory was met with cries of "Indian time ah come"—as the second Indian Trinbagonian and first woman assumed the nation's highest office—it was the confluence of disparate factions that crossed racial, geographic, and apparent ideological lines that prompted a shift in the national electorate.[20]

Under Persad-Bissessar, the principal theater of the petro-state masquerade shifted from the Port of Spain cityscape that had transformed under Manning to the neglected regions of central and south Trinidad. Rather than tall buildings, her government carried out its masquerade of permanence through highways, hospitals, and satellite university campuses. By January 2011, Persad-Bissessar's government ratified a TT$5.2 billion contract for the entirety of the highway project including the disputed segment. Less than a year after the formation of the partnership, the UNC reversed its commitment to the principles of the Fyzabad Declaration. Instead, the highway served as a convenient remedy for the political frictions inherited by her administration, promising to alleviate gridlock and bring spectacular development to an underdeveloped region of her party's electoral base in south Trinidad. The highway exemplified her retreat from the governing accord, setting the stage for a yearslong standoff between Persad-Bissessar and Kublalsingh's organization.

Kublalsingh brought with him an itinerant roster of friends accumulated from previous anti-smelter campaigns that included university students, trade union cadres, and residents of impacted regions on the southwest peninsula. His tactics drew on long-standing traditions of protest perfected by trade unions and grassroots student organizations in the postindependence period. They established protest camps—replete with tarpaulin canopies, protest signs, and propaganda literature—and courted media personnel to serve on the campaign beat. In the long shadows of the glass-and-steel behemoths that underwrite the spectacle of the state's masquerade, Kublalsingh marshaled the HRM and its sympathizers to fashion petty spectacles—occupations, prayers, marches, and hunger strikes—to command the attention of the national press.

In June 2012, police and military forces raided the original protest camp in Debe, forcibly evicting HRM members and demolishing the occupation. Police dragged Kublalsingh away from the build site after he stood firm in the path of a bulldozer. Under the command of National Security Minister (and onetime FIFA Vice President) Jack Warner, deputies razed a makeshift prayer room and movement tents. The HRM, displaced from their south Trinidad base, regrouped by establishing a semipermanent encampment on the roadside opposite the Office of the Prime Minister in Port of Spain. Shifting the location of their protest from the south Trinidad highway route to the seat of executive power in the capital, the HRM recruited newfound audiences to support their cause. Friends emerged on the road. Every morning, HRM members joined the northward pilgrimage of daily commuters from south Trinidad, erecting their tent at the corner of Gray Street and St. Clair Avenue. Posted between the Office of the Prime Minister and the local headquarters of the British oil and gas multinational BG, the protest camp enjoyed frequent visitors in the coming years that included members of the youth organization Project 40, the renowned masman Peter Minshall, members of the media, and students, including an anthropology graduate student completing his degree in the States.

The shift in location from Debe to Port of Spain drew from the masquerade toolkit of Minshall. Rather than a deference to state power and its consolidation in the brick-and-mortar edifices of government halls and offices, the strategy deliberately made use of the state's own ceremonial bombast. Just as Persad-Bissessar blazed a trail from her home constituency in Siparia to the sovereign seat in Port of Spain, Kublalsingh and the HRM trailed behind to mock and unsettle Persad-Bissessar's masquerade of power. Shireen Ramsingh, a recent university graduate and lifelong resident of an area of San Francique zoned for highway development, laid out the terms of the HRM's own masquerade:

> The only way Trinidad moving is when Port of Spain moving. Something happening in Port of Spain then is get bubbling in the country that, you know, is something serious. If it happening in south, deep south, cameraman don't even want to come, media don't even want to come. Because of this Highway Reroute Movement, the media personnel in the country learn a lot about south, you know. Honest to god. Because of the movement they've learned roads they never knew existed, communities they never knew existed because of the movement. And the reason why [Kublalsingh] moved that camp from Debe to Port of Spain is because that is where things happening. Port of Spain. Right in front of the Prime Minister. She doesn't have to come to south. We coming to Port of Spain.

Kublalsingh's tactics intensified with the declaration of a hunger strike on November 15, 2012. In Port of Spain, Kublalsingh enjoyed the company of HRM petitioners and a recurring cast of media observers and sympathizers. Calling for an independent review of the highway project in its entirety, Kublalsingh took to social media after nearly two weeks of hunger to circulate the movement's demands:

> On March 16th 2012, the Prime Minister met with the HRM led by Dr Kublalsingh, and by calling for a halt on all construction and a technical review, acknowledged that there were legitimate technical concerns that needed to be addressed. Today, Dr Kublalsingh is on the 13th day of the hunger strike, to protest the Government's failure to provide the independent review.
>
> The HRM was subsequently called to two meetings. At the first meeting, the HRM was prevented from bringing their own technical team to meet with the Government's technical team and it is because of this that the HRM left the meeting. At the second meeting the HRM was given a five-page document with photographs and one-line statements. At no stage have the technical reports been produced in the areas of hydrology, environmental and social impact, or cost benefit. Although construction works were slowed for a while it has never stopped.
>
> The Government claims to have satisfied the promise of the technical review. The HRM has called the process a farce and a public relations gimmick.[21]

The language of gimmick gestures at the terms of Kublalsingh's own masquerade. As the cultural theorist Sianne Ngai reminds us in her critical archaeology: "While the subject who finds the aesthetic object gimmicky is not taken in by its promises, there exists another subject who is."[22] In other words, to declare the government's claims a gimmick is to interrupt the state as a masquerade that cannot be passively taken at its word, but contains within it the very real power to enchant and command audiences of subjects. Likewise, as Kublalsingh's hunger strike continued, many commentators began to doubt the sincerity of his protest. Jokes abounded on social media as many claimed to have witnessed Kublalsingh in line at local doubles stands or KFC drive-through windows. In the standoff between Kublalsingh and Persad-Bissessar, his emaciated body constituted the grounds of the confrontation between competing masquerades of the state and its critics. Again, the success of each is determined by the extent to which its masquerade veils the conditions of its production. The historic triumph of the state masquerade lies in our inability to identify it as a mas — a gimmick whose promises we are not taken in by.

Kublalsingh's masquerade prevailed in the first round. On December 5, after twenty-one days without food, Kublalsingh accepted the terms of a mediation session between the government and the Joint Consultative Council headed by the chartered surveyor Afra Raymond. Raymond appointed Dr. James Armstrong as chair of a committee to undertake a feasibility study and independent review of the disputed highway segment. While awaiting those findings, the government pledged to halt additional road works on the Debe–Mon Desir highway and suspend the compulsory acquisition and removal of homes along the intended route.

In March 2013, Armstrong returned the 265-page *Report of the Independent Review Committee of the Debe to Mon Desir Segment of the San Fernando to Point Fortin Highway*, more commonly known as the "Armstrong report." The summary of the report included recommendations that no further work be undertaken on the Debe–Mon Desir segment until environmental and water management plans had been submitted to and approved by relevant agencies and a social-impact assessment completed to anticipate "severe adverse impacts to the resident population" of the regions in question. Moreover, the report condemned the procurement process that awarded the highway construction contract to the Brazilian conglomerate Construtora OAS. Embracing the turnkey approach to large publicly funded infrastructure projects spearheaded by the Manning administration, Persad-Bissessar's government extended a design-build agreement to the Brazilian outfit. The Armstrong report concurred with its counterparts from the Uff Commission three years prior:

> The Design-Build approach is considered suitable for well-defined projects with a clearly defined scope of works and list of requirements e.g. buildings. In the case of infrastructural works, such as highways, Design-Build should only be applied in cases where detailed designs and plans are already available at [the] Tendering Phase, and the design tasks will be limited mainly to value engineering.[23]

Following the lead of Manning and Hart in the decade prior, the design-build contract for the highway upheld the values of state building as a practice of rapid and spectacular development directed to key constituencies. At the same time, the design-build contract recalled the hasty expenditure of public funds on vanity projects championed by previous governments.

Aside from this, however, the Armstrong report assumed a social life of its own as a barometer of Persad-Bissessar's aborted pledges to adhere to the findings of the independent review. Shortly after I returned to Trinidad for fieldwork in September 2014, I received a Facebook message from Kublalsingh calling on members of the public to join him the following day outside the Office of the Prime Minister in Port of Spain. In an open letter circulated on a print flier and delivered to the prime minister, Kublalsingh announced his intention to resume the hunger strike if the government refused to abide by the findings of the Armstrong report and discontinue construction pending further review:

> Honourable Prime Minister, we strongly advocate that you keep your promise to put on hold and review the Debe to Mon Desir highway; a position reiterated in the Armstrong Report. A failure to keep your promise will lead to a repeat hunger strike, the consequences and risks of which are unknown.
>
> The hunger strike will start fourteen days from the date of this letter. The hunger strike will stop Madame when you agree to keep your promise to put on hold and review the Debe to Mon Desir Highway. And when you and your government agree to meet with our team of independent experts and professionals to determine the terms of this review and by whom and how it shall be executed.

Early the next morning, I climbed aboard a westbound route taxi to join a small contingent of HRM stalwarts seated on the curb outside the Office of the Prime Minister. As we waited for stragglers to arrive, I spoke with Kublalsingh about my progress since our initial introduction the year before. I rehearsed a short description of my research on fossil fuel development and grassroots politics before he cut my statement short. "*This* is politics," he interjected, gesticulating imprecisely around us. Initially, it was unclear whether he meant to refer to the street in front of us, the government offices on the opposite roadside, or the small group of concerned citizens gathered at our side. Timidly, I abandoned my summary and sat quietly on the edge of the roadside box drain.

Soon, we assembled to gather instructions for the demonstration. After flags and placards were distributed to the approximately two dozen in attendance, we formed a line to display the placards to the Office of the Prime Minister and passing pedestrians and motorists. We proceeded to march up and down the curb in a tight oval, and chanting demands in a collective call-and-response. To calls of "Do the review," we shouted, "Now!" To calls of "Abide by the," we replied, "Armstrong report!" To calls of "Keep your promise," we replied, "Prime Minister!" And so on. On occasion, some would break form to replace "Prime Minister" with

"Drunk Prime Minister," supplementing their pleas with accusations of Persad-Bissessar's alcoholism that jabbed at a supposed incapacity to govern. Later, members of the national media arrived to capture photographs and video as we circled up and down the road. As the cameras rolled, members of the movement held unequivocally to the ideals of technical review procedure and parliamentary due process.

Persad-Bissessar—often referred to by her given name as simply Kamla—emerged as a constant object of gossip and playful derision. But while typical gossip revolved around her deaf-eared temperament and rumored penchant for alcohol consumption, the response to her glib indifference centered on her ties to the rural, predominantly Hindu communities in south Trinidad. Indira Rampersad, one of many south Trinidadians who completed the daily pilgrimage to Port of Spain, reasoned, "She from down south, down Siparia. She should know better to say [the highway] ain't going through a wetland." But to the contrary, on the forty-fourth day of Kublalsingh's second hunger strike, *Trinidad Express* reporters pressed Persad-Bissessar to clarify her position on the HRM. She adeptly deflected the line of questioning, closing with a dismissive quip: "Those matters are not important to me, I have a country to run."[24]

At a public demonstration held in Port of Spain during Kublalsingh's hunger strike, an HRM spokeswoman—in her capacity as a licensed barrister and Debe resident—clarified the debate over environmental impacts and assessment:

> On the news, government ministers are saying it's skirting the Oropouche Lagoon. That is not correct, because the Oropouche Lagoon extends all the way beyond what we see on the map. If you look at the map of Trinidad, you will see a blue area and it says it represents the Oropouche Lagoon. But the truth is, if you live in that area, if you're familiar with the rivers and how they flow into the area, you will know that the Oropouche Lagoon extends far beyond that, into the area called Barrackpore.[25]

A proverbial daughter of the sugar belt, Persad-Bissessar personified the practices of state simplification that accompany the consolidation of a postcolonial bureaucracy.[26] The appeal to local knowledge against the detached methods of state planning cast the prime minister as a corruptible body subject to the whims of transnational capital and local elites. My friend Shireen again made this clear when we discussed the matter at the Gulf City Mall in San Fernando.

It's blatant to see that [the highway project] is [proceeding] because of money. Is because of kickbacks. Is because of how much jobs they going to get out of this, how much people and how much of they family and friends it going to help. Financiers like that, people that they going to give big contracts to, so when election time roll around, these are the people that are going to finance them. And to see it from that perspective, to see that these are the same people, these are the same ministers who led the people in opposition.

And Kamla herself said there would be no highways, no byways through these communities. Today is different. Is totally opposite—she wants it. But to a certain extent, I think she doesn't have the authority even if she wants to say something like, *Let us give in to a certain amount*, because she probably can see that is not really logical to put two highways five minutes apart taking you to the same destination. She knows there are things that are flawed. But because, like I say, I believe she does not have that final say, she like a puppet and people pushing her around.

In Trinidad and elsewhere, it is commonplace to decry the influence of money in politics. Less remarked upon are the ways in which an enforced separation of the state from the economy—its "isolation effect"—preserves understandings of the state as an institution divorced from the exigencies of capital and social reproduction.[27] Vernacular narratives of corruption, by contrast, resist this isolation effect by implicating the state in the operations of a shadow private sector that is tolerated in official discourse but informally decried across diverse segments of Trinbagonian society.

Following Antonio Gramsci, critics mobilize the concept of hegemony to apprehend the state as a contested arena through which the relationship between political and civil society is negotiated.[28] Rather than a synonym for brute domination, hegemony comprises an "entire complex of practical and theoretical activities with which the ruling class not only justifies and maintains its dominance, but manages to win the active consent of those over whom it rules."[29] In other words, the state is produced equally in the halls of Parliament and on the road in its construction, blockade, or the Carnival masquerade.

When the government refused to suspend highway works, Kublalsingh resumed his hunger strike and the movement reprised its makeshift camp from two years prior. While some traveled daily from their embattled homesteads to Port of Spain, the camp attracted sympathizers otherwise disillusioned with the incumbent government. Members of the local press made regular visits to the camp, as those present rehearsed the core objectives of the movement to abide by the recommendations of the Armstrong report and halt construction of the disputed segment. Conversations took on a decidedly different tenor when the curious reporters and their cameras left.

For some, the executive role of prime minister constituted a "dictatorship on a five-year lease," in which national elections nominally shift political power from one faction of elites to another. As a septuagenarian from Debe reasoned, "When the five years finish and she pockets full, she go leave the highway." Many echoed this view, ascribing accusations of a government land grab and fiscal malfeasance to the highway extension. While the camp was strategically positioned adjacent to her executive office, the prime minister never appeared at the camp to respond directly to any demands. As days turned to weeks, it became clear that few expected her to do so. Why, then, do those skeptical of the state and its dubious commitment to democracy nonetheless stand at the feet of its cathedrals of political power?

Although party politics are a constant preoccupation of everyday talk in Trinidad, a undercurrent of skepticism toward parliamentary democracy flows aplenty. Corruption, or in Trinbagonian creole, *bobol*, is a constant preoccupation of media commentaries and popular discourse. As the late Guyanese historian Walter Rodney observed, "The populace [of Trinidad] has become conditioned to the existence of widespread corruption. It is the butt of jokes; it provides the subject matter for calypsos.... It is recognised that corruption is now endemic to the political system."[30] On the one hand, corruption is an accepted feature of Trinbagonian social life, in which bribes and political nepotism are accepted as a "way of getting business done."[31] On the other, it is derided as an abdication of the social contract and a cause célèbre of disenfranchised classes and the political opposition.

Even as the ranks of Kublalsingh's skeptics grew once his hunger strike eclipsed one hundred days, homegrown theories proliferated the camp. On an ordinary day, a small group of fewer than a dozen would sit quietly under a makeshift awning to seek respite from the harsh sun. Unlike the publicized demonstrations that attracted scores of trade unionists, opposition party loyalists, and retrenched workers, the camp typically featured a handful of affected residents engaged in casual talk. Copies of the local *Guardian* and *Express* newspapers circulated about, spreading relevant news. Reports of a corruption indictment involving Construtora OAS—the Brazilian construction company awarded the contract for the highway— and the premature erosion of the new highway during heavy rains stirred condemnations of its procurement and structural integrity.

As I have detailed in the previous chapter, incomplete or defective infrastructures such as the Brian Lara Stadium, the National Academy for the Performing Arts, and the Las Alturas housing complex index failures of governance in accordance with flawed planning, fiscal troubles, or neglect by political opposition. Suggestive commentaries on the highway similarly aligned flaws of technical implementation with the shrouded intentions of the state and private business. Rumored tar-sands oil development in the vicinity of the disputed highway fueled one prominent theory and acquired considerable attention in the form of a pamphlet authored by the Canadian activist Macdonald Stainsby.[32] More than simply a failed infrastructure, the highway appeared suspended in its initial planning stages as a convenient guise for the extractive designs of an elite petrostate bureaucracy.[33]

Discourses of corruption provide vital measures of the perceived legitimacy of state institutions and activities.[34] In T&T, a dualistic view of the state pervades: as a sanctified body corrupted by deceitful politicians, in one sense; in another, as an intrinsically corrupt body beset by inherited colonial governing structures and sustained economic dependence. The postcolonial state is simultaneously repressive and productive. It cannot be reduced to an assembly of repressive ideological apparatuses or a guarantor of liberal rights and privileges.

Inspired by Gramsci, political theorists and social critics trouble an instrumentalist approach to the state.[35] The concept of hegemony, in its insistence upon the contingency of all sovereign formations, lends itself to an analysis of road work as a grammar of political critique. From this vantage, it matters little whether accusations of political corruption are corroborated. Instead, while the state claims an absolute monopoly on the legitimate carriage of governance, road work unsettles this monopoly through its mobilization of popular discourses of corruption to interrupt the state's masquerade. As a masquerade fashioned out of technical works and bureaucratic institutions, the state is susceptible to failure, deterioration, and sabotage. Put differently, the state's masquerade must continually be propped up, reinforced, and retrofitted at moments of breakdown and crisis.

Roads are quintessentially unfinished objects. Even upon completion, they require frequent maintenance and repair to address seasonal wear or periodic breakdowns. And the construction of roads precipitates more road through the construction of tributary routes. In turn, roads are vibrant archives of state planning. Unlike pipelines and electric grids—which ostensibly function surreptitiously beneath the field of view—roads are eminently visible and endowed with aesthetic intent.[36] It is unsurprising, then, that roads often emerge as an insurgent ground for practices of citizenship.[37]

It is not unusual to hear Trinbagonians proclaim in exasperation, "Nothing works in Trinidad." A 1981 pamphlet circulated by the Organisation for National Reconstruction (ONR) fittingly bears the title *Why Nothing Works in Trinidad and Tobago*. Mobilized behind the political leader Karl Hudson-Phillips, the onetime heir apparent to Eric Williams, the ONR staked its facetious claim to the matter of roads: "The condition of our roads is a living testimony of this real waste down government.... Millions of our precious petro-dollars are being spent to dig up roads on a weekly basis for the laying of pipes and electricity cables and the more they dig, the more power cuts, water lock-offs and the more telephones out of order."[38] Calling attention to the blackouts that persisted after the installation of electric cables and pipeline infrastructures, the colloquial dig at frequent power outages suggests that neither the electric current nor the power of the state can be taken for granted. Rather, its precarious networks of roads and power lines take shape by way of the opportune alliances of bureaucrats and private contractors under which contracts are awarded, campaigns are funded, and highways are built. But it is precisely when "nothing works" that the state is demystified and opened to popular critique.

The people's masquerade flourishes in these moments when the state's claims to power are demystified as a masquerade of its own. That the ordinary repertoires of protest I call road work also adopt the form of a masquerade—in their deliberate fashioning of public spectacles, occupations, and hunger strikes—should not be taken as evidence that it is lacking in substance. Just as the state masquerade deploys its very real arsenal of violence to endorse its claims to legitimacy, the people's masquerade draws its power from the fact that at any moment the staging of public spectacles can erupt into a genuine uprising. Just as Captain Baker could not discern whether the Carnival revelers in 1881 were merely playing a mas or launching an insurrection against colonial authorities, road work exposes the fragility of sovereign authority. In other words, in its clashes with the postcolonial state, the vernacular register of road work invites state actors and their deputies to confront the people on the road. When the state is revealed as a masquerade, it is compelled "to recognize its arbitrariness, reveal its contingent dimension."[39] Likewise, it demonstrates how power can be seized by a popular masquerade that does not stop—one that does not anticipate the return of state-sanctioned order and discipline. The state's monopoly on legitimate violence is not a natural or inevitable order of things. Even as we insist otherwise, there is a tendency to assume that the state is a thing that conforms to a prescribed set of instrumental functions. Admittedly, it sometimes appears to do so. But how a given state works—or does not—remains an open question informed by its own historical particulars. Such is the case in T&T.

Highway Mas

In the final months of 2014, a decline in oil prices triggered fears of economic recession in T&T. When markets contracted, the government altered the national budget, initially pegged to an oil price of $80 per barrel, to a revised estimate of $45. Nevertheless, as the government prepared for parliamentary elections, its representatives assured the public that there would be no cutbacks to its signature development projects such as the Couva Children's Hospital and Point Fortin Highway. In a national address, Prime Minister Persad-Bissessar chipped away at her detractors for "using a period of challenges to promote fear and panic," and later proclaimed, "We can withstand the lower oil prices and the right Government is in place at the best possible time."[40]

In June, following the assurances of government ministers and technocrats, the HRM and allied trade union outfits, including the Oilfields Workers' Trade Union, Amalgamated Workers Union, and Steel Workers Union of T&T, convened to tour the route of the disputed segment and survey construction progress. We gathered at the home of one of the movement's long-standing members, which stood at the intended site of the Mon Desir interchange. When I arrived, Vidia Seepersad, a retired oilman and familiar presence at the movement camp in Port of Spain, gestured in my direction and continued down a path overgrown with brush. I traced his steps through the tall grasses to an open clearing that marked the proposed site of the interchange. Despite claims by government ministers that construction had proceeded past a proverbial point of no return, we encountered only scattered patches of tilled earth (figure 5.1).

As we surveyed the landscape, Mr. Seepersad began, "Well the government people, they saying that they progressing and the people are cooperating and they being handsomely compensated. It is not so." We traded sarcastic barbs about the sitting government's desperation to win votes in the upcoming election. Then, in a more serious tone, he recalled, "Now, I've seen in the NIDCO [National Infrastructure Development Company] office a drawing, you know, of what they say is Petit Morne. But when I looked at it, you know, they sketch it out like a development. And what I

FIGURE 5.1. The proposed site of the Mon Desir interchange. Photograph by the author.

tend to believe is they want to get rid of all the people who are scattered and put them there and seize the lands. That the whole idea behind the highway." The scheme he referred to—a public housing project in the nearby community of Petit Morne—was no secret. NIDCO press releases openly advertised subsidized land and housing for relocated homeowners. He cast doubt, though, on the purportedly benevolent displacement of citizens.

When we returned to the adjacent homestead, I claimed a seat next to my friend Shireen. We joined Sheldon Phillip, another retired employee of the state oil company, Petrotrin, beside the front door. As we waited for a bus to arrive from the OWTU headquarters in San Fernando, our conversation generated more speculation.

"You see how flawed the process is?" Shireen interjected as I returned to the spirited exchange.

"Well, if you a businessman, you don't think about that until after the fact. Is the money first, is the planning later," I added, attempting a dig at the contractors at the helm of the highway.

Phillip chimed in: "The first thing that happened—you have to know this—there was a road on the creek and for some reason they never repair it because the creek always sinking."

"And it end up like the road in Manzanilla?" I probed. Earlier in the rainy season, a section of the Manzanilla–Mayaro Road in eastern Trinidad collapsed into the sea. The fate of this road resonated with his assessment of the South Trunk Road in San Fernando.

"You understand?" Phillip replied, confirming my observation. "And that was the first part of the road they start, ent? They had to send for American engineers to come and say well, what we should do?" We shared a laugh. Over several drives through the floodwaters from Mosquito Creek, I observed the deficiencies of the retaining wall that countless locals knew already. Our laughter signaled a collective recognition of the problems that the government had inexplicably failed to account for.

"That's five billion dollars gone, enuh!" another voice chimed in, rounding off the reported cost of the highway. "And you know what? At the end of the day they'll come back and say the contractor want more money."

"They want more money already," Phillip countered. "What I saying is this: if you signing a contract, once you say *design and build—design and build*, it means that when you going up the road, you could meet any kind of thing ahead of you and decide then that we can't build here."

"Because they allocate the whole contract to one company," I concluded.

We debated the particulars of construction contracts before Phillip resumed his narrative: "Now, the next part about that is this: What has happened is that Eric Williams promised to build the San Fernando–Point Fortin highway from 1956. But because of inconveniences and probably money, he didn't do it. But he went—the PNM went ahead and did the feasibility study from San Fernando to Mayaro. To Princes Town. And they got all the people off, bought all the properties and everything. So that was the highway to be built! Because they did everything there. But when you watch and you see how much money you could have make building it, they decide, *I go build here. Nobody can tell me nothing, I go build here.* Them didn't realize we would've stand up and say no, you know?"

As he recalled, an earlier route for the highway was proposed and cleared decades prior. The plan for an additional highway from Debe to Mon Desir, in his version of events, was invested more in land grabbing than road building. It was unclear whether this land grab was motivated by oil-sands reserves or the infamous kickbacks associated with construction contracts. In either case, the function or direction of the road mattered little. All that was needed was more road.

Once the bus and its occupants arrived, our group of approximately two dozen gathered to canvass the highway route and review the construction underway. We stopped at the proposed locations of several interchanges,

FIGURE 5.2. Construction of the Debe–Mon Desir highway at Gandhi Village, Debe. Photograph by the author.

none of which showed any signs of road work. Only as we neared the junction in Debe did we encounter a single stretch of turned soil flanked by two idle bulldozers (figure 5.2).

During one stop on our tour, OWTU President General Ancel Roget briefed reporters on his findings: "Their justification for continuing this or wanting to complete this segment of the highway is built on a lie. That is that it is some 60 or 70 percent completed. When you hear their supporters say, 'Build the highway,' they are talking about build up their pockets. And that is what we're against." His words resounded against the backdrop of the open clearing that supplied evidence of this deceit. The money had been spent. For what was billed as a TT$5.2 billion project, more than TT$5 billion had been paid out. Yet, there was no road.

Less than a month before national elections, the Debe interchange opened to the public. At the ribbon-cutting ceremony, Prime Minister Persad-Bissessar stood on the pristine asphalt in front of a large banner that read MA, KAMLA, THANK YOU FOR THIS HIGHWAY. White, red, and black confetti showered down on the prime minister and the stilt walkers arranged beside her before coming to rest on the finished pavement. While the highway remained far from complete, the interchange was called upon to ease any doubts regarding its timely completion. In the spirit of Carnival, the Debe interchange masqueraded as the highway in its entirety. The deteriorating public coffers and long stretches of untouched land along the route of the highway told another story. The road remained unfinished. Its destination remained unclear. Instead, the fetish of the road was rendered in its purest form. It was simply more road.

Good Sense

In its commonplace usage, *road work* describes the expansion of the power of the state through the construction of streets, highways, and thoroughfares that bolster its administrative reach and permit access to new markets. Karl Marx echoed this view in the *Grundrisse* (1939) when he supplemented his diagnosis of capitalist expansion as "the annihilation of space by time" with a brief aside on the building of roads.[41] In its pursuit of new markets and productive enclaves, he reasoned, capital "will produce roads only when the production of roads has become a necessity for the producers . . . a condition for the capitalist's *profit making*."[42] In his insufficient theorization of the state, Marx did not consider roads apart from their value to the reproduction of capital. The aesthetic dimensions of incomplete highways and roads that lead nowhere demand a more nuanced view. In such instances, it matters little whether the road works as an avenue of transport. As a spectacular venture in which the "means are simultaneously its ends," the construction of more road matters even when it does not serve the immediate interests of capital.[43]

Roads are neglected instruments of common sense. They collapse spatial and temporal distances and inaugurate relations between peoples and communities. However, just as colonial administrators equated civilization with "Roads, Roads, and again Roads," the commonsense values of the postcolonial state champion roads as markers of social progress.[44] By this calculus, the spoils of citizenship can be reduced to the construction of more roads irrespective of their location or utility.

Likewise, Gramsci regards common sense as a "chaotic aggregate" of vernacular knowledge and superstitions that reproduce the ruling class as a hegemonic bloc.[45] In a state of incoherence and naïveté, common sense upholds the provincial interests of the ruling class. Nonetheless, common sense contains elements of what Gramsci calls "good sense" that must be "made more unitary and coherent."[46] In this respect, common sense is the foundation of all revolutionary transformations. The movement from common sense to good sense is a matter of "making 'critical' an already existing activity" of vernacular philosophy and immanent critique.[47] To grant common sense an ideological coherence disrupts the process by which a contingent political order comes to be represented as "natural and interminable."[48]

The Caribbean is not the principal subject of Gramsci's political writings. We can only speculate as to why the concept of hegemony was elaborated in Italy rather than the Caribbean. While I am hesitant to do so, it is often the case in the Caribbean that this hegemony is less coherent than in Gramsci's commentaries on Italian situation. Political leaders are casually addressed by their given names—"Kamla," "Keith," "Jack." Infrastructural failings are laid bare by shared laughs of recognition. In the Caribbean, the concept of hegemony is already self-evident. When politics are practiced on the road, the hegemony of the state fragments alongside cracks in its auxiliary infrastructures such as highways, retaining walls, and cataleptic bureaucracies. If we borrow the language of Gramsci, it is at moments when the state's masquerade of permanence is interrupted by the popular register of road work that good sense prevails.

For the anthropologist Kathryn Takabvirwa, the road is where prevailing theories of the state and disciplinary power melt into air. Revising a Foucauldian genealogy in which the deputies of the state progressively disappear from view in favor of a panoptic condition of self-discipline and docility, Takabvirwa turns to the roadblocks that pervaded the final years of Robert Mugabe's reign in Zimbabwe not as a failure of the African state to embrace a model of disciplinary power but an enduring testimony to the failure of the nation-state in general to transgress its material infrastructures and petty sovereign agents. Roadblocks persisted in Zimbabwe "not because the Zimbabwean police fail[ed] to 'discipline' the mobile citizenry.... Rather, power is deeply personal, and policing depends for its success on the continued presence of the people through whom the state appears."[49] Where some scholars attempt to rescue a Foucauldian frame by contrasting the repressive dimensions of postcolonial power to the liberal modalities of sovereign power in the North Atlantic, Takabvirwa unveils the false distinction between the geographies of repressive and disciplinary power.[50] If a North Atlantic common sense holds that the state does indeed achieve "perfection" in the form of "a power relation independent of the person who exercises it," the good sense fostered in the postcolony reminds us that the state does not operate in a depersonalized register.[51] In confronting the state as an assembly of personal relations that unfold on the road, we are indeed reminded that the state is a relation and not a thing.

As inheritors of British colonial norms of parliamentary governance, the postcolonial states of the anglophone Caribbean are characterized by a strikingly duplicity. On the one hand, a ritualistic adherence to bureaucratic procedure is revered as a marker of postcolonial respectability. On the other, bureaucracy is a constant object of popular derision, one that insists that nothing works as it should. Again, as Michel-Rolph Trouillot tells us, in the postcolonial Caribbean the equation of civil society with political society, registered in the hyphenated compound *nation-state*, is often disarticulated.[52] In this respect, Caribbean sovereignty is defined by its incompleteness—its suspension between colonial governance and the unfulfilled promise of postcolonial sovereignty.

Political theorists typically regard the Caribbean as an exceptional geography marked by distinctively plural demographics, forms of governance, and circuits of violence.[53] Perhaps it is for this reason that "in studies of the Caribbean, the state has always fallen just outside the line of anthropological vision."[54] Just as anthropological approaches to the state have benefited greatly from a turn toward its constitutive margins that refuses a static definition of the state as a prescriptive set of governing practices, a more thoroughgoing engagement with the Caribbean directs us toward neglected theaters of statecraft where its powers of rule cannot be taken for granted.[55]

Road work encompasses an array of practices that unsettle the presumed hegemony of the state through blockades, occupations, strikes, and propaganda. While the Caribbean is often dismissed as a region of small states, quasi-states, and dependencies that fail to conform to the normative expectations of modern sovereignty, road work demands that we draw lessons from such small places—where the state appears less transcendent as a palpable assembly of social actors and institutional structures.[56] From the vantage of the Caribbean, suspension and incompleteness appear as operative conditions of the practice of sovereignty in general. In ordinary encounters on the road, the fact of the state as a masquerade is laid bare.

Not unlike the fleeting temporality of Carnival, roads are transient structures that are nonetheless reified as timeless and objective features of the social landscape. All reification is, indeed, "a forgetting" by which the labor that laid the road is purged from memory.[57] In its masquerade, the state depicts itself as a permanent arrangement of infrastructural power. Road work, on the other hand, "fights reification by making the petrified world speak, sing, perhaps dance."[58]

And in Trinidad, the road overflows with talk, song, and dance.

CODA

Play a Mas

You never know when it is going to explode. The revolutionary movement is a series of explosions when the regular routine of things reaches a pitch where it cannot go on. To me that's a philosophical question based on history and I am never in any doubt—I am in doubt for tomorrow, maybe—but I am never in any doubt for the day after tomorrow. It has been a fundamental part of my outlook, a statement of Marx early on, that the revolution comes like a thief in the night.—C. L. R. James (1989)

The political philosophy of C. L. R. James bookends this study. Regarded imprecisely as a dissident Marxist or a "paradoxical Pan-Africanist" by his contemporaries and critics, the James I am indebted to most closely resembles the figure eulogized by George Lamming in Tunapuna, Trinidad, in 1989.[1] "James," Lamming recalled, "was an evangelist."[2] The word of James's political gospel was not sovereignty in the Hobbesian sense. His oeuvre confirmed instead the creative dimensions of working-class life, from his earliest barrack yard fiction to his manifestos on workers' councils, wildcat strikes, and West Indies cricket.[3]

In 1958, "Nello" James returned to Trinidad at the invitation of Eric Williams. Williams himself had returned to Trinidad to assume a post as political leader of the PNM. His position at the vanguard of the anticolonial movement in the West Indies was secured only by the unyielding agitation of working people against colonial rule. For the moment, the leader aligned with the masses. They gathered by the hundreds to receive addresses delivered by Williams at the University of Woodford Square. In this open-air forum, the Dionysian audience made its desires and dissent known. Politics spilled onto the road.

James accepted a role as a political deputy to his protégé, serving as an editor of the party newspaper the *Nation*. In his view, the *Nation* represented more than an organ of party decrees and resolutions. A newspaper, emulating the popular forum of Woodford Square, formed the material basis of a mass party for the West Indies: "Independence must mean the independent production of ideas to whatever degree adapted from elsewhere, their independent printing and publication in the West Indies. This is no ideal. It is a necessity."[4] In the prelude to independence, the *Nation* embodied his evangelism of direct democracy and the self-governing capacities of ordinary people in the Caribbean.[5]

This vision took shape in James's regular contributions to the paper on deceptively mundane matters such as the exclusion of Black all-rounders from the captaincy of West Indies cricket. His entries for the *Nation* reflected the popular desires of a Caribbean nation simmering below the political surface: "Once more the general public read with deep satisfaction. It saw in print what it wanted expressed."[6] James understood that the spectacle of athletics could not be dismissed as apolitical. His role as a Caribbean intellectual, instead, was to distill and cultivate the popular will that rests in the crowds of spectators that line the stands for test matches at Queen's Park Oval. More than simply echoing their sentiments in print, the party newspaper exalted the creative potential of the Caribbean masses. James wept, "People of the West Indies, you do not know your own power."[7] Far from mere cults of distraction, cricket and the arts formed the basis of his proselytism.

Alongside his more numerable and celebrated reflections on cricket, James dedicated his platform in the *Nation* to reasonings on Carnival.[8] As opposed to the demarcated boundaries of cricket pitch, where a batsman takes his turn standing in the crease where for "all intents and purposes, he is his side," the Carnival road march clears a space of creative abundance beyond prescriptive rules and conventions.[9] James venerates the seasonal preparations for Carnival as something of a dress rehearsal for true independence, where ordinary people display the capacity to govern themselves and enter political life on their own authority:

> Hundreds of people get together in order to organize a display of a certain kind, put themselves under a leader, make all the necessary preparations, make their displays for two days and then, after a period, settle down to do it again. The thing to note is that it is self-organisation.[10]

The meticulous preparation for Carnival—the design of costumes, the gathering of bands, the parade of trucks, and the revelers of the road march—are not a diversion from the realm of politics. Here we observe the greatest demonstration of power among the Caribbean people. The role of the Caribbean intellectual is not to dispense power by decree, but to testify to the immanent capacity for power that the Carnival masquerade beholds.[11]

In James's day and our own, conservative critics have chastised Carnival goers for their conspicuous expenditure of personal savings or withdrawal of bank loans to participate in the annual bacchanal. James is firm in his retort: "Let the heathen rage."[12] Power does not emanate from individual scrounging or restraint. Rather, it is precisely the commitment of the Trinbagonian people to gather year over year for a fleeting masquerade that confirms their capacity for power:

> Or if the Government is able, as it may have to do, to impress the people with the necessity for some great national effort, then once the people are convinced that the effort that they are being called upon to make is worth making, that it is for a good cause, and is led by people they can trust, then we can be certain that *the energy, the creativity and the capacity for independent organization which they show in Carnival will very easily be transferred to another object*. We can see in the Carnival the possibility (we do not go any further than possibility) of such a national mobilisation, as would put to shame all efforts that have hitherto been made in industrial and social activity.[13]

In 1959, James maintained faith in his protégé, Williams, to impress this necessity upon the people to marshal their power. The following April, he would see his faith rewarded with the march on Chaguaramas to demand the return of the US naval base. But Williams did not observe this mobilization of the Caribbean people as a basic condition of democracy rather than an accessory to his own masquerade of power. In confusing his personalization of the party for the party itself, Williams's state masquerade diverged from the people's mas. When James laid out his proposal for the reorganization of the PNM into a mass party in *P.N.M. Go Forward*, Williams demurred. As Roy Augier would presciently observe in his review of James's proposal after its eventual publication in the tract *Party Politics in the West Indies* (1962), "instead of performing a root and branch operation, [Williams] *mounts a masquerade*."[14] Rather than placing power in the hands of the masses, Williams consolidated power in a mas of middle-class leadership and an authoritarian police state.

In his failure to heed his estranged tutor in matters of the political, Williams did not foresee the explosion of Black Power in February 1970. The masses returned politics to the road. By 1973, Williams could not prepare to depart from political life without landing a final blow against the power of the people's masquerade. The "Doctor Politics" of the professional middle class prevailed over a Jamesian vision of the mass democracy and workers' self-management. In the account of another James acolyte, Franklyn Harvey, "Power was *not* to be in the whole class, but in the leader—the 'doctor.'"[15] In his soon-to-be-aborted retirement address, we might recall that Williams decried the ills of rampant individualism and shared his regret that any "national movement as there is does not go beyond increased participation in Carnival."[16]

Williams could not appreciate the Carnival masquerade as an example of what the anthropologist of Trinidadian obeah Brent Crosson calls an "experiment with power."[17] While Crosson is concerned principally with the repertoires of "healing" and "science" carried out by spiritual workers glossed by the colonial archive and postcolonial authorities as "obeah," his work *Experiments with Power* (2020) provides an unheralded theory of the state as an occulted form of the same order as the obeah it condemns. As he reminds us, Hobbes's theory of sovereignty made his aversion to the "occult properties" of spirits and magic evident.[18] Furthermore, Hobbes insists that the sovereign alone decides what constitutes a miracle and who is capable of performing one. This is precisely why the experiments with power of ordinary people draw the ire and even the ban of the state. In illicit spaces of experimentation, spiritual "workers' theories of balance present an alternative conception of virtue in which the interplay of contrasting forces is the basis for an ethics of justice, responsibility, and power."[19] To restate my thesis in the terms of Crosson's comrades in *science*, the apparent success of the Trinbagonian sovereignty lies in its occult fusion of political power with carbon fuels. Enshrined in the hyphenated compound of the petro-state, this relation appears to us deceptively as permanent and indivisible rather than a contingent experiment with power.

Against Leviathan!

Today, the habitability of the Caribbean is threatened by warming temperatures, rising coastal sea levels, and the intensification of hurricanes and severe tropical storms. Since the commercial discovery of petroleum deposits in the nineteenth century, the political futures of T&T have been staked to the exploitation and expansion of markets for this precious resource. *The Petro-state Masquerade* is concerned with the ways this series of historical events came together for a brief geological moment to derail alternative models for Caribbean political life.

Never has the necessity of evangelizing alternatives been more urgent. David Hughes sounds this alarm in his ethnography-cum-manifesto of a "national intelligentsia of climate change" in T&T.[20] Under the protective guise of climate vulnerability, enterprising technocrats flout the existential threat of climate change. This move to climate innocence is an enduring feature of the masquerade of permanence that led Prime Minister Keith Rowley to insist that T&T is "in the business of hydrocarbons and will remain there as long as there is a market in the world."[21] At precisely the moment when the age of fossil fuels reaches its critical tipping point in the form of ecological collapse, the hyphenated form of the petro-state grounds itself again in a deceptive masquerade.

If I have demonstrated how the two sides of this hyphenated form came together, the survival of the Caribbean people demands that we drive them apart. To do so requires that we intervene in the petro-state masquerade to play masquerades of our own. Where the state shrouds the terms of its masquerade by retreating from the road into its glass-and-steel edifices, offices, and boardrooms, Sylvia Wynter's prophesized confrontation "between those who justify and defend the system; and those who challenge it" will compel the state to reveal the inner workings of its own masquerade by returning the domain of politics to the road.[22]

James's faith in the ordinary people of the Caribbean is stoked by his meticulous study of history. As he observes, the contours of the people's masquerade take shape in the formative decades of the plantation complex in the Americas. In "The Making of the Caribbean People," a lecture delivered in Montreal in 1966 to the second Conference on West Indian Affairs, he deploys Richard Ligon's seventeenth-century *True and Exact History of the Island of Barbados* against its own triumphant christening of Bimshire as a "Leviathan, a well governed Common-wealth."[23] James quotes at length from Ligon's recollection of the aborted plot by enslaved Africans to seize power by force. This, he writes, "is the very beginning (and the continuation) of West Indian history. They wanted not only their freedom but to remove their masters and make themselves masters of the island."[24] In Ligon's estimation, this desire for freedom is incompatible with his Hobbesian endorsement of plantation order and discipline. The masquerade of power inherited by contemporary statesmen from planters, their overseer deputies, and colonial militias of yesteryear adorns itself in the image of the monstrous, sea-dwelling Leviathan.

At every instance, the Leviathan is confronted by another masquerade. The same immanent tradition that compelled enslaved Africans to "make themselves masters of the island" in seventeenth-century Barbados recurs in Bois Caïman in 1791 and Morant Bay in 1865. In Trinidad, it presents itself in the Kambule rebellion of 1881, the Hosay riots of 1884, the general strike of 1937, and the Black Power Revolution of 1970. As James underscored in his address to the Oilfield Workers' Trade Union conference of delegates in 1982: "The mass movement creates power for anybody to take it; the power is right there lying about in the streets, and it has been lying about in the streets in Trinidad for some time."[25] Lloyd Best, in his bad-faith reading, cynically gags that "[you] can't seize no power in the Caribbean: the Americans will put you out the next morning."[26] Best is unable to grasp what James means by power; power lies in the streets, not in White Hall or the Red House. The seizure of power proceeds not from above, but below. Turned against Leviathan, this masquerade is less concerned with the storming of palaces and statehouses than the "dwelling in unity" that the anthropologist Connie Sutton observed during the wildcat strikes of sugar workers in late colonial Barbados.[27] Rather than the singular moment of the coup d'état, this impulse grounds itself in the creative fount of the riot, the mob, and the road march not as a means but as an *end*. In disputing the presumed location of power in the state and its edifices, this masquerade does not anticipate a moment when it retreats from the road to consolidate a new class of rulers who sit above society. The practice of mass politics must embrace the politics of mas.[28]

Again, James locates this capacity for power in the Carnival masquerade. Ordinary people make preparations of their own accord to play a mas. This same sensibility extends to his other writings directed toward an industrial working class in North Atlantic metropoles: "The task today is to call for, to teach, to illustrate, to develop *spontaneity*—the free creative activity of the proletariat."[29] We might argue that a Jamesian dialectic is less indebted to Hegel than it is to the Mighty Sparrow. Rather than a retreat from the Carnivalesque—and with it, an end to the dialectic of spontaneity and organization—the seizure of power is a call to mas.[30] As Mical Teja and Freetown Collective sing in their 2022 Carnival benediction, "MAS," this dialectic is charged with "a spirit to bring the power down" from the parliamentary chambers of the Red House to the road.[31]

Touch Road

The insurgent character of James's criticism appears a far cry from a Caribbean political present that appears conditioned by a neoliberal consensus and the foreclosure of political alternatives to Westminster democracy. For David Scott, the tragic implosion of the Grenada revolution in 1983 entered the Caribbean into a crisis of political time in which the anticipated "eschatological moment" of Hegelian–Marxist revolutionary transcendence is aborted prematurely, leaving us to wade in the muck of an "endlessly extending present,"[32] Indeed, the certainty that guided earlier generations of Caribbean radicals registers as a utopia disavowed, one scarcely recognizable to those of us born in the moment after. After Grenada. After the end of history.

"You never know when it is going to explode."[33] These were the parting words offered by James in the months before his death in 1989. James flew away home as the "end of history" began with the fall of the Berlin Wall.[34] We might consider, then, what fueled his undying conviction in an impending confrontation. In 1970, James addressed a cohort of Caribbean students at Howard University in Washington, DC. He insisted that his audience begin to "think in terms of the seizure of power" to prepare for the imminent clash between the majority of the population and the professional middle classes who had retreated from the necessity of mass democracy. The students listened intently but did not take James at his word. History, though, would absolve him:

> On the following Wednesday, I went to the University to take my class. I was met by a body of West Indian students who told me that the confrontation had taken place in Trinidad. I hadn't read the papers that morning but they told me here it is in the paper; they had revolted; they had made the revolution, and that confrontation you had told us about, that had taken place. And they talked in a way that made it quite clear that when I had spoken to them about the impending confrontation they hadn't believed me. Some of them were saying, "James loves the revolution so he thinks that there is going to be a confrontation; so if he loves the revolution and thinks there will be a confrontation we don't mind; it doesn't trouble us at all." But they were there the next morning, a few days with the papers. They said, "Dr. James, the confrontation has taken place."[35]

The definitive historian of world revolution understood revolution not to be a singular event but an opening. In lieu of a "longing for total revolution" that characterized a self-professed vanguard of Caribbean revolutionaries, James understood the impending confrontation as a series of explosions that do not stipulate an end to their movement.[36] In his heterodox synthesis of Hegel and Marx, the dialectic does not reach an end. The confrontation is less a moment than a masquerade—a multiplication of smaller eruptions that persist in the Caribbean today. To break apart the masquerade of the petro-state requires that we all become evangelists of the free, creative activity of the masses.

Don't Stop the Masquerade

In June 2020, a series of explosions gripped urban centers across the Atlantic World. Sparked by the murder of George Floyd by Minneapolis police that May, the spontaneous uprising and burning of the Minneapolis Third Precinct police station reverberated elsewhere. More than demonstrations in solidarity with the Minneapolis uprising, parallel mobilizations against the police state adopted a local tenor including those following murder of Breonna Taylor in Louisville, Kentucky, and #EndSARS protests against the Special Anti-robbery Squad once again took hold across major cities and municipalities in Nigeria.

This wave did not miss the Caribbean. On June 26, T&T police officers murdered three men—Joel Jacob, Noel Diamond, and Israel Moses Clinton—in the community of Second Caledonia, Morvant. Seeking retribution for the shooting death of a fellow officer, the police intercepted a Nissan Tiida hatchback on Juman Drive. Jacob and Diamond exited the car with their hands raised; the driver, Clinton, held his hands above the steering wheel. Police opened fire, killing all three. The incident, captured by CCTV cameras, triggered protests from residents of Morvant and nearby communities of East Port of Spain. Residents blocked roads with burning tires and debris to upset the movement of police and military troops deployed to the scenes. In Beetham Gardens, protesters clashed with police and three more civilians were shot. One, a pregnant thirty-year-old woman named Ornella Greaves, later died from gunshot injuries while receiving treatment at Port of Spain General Hospital.

Greaves's murder indexed a disturbing pattern of state violence in areas targeted as "crime hotspots" by state-led anti-gang and narcotics-trafficking interventions. In the first six months of 2020, the tally of killings by police in Trinidad and Tobago reached a stunning total of forty-three.[37]

The state's license to kill with impunity rested in no small part on the distorted image of impoverished Black Trinbagonians as morally depraved "badjohns" or "zessers" who inhabit an irredeemable culture of violence. Therefore, when the Trinbagonian anthropologist Leniqueca Welcome places this moment in a longer arc of anti-Black state violence in the Caribbean, she instructively adopts the language of masquerade to describe the state's claim to a monopoly on legitimate violence: "[Police Commissioner Gary] Griffith attempted to silence the protest and redirect attention away from his officers by stating that the mass action was part of an elaborate plot led by several gang-leaders to destabilize the country.... With this rhetorical move, Griffith attempted to masquerade protest suppression as crime prevention policing."[38]

As Welcome contends, the confrontation was sparked by the unexpected failure of Griffith's masquerade. Armed with CCTV footage that contradicted the official narrative Griffith had circulated, the protests received unprecedented support from the Trinbagonian public on the road and social media outlets alike. The circum-Atlantic rallying cry in defense of Black life lent itself to the local contours of predominantly Black urban geographies in the Caribbean that are coded as inherently criminal or cast outside the confines of civil society. However, even those who decried the overreach and abuse of power by police on Juman Drive and the Beetham Highway did not identify the road work of Greaves and her compatriots as the basis for another order of things. Even as trade union leaders and civil society organizations defended the right to nonviolent protest, they continued to fuel narratives of the urban poor as an unruly mob in need of proper leadership or a renewed politics of respectability. They did not conceive of the mob's road work as an effort to block the procession of the state's masquerade of police and military through the hills of East Port of Spain. In doing so, the mob dared to organize the world anew.

Another James protégé, Walter Rodney, dared to venerate the mob as the foundation of a new society: "The regime considers us a mob when we come together in big numbers. They call us a mob. We say, come together to draw strength from the traditions of resistance which have come down from the tradition of slavery and indentureship and anticolonialism to the present time. And there is no force that has stopped it in any other part of the world."[39] Others were not as perceptive. In 1937, Captain Cipriani did not recognize that the working masses of south Trinidad—rather than the labor leaders of Port of Spain—constituted the vanguard of the movement for self-government in the West Indies. In 1970, Williams could not comprehend that the groundswell of Black Power—rather than the PNM—represented the same. Today, we might ask the same question when a Caribbean intelligentsia fails to defend the people's masquerade as it confronts the state's masquerade on the road. Indeed, "you never know when it is going to explode."[40]

The petro-state masquerade gathers power from its presumptive monopoly on legitimate violence. The ability of the petro-state to preserve itself against failed bid rounds, deepwater dry holes, and shuttered industrial plants requires that the state dole out its brute force to contain the masses of people made redundant by the decline of oil as a pathway to mobility beyond the plantation. As the state retreats behind concrete walls and glass windows, however, it commands ordinary people to "band they belly" through long cycles of austerity, cutbacks, and self-discipline. While the petro-state maintains its pursuit of new reserves of carbon power through offshore and deepwater plays, the people are expected to suspend their power to play a mas. Our preparations for the impending confrontation cannot shepherd ordinary people toward statutory avenues of political participation and redress. Instead, there must be a call to evangelize our own masquerades of power.

Let the heathen rage. Don't stop the masquerade.

Acknowledgments

My greatest debt as the author of this book is owed to the people of Trinidad and Tobago who made it possible. I arrived in Trinidad for the first time as a twenty-year-old Caribbean American undergraduate to conduct research for a senior honors thesis. Nearly a decade and a half later, I am proud to call Trinidad one of my many homes. Over the years countless friends and collaborators have shared their time and opened their doors armed with patience and conviction in the value of this work.

My research allowed me the luxury of rekindling relations with maternal cousins and kin more than a century after our ancestors emigrated from Barbados to New York and Trinidad, respectively. Thank you to my uncle, Stephen Callender, for putting us in touch. To my family in Arima, but especially my dear cousin Joan Foster and her late parents Franklin and Gale, thank you for making sure I always have a home in sweet T&T. I will always cherish our memories with "Mummy" and "Daddy" and our Scrabble competitions most of all.

The elemental form of what became this research took shape on the campus of the University of Pennsylvania. I am grateful to Deborah Thomas for everything, but most of all for introducing me to the field of anthropology and insisting upon the central place of the Caribbean within it. I learned crucial lessons, too, from John Jackson, Peggy Sanday, and Salamishah Tillet, who brokered an introduction to her own Trini family by connecting me with Mariamma and Khafra Kambon in 2010. My development as a scholar and pedagogue was shaped immeasurably by my involvement with Ase Academy and the Makuu Black Cultural Center thanks to Brian Peterson and Daina Troy. Herman Beavers, Patricia Ravenell, and Valarie Swain-Cade McCoullum ensured I was nourished in body and mind alike. The scholarly communities in the Departments of Africana Studies and Anthropology continue to shape the scholar I am today. I am especially thankful to the Mellon Mays Undergraduate Fellowship, Penn Humanities Forum, and University Scholars for supporting my research in Trinidad, as well as to a group of doctoral students who welcomed this eager undergraduate into the fold with open arms: Brittany Webb, Julius Fleming, Keon McGuire, Krystal Smalls, Savannah Shange, and Wilfredo Gomez.

At Yale, this intellectual community grew beyond my wildest imagination. I am so proud to call Jafari Allen my adviser, collaborator, and friend. Doug Rogers and Inderpal Grewal encouraged me to stretch my scholarship further than I ever thought possible. The opportunity to study under Hazel Carby was, and remains, an incredible gift. Likewise, seminars and conversations with faculty members in the Departments of Anthropology and African American Studies, including Bill Kelly, Elizabeth Alexander, Erica Moiah James, Erik Harms, K. Sivaramakrishnan, Kamari Clarke, Karen Hébert, and Sean Brotherton, remain with me to this day. My fellow students at Yale also became lifelong friends. Andrew Dowe, Annette Walton, Ashley James, Chris Johnson, Dana Asbury, Danielle Bainbridge, Nicholas Forster, Sebastián Perez, Tyler Rogers, and Wendell Adjetey— thank you for everything. Andrew, we miss you.

When I joined the faculty at the University of Chicago, I was lucky enough to be welcomed by several familiar faces from New Haven: Adom Getachew, Edgar Garcia, and Sean Brotherton. Thank you for paving the way for me. Destin Jenkins and I became fast friends and inseparable comrades. In the Department of Anthropology, François Richard and Stephan Palmié generously offered their time and energy as professional mentors. Throughout, I enjoyed the support and friendship of a remarkable cohort of young scholars: Darryl Li, Kamala Russell, Kathryn Takabvirwa, Natacha Nsabimana, Sarah Newman, and Teresa Montoya. I have sought counsel from my incredible senior colleagues at several moments during the process of writing this book, including Alan Kolata, Alice Yao, Costas Nakassis, Hussein Agrama, Jim Fernandez, Joe Masco, John Kelly, Judith Farquhar, Julie Chu, Justin Richland, Karin Knorr Cetina, Kaushik Sunder Rajan, Mareike Winchell, Michael Fisch, Mickey Dietler, Shannon

ACKNOWLEDGMENTS

Dawdy, Sue Gal, Summerson Carr, and William Mazzarella. Anne Chien, who kept the department's engine running, and the incomparable Trilbe Wynne and Americia Huckabee work miracles at Haskell Hall. I cannot forget the gift of my late colleagues, Marshall Sahlins and Michael Silverstein, who shared their wisdom over many lunches at the Quadrangle Club. The late Nancy Munn was a treasure. Thank you, Nancy, for your generous handwritten comments that I continue to hold dear.

To my family in the Department of Race, Diaspora, and Indigeneity, thank you for sharing with me a clarity of purpose. It is a joy to have shaped this department with Adam Green, Adom Getachew, Adrienne Brown, Cathy Cohen, Eve Ewing, Joyce Bell, Leora Auslander, Matthew Kruer, Michael Dawson, Omar McRoberts, Reuben Miller, Riley Snorton, Salikoko Mufwene, and Sophia Azeb. Elsewhere, Alexander Arroyo, Ally Field, Dan Morgan, Danielle Roper, Fredrik Jonsson, Gabe Winant, Jessica Baker, Liz Chatterjee, Michael Dawson, Neil Brenner, and Victoria Saramago have offered ports in many a storm.

One of the great privileges of my employment at the University of Chicago is to benefit from the genius of my undergraduate and graduate students. I am especially grateful to Adriana Gonzales, Alyssa Mendez, Angela Romea, Ashley Jackson, Caressa Franklin, Carol Iglesias Otero, Daliyah Killback, Dinayuri Rodriguez, Emma Pask, Gabby Mahabeer, Jacob Siegel, Jolen Martinez, Jordan Cooper, Josh Babcock, Kasia Kaczowka, Kiara Houston, Lorenzo Granada, Maya Singhal, Michael Clevenger, Misha McDaniel, Navid Mazidabadifarahani, Noah Powell, Noah Tesfaye, Paulina Gomez, Phoebe Beckett Chingono, Rayna Acha, Reed McConnell, Roxanne Dobson, Sabena Allen, Sarah Shaer, Sophia Abuabara, Stasha Wong, and Zaria El-Fil for their insights or comments on the manuscript.

Many friends and colleagues contributed early and often to the making of this book. Adriana Garriga-López, Alissa Trotz, Alyssa Paredes, Braxton Shelley, Christien Tompkins, Cymene Howe, Damien Sojoyner, David Scott, Dominic Boyer, Eusi Kwayana, Fadeke Castor, Gisa Weszkalnys, Greg Beckett, Hannah Appel, Jay Grimes, Jemima Pierre, Jessica Smith, Jon Connolly, Jonathan Rosa, Jovan Lewis, Karin Ahlberg, Krystal Strong, Louis Römer, Lucia Cantero, Lyndon Gill, Lynn Bolles, Martin Michaels, Matthew Quest, Michael Ralph, Natasha Lightfoot, Omolade Adunbi, Orisanmi Burton, Peter Hudson, Regine Debrosse, Shanya Cordis, Stefanie Graeter, Vanessa Agard-Jones, William Balan-Gaubert, Yarimar Bonilla, and Zophia Edwards are the best interlocutors anyone can ask for.

This book also benefited from invited talks delivered at Cambridge University, Massachusetts Institute of Technology, Northwestern University, Rice University, Rutgers University, University of Michigan–Ann Arbor, and University of Pennsylvania. In conducting research for and writing this book, I enjoyed support from the Center for International Social Science Research at the University of Chicago, Ford Foundation, Fulbright US Student Program, MacMillan Center for International and Area Studies, Mellon Mays Graduate Initiatives, and National Science Foundation. Cally Waite, thank you for always keeping us on time and on track.

My time in Trinidad fostered lasting intellectual connections and friendships as well. Alex Rocklin, Brent Crosson, Dan Castilow, Kelvin Ferguson, Keston Perry, and Leniqueca Welcome have left their indelible marks on this work. Jay John, Keisha Edwards, Krystal Ghisyawan, Richie Daly, Sue Ann Barrett, Tivia Collins, and Zeleca Julien created a lasting community of genuine joy and occasional masquerades. Chris Cozier, Nicholas Laughlin, and Sean Leonard deserve special thanks for their artistic and curatorial genius. I thank Georgia Popplewell for granting permission to reproduce her photo of Nicholas in this book. The National Workers Union in Barataria provided an entry point into the contemporary labor politics and radical histories of the Caribbean. Cecil Paul, Dave Smith, Gerry Kangalee, and Sylvan Wilson extended their generosity beyond what I deserved. I reserve my deepest thanks and gratitude for the Highway Re-route Movement, especially Wayne Kublalsingh, Mr. Ram, Gitana Boodhai, and the Boodhai family.

Special thanks are due to Uche Ogbue and Mark Raymond for opening their home to me on many occasions and supporting my research. Uche, Dax Driver, Gregory McGuire, and Tony Paul patiently walked me through the technical particulars of the energy sector. Afra Raymond clarified the inner reaches of the construction industry in Trinidad. At the University of the West Indies–St. Augustine, Amilcar Sanatan, Angelique Nixon, Dylan Kerrigan, Gabrielle Hosein, Keith McNeal, Maarit Forde, Matt Bishop, and Rhoda Reddock served as guides, friends, and confidants. Lorraine Nero and Darron Small fostered another home for this work at the West Indiana and Special Collections Division at UWI, where I often crossed paths with the late Brinsley Samaroo during long stretches in the archives. I must also thank the staff at the National Archives of Trinidad and Tobago, the Oilfields Workers' Trade Union Library in San Fernando, and the National Archives of the United Kingdom in Kew.

At the University of Chicago Press, Mary Al-Sayed arrived at the perfect moment to push the manuscript forward. I will never take for granted

ACKNOWLEDGMENTS

the hours you spent poring over my writing and mustering the exact advice I needed to tackle what came next. Dylan Montanari joined the fold soon after and hit the ground running. Your generosity is matched only by your editorial eye and attention to detail. I am very pleased to be a member of Hyde Park's cast of characters with you both. Kate Blackmer prepared the stunning maps included in this work. Fabiola Enríquez Flores lent a steady hand to guide this book into production. The two anonymous reviewers selected by the press provided invaluable comments on the structure and contents of the manuscript. I thank the *Journal of Latin American and Caribbean Anthropology* for granting permission to republish a revised version of my 2018 article "Road Work: Highways and Hegemony in Trinidad and Tobago" (https://anthrosource.onlinelibrary.wiley.com/doi/10.1111/jlca.12345) as chapter 5 of this book.

None of this would be possible without the support of my family. My in-laws, the Parsards—Keston, Sheryl, and Kyle—have offered material and emotional support during my highest and lowest moments. My siblings, Elizabeth and Ethan, remain sources of strength and intellectual inspiration. My parents, Mark and Lisa Jobson, provided a life that fostered the diligence and creativity I needed to complete the arduous labor that made this book what it is. You instilled in me a love of your homes—Malvern, Jamaica, and Brooklyn—and raised me in another vibrant landscape of Woodstock, New York, where I was confronted daily with the dynamic relations between the country and the city.

My wife, Kaneesha Parsard, has stuck with me on every step of this journey from our earliest encounters in Philadelphia, our doctoral studies in New Haven, and our present stomping grounds in Chicago. Nothing could be more special than to indulge our mutual love for the Caribbean through our life's work. You are the person and intellectual who I strive to be. Thank you for everything. I love you.

Notes

Prologue

1. Peter R. Bacon, *Flora and Fauna of the Caribbean: An Introduction to the Ecology of the West Indies* (Port of Spain, Trinidad: Key Caribbean Publications, 1978), 23.
2. See Irving Rouse, *The Tainos: Rise and Decline of the People Who Greeted Columbus* (New Haven, CT: Yale University Press, 1992).
3. V. S. Naipaul, "Power to the Caribbean People," *New York Review of Books*, September 3, 1970.
4. For historical surveys of the Caribbean sugar-plantation complex, see Michelle Harrison, *King Sugar: Jamaica, the Caribbean and the World Sugar Industry* (New York: New York University Press, 2001); Sidney W. Mintz, *Sweetness and Power: The Place of Sugar in Modern History* (New York: Penguin, 1985); and Eric Eustace Williams, *Capitalism and Slavery* (Chapel Hill: University of North Carolina Press, 1994).
5. Bridget Brereton, *A History of Modern Trinidad, 1783–1962* (Kingston, Jamaica: Heinemann, 1981), 4.
6. Governor Woodford's views on the removal of slaves to Trinidad, February 7, 1824, National Archives of the United Kingdom, Kew (hereafter cited as NA), Colonial Office (hereafter cited as CO) 295/62.
7. Lyndon Kamaal Gill, "Transfiguring Trinidad and Tobago: Queer Cultural Production, Erotic Subjectivity and the Praxis of Black Queer Anthropology" (PhD diss., Harvard University, 2010), 17.
8. See Maureen Warner-Lewis, *Trinidad Yoruba: From Mother Tongue to Memory* (Kingston, Jamaica: University of the West Indies Press, 1997); and Kumar Mahabir, "The Impact of Hindi on Trinidad English," *Caribbean Quarterly* 45, no. 4 (1999): 13–34.
9. Trinidad, in this respect, holds much in common with other geographies where the histories of African slavery and petroleum extraction overlap, such as

Louisiana and Texas in the United States, as well as Angola, Nigeria, Venezuela, and Brazil. Robin McDowell, for instance, points us to Louisiana's "Cancer Alley" as a location where the corporeal politics of energy transitions come into view: "In the eighteenth and nineteenth centuries, this region was home to the largest sugar plantations in the Americas outside of the Caribbean. Today, the same land on either side of the river is riddled with natural gas pipelines, oil refineries, plastic manufacturing plants, and shipping terminals that pollute the air, water, soil, and bodies of the many Black communities descended from enslaved people who had worked the land for generations before them." Likewise, Omolade Adunbi directs our attention to another circum-Atlantic theater 100 kilometers (62 miles) southeast of Lagos, Nigeria: "Some of the creeks of the Niger Delta are tributaries of the Escravos River, on which Chevron has an oil terminal. The Escravos is historically connected to two different forms of extraction prevalent in the Niger Delta region before the discovery of oil: the extraction of the human body (slavery) and the extraction of palm oil. Escravos is the Portuguese word for 'slaves.'" McDowell, "'There Are Lives Here': The African and African American Cemeteries of the Bonnet Carré Spillway," *Radical History Review* 147 (2023): 37; Adunbi, *Oil Wealth and Insurgency in Nigeria* (Bloomington: Indiana University Press, 2015), 168.

10. See Jamaica Kincaid, *A Small Place* (New York: Farrar, Straus and Giroux, 1998).

11. C. L. R. James, "George Padmore: Black Marxist Revolutionary—a Memoir," in *At the Rendezvous of Victory: Selected Writings* (London: Allison and Busby, 1984), 251.

12. V. S. Naipaul, *The Middle Passage* (1962; New York: Random House, 2010), 20.

13. C. L. R. James, "Interviews with Kenneth Ramchand," September 5, 1980, accessed October 1, 2023, at Marxists Internet Archive, https://www.marxists.org/archive/james-clr/works/1980/09/banyan.htm.

14. C. L. R. James Papers, Columbia University, Rare Book and Manuscript Library, MS 1529, box 11, folder 25.

15. See Sidney W. Mintz, *Caribbean Transformations* (Chicago: Aldine, 1974).

16. Michel-Rolph Trouillot, *Peasants and Capital: Dominica in the World Economy* (Baltimore: Johns Hopkins University Press, 1988), 21.

17. In his ethnographic inquiry into deep south Trinidad, Brent Crosson describes this perspective as one of "rural cosmopolitanism." See Crosson, *Experiments with Power: Obeah and the Remaking of Religion in Trinidad* (Chicago: University of Chicago Press, 2020).

18. Trouillot, *Peasants and Capital*, 17.

19. Laurence Ralph concurs in his ethnography of "gangland" Chicago, where the isolation of small-island geographies in the anthropological imagination is paralleled by the isolation of urban enclaves in scholarly and popular accounts of the Black geographies of ghettos, garrisons, and favelas. As Ralph observes, accounts of this sort remain "at work, efficiently reproducing the enduring trope of

the 'socially isolated' ghetto, over and over again." See Ralph, *Renegade Dreams: Living through Injury in Gangland Chicago* (Chicago: University of Chicago Press, 2014), quotation on 172.

20. On Trouillot's methodological play with scale and form, see also Vanessa Agard-Jones, "Bodies in the System," *Small Axe* 42 (2013): 182–92.

21. I expand on this point in my own sketch of Melville and Frances Herskovits's Trinidad fieldwork in the summer of 1939. Again, I consider how the methodological conventions and professionalization of anthropological research led the Herskovitses to neglect other emergent histories and repertoires circulating in the aftermath of the 1937 general strike: "Where [Melville] Herskovits failed to face the flames of workers' agitation in south Trinidad in the name of anthropology, we should consider what anthropology permits and what we fail to confront in the name of disciplinary survival. When anthropology finds itself on the chopping block as a casualty of university budget cuts—as many departments of anthropology have in recent years—it is not a classical investment in culture and relativism that will rescue us from bureaucratic retrenchment. Here, I am inviting us to be unabashed in our rejection of a stable object that we often adopt as a shorthand for our contributions to university curricula and the credentialing circuit of higher education." See Ryan Cecil Jobson, "Facing the Flames: The Herskovitses, Trinidad, and the Anthropological Imagination," *American Ethnologist* 50, no. 3 (2023): 368–74, quotation on 372.

22. James, "George Padmore: Black Marxist Revolutionary," 251.

Introduction

1. Rex Tillerson, "Energy Leading the Way: From Investment and Innovation to 21st Century Economic Transformation," in *Business in a Changing Society*, ed. A. Koopmann (Zurich: Neue Zürcher Zeitung, 2014), 31.

2. For a critical study of the US peak oil movement and its attendant ideologies of right-wing libertarianism, see Matthew Schneider-Meyerson, *Peak Oil: Apocalyptic Environmentalism and Libertarian Political Culture* (Chicago: University of Chicago Press, 2015).

3. "Sheikhs v Shale: The New Economics of Oil," *Economist*, December 6, 2014.

4. Cameron Hu's ethnographic research on shale operators in West Texas details the geological features that support the short-cycle temporality of shale extraction. For industry insiders, "West Texas fracking requires no exploration time—because they represent the well-known and leftovers revealed by a previous area of extraction—they present the possibility of a 'short cycle' of rapid investment and return." See Hu, "Knowing Destroying: The Geopolitics of Fracking and the Metaphysics of Imperialism" (PhD diss., University of Chicago, 2021), quotation on 149.

5. "Oil Markets on Edge amid Trump's Dubious Energy Tweets," *Politico*, September 16, 2019, accessed June 14, 2022, https://www.politico.com/story/2019/09/16/donald-trump-oil-pices-1734085.

6. In his ethnography of unemployed young men in Dakar, Senegal, Michael Ralph theorizes "killing time" as a repertoire that emerges out of the "conspicuous absence" of opportunities for gainful employment, or "opportunities available to improve one's chances of securing a job." The repertoires of oil industry technocrats represent the opposite side of this coin, wherein they must demonstrate their capacity to traverse declining productivity and widespread layoffs to an audience of shareholders and partners. See M. Ralph, "Killing Time," *Social Text* 26, no. 4 (2008): 1–29, quotation on 16.

7. David Wethe, "Mothballing the World's Fanciest Oil Rigs Is a Massive Gamble," Bloomberg.com, September 9, 2016, accessed February 8, 2024, https://www.bloomberg.com/news/articles/2016-09-19/at-500-million-a-pop-it-s-an-oil-gamble-that-has-no-precedent.

8. Wethe, "Mothballing the World's Fanciest Rigs."

9. World Bank, "The World Bank in Trinidad and Tobago: Overview" (n.d.), accessed February 5, 2023, https://www.worldbank.org/en/country/trinidadandtobago/overview#1.

10. Scott MacDonald, *Trinidad and Tobago: Democracy and Development in the Caribbean* (New York: Praeger, 1986), 191.

11. On Trinidad and Tobago as a candidate for the role of "regional paymaster" in the Caribbean Single-Market Economy, see Rachel Simms and Errol Simms, "The Building Blocks of Successful Regional Integration: Lessons for CSME from Other Integration Schemes," *Social and Economic Studies* 56, no. 4 (2007): 255–85.

12. On the concept of "expectations of permanence," see James Ferguson, *Expectations of Modernity: Myths and Meaning of Urban Life on the Zambian Copperbelt* (Berkeley: University of California Press, 1999), 38.

13. The distinct temporalities of long-cycle deepwater extraction and short-cycle shale extraction call to mind the insights of Elizabeth Ferry and Mandana Limbert on "resource temporalities." While Ferry and Limbert direct their attention to three distinct moments in the making of resources as socially consequential categories, I am most preoccupied here with the third and final moment they flag, of "the future orientation of resources . . . that lay claim to them or grapple with their limits or scarcity." As they demonstrate in their inquiries into Mexican silver mining and Omani oil production, respectively, such future orientations are guided equally by material conditions and regimes of popular representation. In turn, the petro-state masquerade points us toward the distance between material uncertainty and the representation of certainty that governs the future orientation of oil and gas production in Trinidad and Tobago. See Ferry and Limbert, eds., *Timely Assets: The Politics of Resources and Their Temporalities* (Santa Fe, NM: School for Advanced Research, 2008), quotation on 6.

14. Jerome Rajnauth and Craig Boodoo, "Trinidad and Tobago's First Deepwater Drilling Campaign," *West Indian Journal of Engineering* 36, no. 2 (2013): 4–14.

15. Kevin Ramnarine, "Statement to Parliament on Energy Policy," Port of Spain, Trinidad and Tobago, April 24, 2015, 2, http://www.news.gov.tt/sites/default/files/Statement%20to%20Parliament%20on%20Energy%20Policy_final%20%2024.4.2015.pdf.

16. Douglas Rogers, "Oil and Anthropology," *Annual Review of Anthropology* 44, no. 1 (2015): 365–80.

17. On the concept of resource curse and its discontents, see Terry Lynn Karl, *The Paradox of Plenty* (Berkeley: University of California Press, 1997); Michael L. Ross, *The Oil Curse: How Petroleum Wealth Shapes the Development of Nations* (Princeton, NJ: Princeton University Press, 2001); and Michael Watts, "Resource Curse? Governmentality, Oil and Power in the Niger Delta, Nigeria," *Geopolitics* 9, no. 1 (2004): 50–80.

18. Hannah Appel, *The Licit Life of Capitalism: US Oil in Equatorial Guinea* (Durham, NC: Duke University Press, 2019).

19. Appel, *Licit Life of Capitalism*, 77.

20. Appel, 305.

21. See Dominic Boyer, *No More Fossils* (Minneapolis: University of Minnesota Press, 2023), 50.

22. Weszkalnys further theorizes the "pause" as a leitmotif of twenty-first-century oil economies in her article on extractive speculation in São Tomé and Príncipe. Here, "in the case of first oil, gestures keep the pause pried open by materializing an absent potential and promising future gain." See Gisa Weszkalnys, "Geology, Potentiality, Speculation: On the Indeterminacy of First Oil," *Cultural Anthropology* 30, no. 4 (2015): 611–39, quotation on 616.

23. See David McDermott Hughes, *Energy without Conscience: Oil, Climate Change, and Complicity* (Durham, NC: Duke University Press, 2017).

24. Keith Rowley, "Prime Minister Rowley's Statement at World Leaders Summit—COP26," Office of the Prime Minister, Republic of Trinidad and Tobago, November 2, 2021, https://www.opm.gov.tt/prime-minister-rowleys-statement-at-world-leaders-summit-cop26/.

25. Darren Bahaw, "Rowley: Trinidad and Tobago Holding On to Hydrocarbon Market," *Trinidad and Tobago Newsday*, November 7, 2021.

26. Thomas Hobbes, *Leviathan* (New York: Penguin Classics, 2017), 236.

27. Thomas Blom Hansen and Finn Stepputat, "Sovereignty Revisited," *Annual Review of Anthropology* 35, no. 1 (2006): 297.

28. On matters of sovereignty in the Caribbean, see Yarimar Bonilla, *Non-sovereign Futures: French Caribbean Politics in the Wake of Disenchantment* (Chicago: University of Chicago Press, 2015); David Scott, "Norms of Self-Determination: Thinking Sovereignty Through," *Middle East Law and Governance* 4, nos. 2–3 (2012): 195–224; Deborah A. Thomas, *Political Life in the Wake of the Plantation:*

Sovereignty, Witnessing, Repair (Durham, NC: Duke University Press, 2019); and Michel-Rolph Trouillot, *Haiti: State against Nation* (New York: Monthly Review Press, 1990).

29. In my insistence on eating my analytical cake and having it too, my approach to the study of the state most closely resembles the methodological ground outlined by Kriti Kapila: "Sovereignty lies in the power to take, but also in the ability to create illusions. The ability to dupe, transform, and self-transform is a singularly divine potency, which cannot be acquired through knowledge, penance (or labor), or merit (or conduct). To create an illusion is to dispossess the other of their discrimination between the real and unreal." Kapila, *Nullius: The Anthropology of Ownership, Sovereignty, and the Law in India* (Chicago: HAU Books, 2022), 155.

30. Philip Abrams, "Notes on the Difficulty of Studying the State," *Journal of Historical Sociology* 1, no. 1 (1988): 82.

31. Here, I take my cues on the theater of the state from Mike McGovern's historical ethnography of "demystification" programs carried out under Guinean state socialism. As McGovern has it, "The cultural and aesthetic facets of statecraft often lead rather than follow those practices more typically studied by political scientists. They are also a rich site for examining the interaction of rulers and ruled. Demystification was (among other things) a dramatic performance of the power and capacity of the state. The dramatic burning of masks and the folkloric performance of the same sacred objects were politics as theater and theater as politics. Whole populations often participate in such cultural struggles, while at the level of elections and party politics, those who have exited the political process become invisible by virtue of the categories of analysis." McGovern, *Unmasking the State: Making Guinea Modern* (Chicago: University of Chicago Press, 2013): 151.

32. Abrams, "Difficulty of Studying the State," 88.

33. For a theorization of the practice of retrofit, see Cymene Howe, Jessica Lockrem, Hannah Appel, Edward Hackett, Dominic Boyer, Randal Hall, Matthew Schneider-Mayerson, et al., "Paradoxical Infrastructures: Ruins, Retrofit, and Risk," *Science, Technology & Human Values* 41, no. 3 (2016): 553.

34. Hobbes, *Leviathan*, 108.

35. Modibo Kadalie, *Pan-African Social Ecology* (Atlanta: On Our Own Authority! Publishing, 2019): 87.

36. Alongside Jamaica Kincaid's formative meditations on Caribbean postcolonial melancholia in *A Small Place* (1988), I am indebted here to the critical insights of my colleague Jessica Swanston Baker on the political and sonic contours of the smallest islands of the Caribbean archipelago. As she reminds us from her epistemological location as an ethnomusicologist of Kittian-Nevisian wilders, her "goal in researching the popular music of St. Kitts and Nevis . . . was to disprove the conceit that the small islands of the Caribbean are historically and musically empty." Baker's work cautions against a persistent view that theory emanates in a flow of one-way traffic from North Atlantic ivory towers to the smallest places of

the Antilles such as Nevis, Saba, Anguilla, Tobago, Barbuda, Vieques, Bequia, and Carriacou, which often remain unmarked on maps of the Americas. Her caution applies equally to tendencies in Caribbean studies to foreground the Antillean vanguard of Hispaniola, Cuba, Jamaica, Puerto Rico, and Trinidad while marginalizing their regional compatriots as sites of theory production in their own right. My objective, following Baker, is to consider how even smaller islands might inform the political realities of Trinidad more so than political theories with provincial, North Atlantic metropolitan origins. See Baker, "Small Islands, Large Radio: Archipelagic Listening in the Caribbean," in *Contemporary Archipelagic Thinking: Toward New Comparative Methodologies and Disciplinary Formations*, ed. M. Stephens and Y. Martínez-San Miguel (Lanham, MD: Rowman & Littlefield, 2020), quotation on 383.

37. Joseph Edwards [pseud. Fundi], *Workers' Self-Management in the Caribbean* (Atlanta: On Our Own Authority!, 2014), 135.

38. Indeed, as the legal anthropologist Lee Cabatingan observes, Caribbean states are often "overexpressed" through the proliferation of state effects—of national symbols, state commemorations, and monumental displays of public investment—that betrays their marginal status in a global hierarchy of nation-states. Cabatingan, *A Region among States: Law and Non-sovereignty in the Caribbean* (Chicago: University of Chicago Press, 2023). 15.

39. Errol Hill, *The Trinidad Carnival: Mandate for a National Theatre* (Austin: University of Texas Press, 1972): 5.

40. Hill, *Trinidad Carnival*, 14.

41. Editorial, *Port of Spain Gazette*, February 14, 1834.

42. Editorial, *Port of Spain Gazette*, February 14, 1834.

43. Here, we might recall David Graeber's provocative claim that modern police have their origin in the classical figures of clowns, who fashioned rules and enforced commands during limited periods of ritual subversion. As he concludes, the "really striking thing about the powers of command that could be exercised only during rituals, though, is that, most often, they were exercised by clowns." Graeber and Marshall Sahlins, *On Kings* (Chicago: HAU Books, 2017), 382. I thank Phoebe Beckett Chingono for directing me to this passage.

44. *Kambule* can refer to both the procession itself (*the Kambule*) and the practice in general (*Kambule*). On commemorations of Emancipation Day on August 1 in the Atlantic World, see J. R. Kerr-Ritchie, *Rites of August First: Emancipation Day in the Black Atlantic World* (Baton Rouge: Louisiana State University Press, 2007).

45. Governor Sanford Freeling to John Wodehouse, 1st Earl of Kimberley, March 7, 1881, 5, NA, CO 295/289.

46. Freeling to Wodehouse, March 7, 1881, 6.

47. See Crosson, *Experiments with Power*.

48. Richard D. E. Burton, *Afro-Creole: Power, Opposition, and Play in the Caribbean* (Ithaca, NY: Cornell University Press, 1997), 259.

49. Burton, *Afro-Creole*, 259.

50. C. L. R. James, "The Seizure of Power," 1975, 3, C. L. R. James Papers, Columbia University, Rare Book and Manuscript Library, box 11, folder 4.

51. Sylvia Wynter, "Novel and History, Plot and Plantation," *Savacou* 5 (1971): 102.

52. In his magisterial work of Caribbean political theory, Aaron Kamugisha also pairs Wynter and James. I am grateful to Kamugisha's insights that move us toward a recuperation of an insurgent tradition that is obscured by the recent incorporation of both thinkers into university curricula and graduate syllabi. As Kamugisha has it, "The scope, provenance, and political urgency of the work of C.L.R. James and Sylvia Wynter (and the radical Caribbean intellectual tradition that lies behind it) help us clarify the questions of the contribution Caribbean thought can make to Caribbean self-determination beyond coloniality." Kamugisha, *Beyond Coloniality: Citizenship and Freedom in the Caribbean Intellectual Tradition* (Bloomington: Indiana University Press, 2019), 10.

53. For a glimpse of this powerful feeling, see Kes, "Savannah Grass," Spotify, on *Savannah Grass—Single*, Ineffable Records, 2019.

54. Kevin Adonis Browne, *High Mas: Carnival and the Poetics of Caribbean Culture* (Jackson: University Press of Mississippi, 2018), 21.

55. Similarly to *Kambule*, the term *mas* is often used without the article as a metonym for Carnival, while *the mas* refers to the procession itself.

56. Max Weber, "Politics as a Vocation," in *From Max Weber: Essays in Sociology*, ed. H. Gerth and C. Mills (New York: Oxford University Press, 1946), 77–128.

57. See Chris Cozier, "Trinidad: Questions about Contemporary Histories," in *Caribe Insular: Exclusión, Fragmentación y Paraíso* (Badajoz, Spain: Museo Extremeño e Iberoamericano de Arte Contemporáneo, 1998), 348–49.

58. Cozier, "Trinidad: Questions about Contemporary Histories," 349.

59. I am indebted to Shayne de-Landè for this crucial observation that appears in her master's thesis on the figure of the Jab Molassie in Grenada Carnival. That many Grenadian migrants, including Uriah Butler, embraced this form of the Jab Jab in their revolts against colonial authority is surely no accident. See de-Landè, "Unveiling Revolutionary Threads: A Thematic Analysis of the Jab Molassie as a Lens into the 1979 Grenadian Revolution" (master's thesis, University of West London, 2023).

60. Gerard Aching, *Masking and Power: Carnival and Popular Culture in the Caribbean* (Minneapolis: University of Minnesota Press, 2002), 9.

61. "Annual Conference of Delegates," *Vanguard* (San Fernando, Trinidad and Tobago), November 26, 1982, 4.

62. As a brief selection of this voluminous literature, see Brereton, *A History of Modern Trinidad*; W. Chris Johnson, "Guerrilla Ganja Gun Girls: Policing Black Revolutionaries from Notting Hill to Laventille," *Gender & History* 26, no. 3 (2015): 661–87; Harvey R. Neptune, *Caliban and the Yankees: Trinidad and the*

United States Occupation (Chapel Hill: University of North Carolina Press, 2007); Ivar Oxaal, *Black Intellectuals Come to Power: The Rise of Creole Nationalism in Trinidad and Tobago* (Cambridge, MA: Schenkman Publishing, 1968); Rhoda Reddock, *Women, Labour and Politics in Trinidad and Tobago: A History* (London: Zed Books, 1994); Selwyn D. Ryan, *Race and Nationalism in Trinidad and Tobago: A Study of Decolonization in a Multiracial Society* (Toronto: University of Toronto Press, 1972); and Brinsley Samaroo, "The Trinidad Workingmen's Association and the Origins of Popular Protest in a Crown Colony," *Social and Economic Studies* 21, no. 2 (1972) 205–22.

63. See Martin Carter, "A Free Community of Valid Persons," *Kyk-Over-Al* 44 (1993): 30–32.

64. James, "Seizure of Power," 21.

65. Eric Eustace Williams, *The Energy Crisis, 1973–1974: Three Addresses by Dr. Eric Williams* (Port of Spain: Public Relations Division, Office of the Prime Minister, 1974), 2.

66. See Rob Shepherd and James Ball, "Liquefied Natural Gas from Trinidad and Tobago: The Atlantic LNG Project," in *Natural Gas and Geopolitics: From 1970 to 2040*, ed. D. Victor, A. Jaffe, and M. Hayes (Cambridge: Cambridge University Press, 2006), 268–318.

67. Michelle Stephens, "What Is an Island? Caribbean Studies and the Contemporary Visual Artist," *Small Axe* 17, no. 2 (2013): 14.

68. Richard Ligon, *A True and Exact History of the Island of Barbados* (Indianapolis: Hackett, 2011), 65.

69. Ligon, *True and Exact History*, 96.

70. Yarimar Bonilla, "Ordinary Sovereignty," *Small Axe* 17, no 3. (2013): 156.

71. From the perspective of the Jamaican economist Norman Girvan, this disenchantment with the postcolonial experiment in the anglophone Caribbean reflects a state of *in-dependence*, in which the aspiration to sovereignty is frustrated by the existential threats of "a world food crisis, an energy crisis and an environmental crisis." Girvan, "50 Years of In-dependence in Jamaica: Reflections" (SALISES 50-50 Conference, University of the West Indies—Mona, Kingston, Jamaica, August 22, 2012), https://www.alai.info/wp-content/uploads/2012/08/girvan-jamaica-in-dependence.pdf.

72. See Bonilla, *Non-sovereign Futures*.

73. See Yarimar Bonilla, "Postdisaster Futures: Hopeful Pessimism, Imperial Ruination, and *La futura cuir*," *Small Axe* 24, no. 2 (2020): 147–62.

74. See Ryan Cecil Jobson, "States of Crisis, Flags of Convenience: An Introduction," *Small Axe* 24, no. 2 (2020): 67–77.

75. Jobson, "States of Crisis," 69.

76. See C. L. R. James, *Every Cook Can Govern: A Study of Democracy in Ancient Greece* (Detroit: Correspondence Publishing, 1956). Furthermore, as Matthew Quest observes, "for James, a socialist society is synonymous with a direct

democracy where working people directly control both the economic and social relations in their workplaces, schools, and neighborhoods. For James, there should be no separation of economic production and government. A regime governing through a separation of mental and manual labor, however much claiming to govern for the people with a democratic, socialist, or revolutionary nationalist veneer, is termed 'state capitalist' and deemed oppressive. Freedom cannot be fashioned on such terms. At his most consistent, this is true whether found in Stalinist Russia and Eastern Europe, the United States during the Age of the CIO, or in the post-colonial Third World." Quest, "'Every Cook Can Govern': Direct Democracy, Workers' Self Management and the Creative Foundations of C. L. R. James' Political Thought," *CLR James Journal* 19, nos. 1–2 (2013): 381.

77. J. Edwards [a.k.a. Fundi], *Workers' Self-Management*, 138.

Chapter One

1. J. D. Henry, *Oil Fields of the Empire* (London: Bradbury, Agnew, 1910), 7.

2. Henry, *Oil Fields of the Empire*, 41.

3. P. E. T. O'Connor, *Some Trinidad Yesterdays* (Port of Spain: Inprint Caribbean, 1978), 86.

4. Arthur Beeby-Thompson, *Oil Pioneer: Selected Experience and Incidents Associated with Sixty Years of World-Wide Petroleum Exploration and Oilfield Development* (London: Sidgwick and Jackson, 1961), 118.

5. Brereton, *History of Modern Trinidad*, 205.

6. "Oilfield Worker Killed," *Trinidad Guardian*, January 17, 1937.

7. "Killed on Eve of Wedding: Tragedy of Oil Worker," *Trinidad Guardian*, May 2, 1937.

8. "Oilfields Precipitate Shortage of Agricultural Labour in South Trinidad," *Trinidad Guardian*, January 31, 1937.

9. See "The Worker and the Land," *People*, February 6, 1937; and "Planters and Labourers," *People*, April 3, 1937.

10. "Reader Advocates: Oil Preference as Unemployment Aid," *Trinidad Guardian*, April 14, 1937.

11. "Oilfields Precipitate Shortage," *Trinidad Guardian*, January 31, 1937.

12. "Unemployment in the Increase," *People*, June 27, 1936.

13. "Oilfields Precipitate Shortage," *Trinidad Guardian*, January 31, 1937.

14. "Unemployment in the Increase," *People*, June 27, 1936.

15. "Oilfields Precipitate Shortage," *Trinidad Guardian*, January 31, 1937.

16. "Sir Lennox O'Reilly on Cocoa and Oil: Trinidad Future Big Oil City," *Port of Spain Gazette*, February 20, 1937.

17. Report of the Labour Disturbances Commission, October 16, 1934, 27, NA, CO 295/585/11.

18. A. Bukka Rennie, *The History of the Working-Class in Trinidad and Tobago in the 20th Century (1919–1956)* (Port of Spain: New Beginning Movement, 1974), 47.

19. Selwyn MacGregor Grier, acting governor of Trinidad and Tobago, to Philip Cunliffe-Lister, July 28, 1934, 68, NA, CO 295/585/11.

20. Report of the Labour Disturbances Commission, 34.

21. "The 'Hunger' Strike," *People*, July 28, 1934.

22. For a contemporaneous political biography of Cipriani, see C. L. R. James, *The Life of Captain Cipriani* (Durham, NC: Duke University Press, 2014).

23. "Capt. Cipriani's May-Day Message to Colony's Workers: Confidence and Patience Urged," *People*, May 5, 1934.

24. Sahadeo Basdeo, *Labour Organisation and Labour Reform in Trinidad, 1919–1939* (St. Augustine, Trinidad: Institute of Social and Economic Research, University of the West Indies, 1983), 122.

25. Basdeo, *Labour Organisation and Reform*, 122.

26. Grier to Cunliffe-Lister, July 28, 1934, 67, NA, CO 295/585/11.

27. Jim Headley, "Some Lessons of the Economic Struggles," *People*, August 18, 1934.

28. Report of the Labour Disturbances Commission, 35.

29. George Padmore, "Imperialism in the West Indies," *International Negro Workers' Review* 1, no. 1 (January 1931): 17.

30. Padmore, "Imperialism in the West Indies," 17.

31. Elsewhere, the literary critic Julius Fleming theorizes waiting and postponement as characteristic of a condition he terms "*black patience* . . . that arises from and sustains a global system of waiting that produces black suffering by compelling black people to wait and to capitulate to the racialized terms and assumptions of these forced performances of waiting." Fleming's inquiries into African American theater and performance productively extend to the theater of twentieth-century labor movements in the Caribbean. Patience, and the insistence on the necessity of patience, is a central tactic of colonial governance and the state masquerade as it marks time between an uncertain present and the certainty of a future yet to come. See Fleming, *Black Patience: Performance, Civil Rights, and the Unfinished Project of Emancipation* (New York: New York University Press, 2022), quotation on 12; emphasis in the original.

32. "Commission Hears Butler's Evidence," *Trinidad Guardian*, October 7, 1937.

33. "Commission Hears Butler's Evidence," *Trinidad Guardian*, October 7, 1937.

34. Rennie, *History of the Working-Class*, 63.

35. See "Resolution by New Party in South," *Port of Spain Gazette*, August 1, 1936; and "Fyzabad Workers State Grievances," *People*, August 8, 1936.

36. Rennie, *History of the Working-Class*, 45.

37. "Big Crowd of Unemployed Workers March to Government House," *People*, August 3, 1935.

38. Neptune, *Caliban and the Yankees*, 42.

39. Nyahuma Obika, *An Introduction to the Life and Times of Tubal Uriah Buzz Butler* (Maracas, Trinidad and Tobago: College Press, 1983), 32.

40. Thanks to William Mazzarella, we need not fear the crowd as a directionless mob destined to succumb to the most elemental of human drives and desires. Mazzarella takes on the formative theorization of the crowd by the French psychologist Gustave Le Bon as that which "cannot appeal to the influence of reason, deprived of all critical faculty." Mazzarella challenges us to upend the classical assumptions of crowd theory to consider how the "mimetic contagion" of the crowd might be imagined as productive of an emancipatory politics rather than merely an organ of stupidity. After all, there is a thin line between the impulse of the anticolonial mob and fascist insurgents inspired to storm capitol buildings in the name of individual freedom. However, to remedy the latter by decrying the productive capacity of the crowd as a political force would be a fatal error—one that liberal critics who favor a technocratic rule of experts appear destined to make time and time again. Le Bon, *The Crowd: A Study of the Popular Mind* (London: T. F. Unwin, 1903), 45; Mazzarella, "The Myth of the Multitude, or, Who's Afraid of the Crowd?," *Critical Inquiry* 36, no. 4 (2010): 718.

41. Mazzarella, "Myth of the Multitude," 707.

42. C. L. R. James, "The Seizure of Power," 3.

43. C. L. R. James, "Walter Rodney and the Question of Power," January 30, 1981, accessed February 8, 2024, at Marxists Internet Archive, https://www.marxists.org/archive/james-clr/works/1981/01/rodney.htm.

44. See Jerome Teelucksingh, *Ideology, Politics, and Radicalism of the Afro-Caribbean* (New York: Palgrave, 2016), 101.

45. Ryan Cecil Jobson, "Road Work: Highways and Hegemony in Trinidad and Tobago," *Journal of Latin American and Caribbean Anthropology* 23, no. 3 (2018): 460.

46. As Brent Crosson reminds us in his ethnography of obeah in Trinidad, power—for obeahmen and statesmen alike—constitutes itself through "embodied performance[s]" of legitimate authority. Though Crosson is preoccupied in his monograph with subaltern repertoires of religious science and spirit possession (rendered colloquially as *catching power* in Trinbagonian English), his ethnography is a reminder of the way all claims to sovereign power constitute occulted practices that represent temporary or incomplete arrangements of power as total or absolute. This masquerade of power is evident equally in the modern state and in the justice-making repertoires of obeah healers and mediums. See Crosson, *Experiments with Power*, quotation on 57.

47. "Sidelights on Labour Claims and the Oil Preference," *People*, February 8, 1936.

48. "Sidelights on Labour Claims and the Oil Preference," *People*, February 8, 1936.

49. "Bright Hopes Foreseen: All Trinidad Trades Begin to Boom," *Trinidad Guardian*, January 1, 1937.

50. "The Oil Industry," *Port of Spain Gazette*, May 19, 1937.

51. "Apex (Trinidad) Oilfields, Limited: Largely Increased Production," *Port of Spain Gazette*, February 7, 1937.

52. "Oil Exploitation: Activities of New Company," *Port of Spain Gazette*, June 12, 1937.

53. "Record Oil Shipment," *Trinidad Guardian*, January 22, 1937.

54. See "Oilfield Boom to Railway," *Trinidad Guardian*, January 26, 1937; and "For the Oilfields," *Trinidad Guardian*, April 2, 1937.

55. "In Quest of More Oil: Increased Drilling Activities," *Port of Spain Gazette*, June 4, 1937.

56. "Oil on the Surface," *People*, February 8, 1936.

57. "Sir Lennox O'Reilly on Cocoa and Oil: Trinidad Future Big Oil City," *Port of Spain Gazette*, February 20, 1937.

58. This language of inexhaustibility surfaces in strikingly similar terms in Victor Seow's magisterial history of surveys of coalfields carried out by Japanese technologists in Fushun, Manchuria, at the turn of the twentieth century. The full dimensions of the petro-state masquerade compel us to look in theaters far beyond the Carnival traditions of the Caribbean. As Seow details, "The staggering figures that experts like [Chutaro] Kido produced circulated widely across official and mass channels. Often, these were accompanied by claims that Fushun coal could be mined for hundreds of years, its eventual exhaustion so far in the future as to have no bearing on behavior in the present. Over time, the size of the reserves and their projected productivity prompted pundits and planners to talk about this coal as effectively 'limitless' or 'inexhaustible.' This rhetoric fostered an idea among many Japanese that continued access to Fushun's carbon resources was a matter of national interest." See Seow, *Carbon Technocracy: Energy Regimes in Modern East Asia* (Chicago: University of Chicago Press, 2022), quotation on 46.

59. "Sir Lennox O'Reilly on Cocoa and Oil: Trinidad Future Big Oil City," *Port of Spain Gazette*, February 20, 1937.

60. "Sir Lennox O'Reilly on Cocoa and Oil: Trinidad Future Big Oil City," *Port of Spain Gazette*, February 20, 1937.

61. "The Oil Industry in Trinidad, by Sir John Cadman," *Trinidad Guardian*, March 16, 1937.

62. "Oilfields Second Annual Dinner," *Trinidad Guardian*, July 28, 1936.

63. "Oilfields Second Annual Dinner," *Trinidad Guardian*, July 28, 1936.

64. "Farewell Party in Oilfield," *Trinidad Guardian*, June 1, 1937.

65. "Fyzabad Workers Complain," *People*, January 18, 1936.

66. "Yet Another Oilfield Complaint," *People*, August 1, 1936.

67. John Forster, *Trinidad and Tobago Disturbances, 1937: Report of Commission* (London: H. M. Stationery Office, 1938), 77.

68. Forster, *Trinidad and Tobago Disturbances, 1937*, 78.

69. "Answer to Oilfield Complaint," *People*, July 26, 1936.

70. "Another Oilfield Complaint," *People*, July 26, 1936.

71. Forster, *Trinidad and Tobago Disturbances, 1937*, 38.

72. Forster, 39.

73. "Fyzabad: Need for a Market," *Port of Spain Gazette*, May 29, 1937.

74. Forster, *Trinidad and Tobago Disturbances, 1937*, 30.

75. "Trinidad 'Home Rulers' Greet N.W.C., S.A. Chief," *People*, February 20, 1937.

76. Rennie, *History of the Working-Class*, 80.

77. Tony Hall, "Interviews with Pioneers of the Labour Movement, Part 2," Banyan Archive, 1986, accessed February 9, 2024, minute 10, at Alexander Street (password required), https://video.alexanderstreet.com/watch/interviews-with-pioneers-of-the-labour-movement-2.

78. Hall, "Interviews with Pioneers of the Labour Movement, Part 3," Banyan Archive 1986, accessed February 9, 2024, minute 8, at Alexander Street (password required), https://video.alexanderstreet.com/watch/interviews-with-pioneers-of-the-labour-movement-3.

79. "Trinidad 'Home Rulers' Stage Mass Meeting," *Port of Spain Gazette*, January 15, 1937; "'Trinidad Home Rulers' at Siparia," *People*, March 27, 1937.

80. "Oilfields Precipitate Shortage," *Trinidad Guardian*, January 31, 1937.

81. Rennie, *History of the Working-Class*, 81.

82. Hall, "Interviews with Pioneers, Part 3," minute 4; and Hall, "Interviews with Pioneers of the Labour Movement, Part 6," Banyan Archive, 1986, accessed February 9, 2024, minute 1, at Alexander Street (password required), https://video.alexanderstreet.com/watch/interviews-with-pioneers-of-the-labour-movement-6.

83. According to MacDonald Stanley, Butler carried out his meetings with Christian iconography: "He always related his activities to Old Testament, biblical, historical figures. He compared himself normally to be the modern Moses who was sent by God as the original Moses was sent by God to save the children of Israel from the exploitations of the Pharaohs. And so he assumed he was sent by God to save the workers of Trinidad from the exploitation of the colonial powers under the British imperial system.... And this worked well because the workers in the oil industry and elsewhere were fully acquainted, if nothing else, in terms of academic knowledge, they were acquainted with the texts of the Bible. And when he quoted certain references why it is that they had to come out and fight and to see that they had proper leadership that was ordained and directed by God—a kind of divine association—they all pandered to that kind of approach. And they accepted Butler as being sent from God and ... prepared to assist him and associate with him as a servant of God." See Hall, "Interviews with Pioneers, Part 2," minute 7.

84. In his sedition trial, *The King v. Uriah Butler*, Butler was asked in sworn testimony to repeat his address of May 9, 1937 "in the same style and manner as he delivered it." "Rex v Butler: for Sedition," June 13, 1938, 70, NA, CO 295/608/5.

85. "Commission Hears Butler's Evidence," *Trinidad Guardian*, October 7, 1937.

86. "May Day Celebrations Opened: March and Speeches in Woodford Square," *Port of Spain Gazette*, May 2, 1937.

87. "Labour Party Celebrate May Day," *Trinidad Guardian*, May 4, 1937.

88. "Labour Party Celebrate May Day," *Trinidad Guardian*, May 4, 1937.

89. "Labour Party Celebrate May Day," *Trinidad Guardian*, May 4, 1937.

90. "Oil Exports Up this Year," *Trinidad Guardian*, June 2, 1937.

91. "Trinidad Seen as R.A.F. Base in West Indies," *Trinidad Guardian*, February 2, 1937.

92. "Oilfield Earth Workers Strike Still Unsettled," *Trinidad Guardian*, April 10, 1937.

93. "Siparia Road-Workers on Strike!" *Port of Spain Gazette*, May 7, 1937.

94. "Major Oilfields Strike: Rioting Reported from Oil Area," *Port of Spain Gazette*, June 20, 1937.

95. Hall, "Interviews with Pioneers, Part 3," minute 15.

96. "Strike Threat in Oilfields," *Port of Spain Gazette*, June 9, 1937.

97. "Commission Hears Butler's Evidence," *Trinidad Guardian*, October 7, 1937.

98. "Commission Hears Butler's Evidence," *Trinidad Guardian*, October 7, 1937.

99. "Labour Problem in the South," *Trinidad Guardian*, June 19, 1937.

100. "Trinidad's Oilfields Go on Strike," *Trinidad Guardian*, July 25, 1937.

101. "Trinidad's Oilfields Go on Strike," *Trinidad Guardian*, July 25, 1937.

102. "Oil Runs to Waste while Labourers Strike: Drillers Work as Rigmen," *Trinidad Guardian*, June 22, 1937.

103. "Butler Before the Unrest Commission," *Port of Spain Gazette*, October 7, 1937.

104. "Trinidad's Oilfields Go on Strike," *Trinidad Guardian*, July 25, 1937.

105. "Butler Before the Unrest Commission," *Port of Spain Gazette*, October 7, 1937.

106. "Eye-Witnesses Account of Fyzabad Disturbance," *People*, June 26, 1937.

107. "Trinidad's Oilfields Go on Strike," *Trinidad Guardian*, July 25, 1937.

108. "Trinidad's Oilfields Go on Strike," *Trinidad Guardian*, July 25, 1937.

109. Oblka, *Introduction to Butler*, 57.

110. "Trinidad's Oilfields Go on Strike," *Trinidad Guardian*, July 25, 1937.

111. "Mobs Shut Down Stores in San Fernando: Carnival Parades on Streets," *Trinidad Guardian*, June 22, 1937.

112. "Trinidad's Oilfields Go on Strike," *Trinidad Guardian*, July 25, 1937.

113. See "3 Killed: 3 Wounded in Point Fortin," *Trinidad Guardian*, June 22, 1937; "Women Join Strike Bands: Demonstration in Palo Seco," *Trinidad Guardian*, June 22, 1937.

114. "Ajax Arrives: Exeter Due Today: Four Platoons Landed at Pointe-a-Pierre," *Trinidad Guardian*, June 23, 1937.

115. "Horse Goes on 'Strike,'" *Trinidad Guardian*, June 26, 1937.

116. "T.L.I.V. Activities Described to Commission," *Trinidad Guardian*, September 8, 1937.

117. "T.L.I.V. Activities Described to Commission," *Trinidad Guardian*, September 8, 1937.

118. "T.L.I.V. Activities Described to Commission," *Trinidad Guardian*, September 8, 1937.

119. "Strikers Burn Sugar Cane Fields at Orange Grove Estate," *Trinidad Guardian*, June 25, 1937.

120. "Strikers March in Mayaro," *Trinidad Guardian*, June 25, 1937.

121. Telegram, governor of Trinidad to the secretary of state for the colonies, June 23, 1937, 154, NA, CO 295/599/13.

122. "Military Headquarters in Apex," *Trinidad Guardian*, June 23, 1937.

123. "Military Headquarters in Apex," *Trinidad Guardian*, June 23, 1937.

124. "All Quiet in San Fernando," *Port of Spain Gazette*, June 23, 1937.

125. "Open Letter by T.L.P. Secretary," *Port of Spain Gazette*, June 23, 1937.

126. "Mr. Roodal Appeals to Strikers to Keep the Peace," *Trinidad Guardian*, June 23, 1937.

127. "Capt. Cipriani's Mid-Ocean Plea," *Trinidad Guardian*, June 24, 1937.

128. Telegram, governor of Trinidad to secretary of state for the colonies, June 25, 1937, 141, NA, CO 295/599/13.

129. Telegram, governor of Trinidad to secretary of state for the colonies, June 30, 1937, 113, NA, CO 295/599/13.

130. Summary of principal events in the Trinidad strike, July 2, 1937, 96, NA, CO 295/599/13.

131. Notes of a meeting between the secretary of state for the colonies and a deputation of the West India Committee, July 3, 1937, 86, NA, CO 295/599/13.

132. "No Resumption of Work, Unless," *People*, June 26, 1937.

133. Zophia Edwards, "Resistance and Reforms: The Role of Subaltern Agency in Colonial State Development," in *Rethinking the Colonial State*, ed. S. Rud and S. Ivarsson (Bingley, UK: Emerald Publishing), 193.

134. Hall, "Interviews with Pioneers, Part 3," minute 13.

135. Franklyn Harvey, *Rise and Fall of Party Politics in Trinidad and Tobago* (Toronto: New Beginning Movement, 1974), 21.

136. See "Butler's Arrival Creates Sensation in S. Trinidad," *People*, May 20, 1939; and "Thousands Throng Savannah for Butler's Celebrations," *People*, May 27, 1939.

137. "Butler Gets Warm Welcome in Siparia," *People*, May 27, 1939.
138. "Federated Workers Welcome Uriah Butler," *People*, June 2, 1939.
139. "La Brea Oil Unionists Again Advised to Resume Work," *People*, August 5, 1939.
140. Obika, *Introduction to Butler*, 82.
141. Obika, 83.
142. See "Unemployed Hunger March," *People*, January 7, 1939; "Sugar Workers Stage Hunger March," *People*, January 14, 1939; "Sugar Workers to Stage March to City," *People*, July 15, 1939; and "Unemployed Workers to March on Port of Spain," *People*, September 2, 1939.
143. Neptune, *Caliban and the Yankees*.
144. "Butler's Party Celebrates Fourth Anniversary: Mass Meeting at Fyzabad," *People*, September 21, 1940.
145. Jean Casimir, *The Haitians: A Decolonial History* (Chapel Hill: University of North Carolina Press, 2020), 351.
146. Adriana Gonzales extends Casimir's framework of counter-plantation futures through her inquiry into the "solidary futures" of Dominican migrants in Villas del Sol, Puerto Rico. The analytic that she devises in her undergraduate thesis compels us to think the Caribbean anew, outside provincial domains of imperial and national citizenships. In her estimation, "as people share food and help each other meet their basic needs through mutual aid, they are participating in an antisystemic, decolonial political act which allows us to imagine what survival could look like outside regimes of state or imperial citizenships (and the violent policing of borders and belonging that come with them)." See Gonzales, "Sowing Solidary Futures: Migration, Land, and Collective Survival in an Ordinary Caribbean Community" (bachelor's thesis, University of Chicago, 2021), quotation on 21.
147. Atilla the Hun, "Commission's Report," Spotify, on *Treasury Scandal*, Caribya Music, 1950.

Chapter Two

1. Eric Eustace Williams, *Convention Documents* (Port of Spain: People's National Movement, 1973), 13.
2. Eric Eustace Williams, "Massa Day Done (Public Lecture at Woodford Square, 22 March 1961)," *Callaloo* 20, no. 4 (1997): 729.
3. Williams, "Massa Day Done," 730.
4. Williams, *Convention Documents*, 17.
5. Williams, 18.
6. On the concept of corporate imperialism, see Norman Girvan, *Corporate Imperialism: Conflict and Expropriation, Transnational Corporations and Economic Nationalism in the Third World* (White Plains, NY: M. E. Sharpe, 1976).

7. Harry Partap, "CLR James: Williams Was No Genius . . . the Oil Saved Him," *Trinidad Express*, April 7, 1981.

8. On the temporality of oil and resources, see Mandana Limbert, *In the Time of Oil: Piety, Memory, and Social Life in an Omani Town* (Stanford, CA: Stanford University Press, 2010).

9. Robin Bunce and Paul Field, *Darcus Howe: A Political Biography* (London: Bloomsbury, 2014), 77.

10. For a series of essays on the Sir George Williams Affair, see Nalini Mohabir and Ronald Cummings, eds., *The Fire That Time: Transnational Black Radicalism and the Sir George Williams Occupation* (Montreal: Black Rose Books, 2022).

11. "The New Mass Movement and the 1970's," *Vanguard*, January 3, 1970.

12. Darcus Owusu, "The Long March to Caroni," *Vanguard*, March 21, 1970.

13. As Khafra Kambon recalls, the late Indo-Trinbagonian historian Brinsley Samaroo played a crucial role in this warm welcome by supporting the Black Power uprising and taking the "struggle to nightclubs, bars and communities, before the infamous Caroni March in 1970." Michelle Loubon, "Tributes Flow for 'Brinz': Prof Brinsley Samaroo—April 14, 1940 to July 9, 2023," *Trinidad Express*, July 15, 2023.

14. Owusu, "The Long March to Caroni."

15. Bunce and Field, *Darcus Howe*, 88.

16. Selwyn D. Ryan, *Eric Williams: The Myth and the Man* (Kingston, Jamaica: University Press of the West Indies, 2009), 387.

17. Raffique Shah, "Reflections on the Mutiny and Trial," in *The Black Power Revolution, 1970: A Retrospective*, ed. S. Ryan and T. Stewart (St. Augustine, Trinidad and Tobago: I.S.E.R., 1995), 515. See also Deryck Brown, "The Failed Coup: The Jamesian Connection," in *The Black Power Revolution, 1970: A Retrospective*, ed. S. Ryan and T. Stewart (St. Augustine, Trinidad and Tobago: I.S.E.R., 1995), 543–78.

18. James Millette, "Toward the Black Power Revolt of 1970," in *The Black Power Revolution, 1970: A Retrospective*, ed. S. Ryan and T. Stewart (St. Augustine, Trinidad and Tobago: I.S.E.R., 1995), 59–96. See also Peter James Hudson, "Imperial Designs: The Royal Bank of Canada in the Caribbean," *Race & Class* 52, no. 1 (2010): 33–48; Johnson, "Guerrilla Ganja Gun Girls;" Brian Meeks, "NUFF at the Cusp of an Idea: Grassroots Guerrillas and the Politics of the 1970s in Trinidad and Tobago," *Social Identities* 5, no. 4 (1999): 415–39.

19. Cited in Millette, "Toward the Black Power Revolt," 636.

20. World Bank, "Trinidad and Tobago—Economic Position and Prospects," July 31, 1974, https://documents.worldbank.org/en/publication/documents-reports/documentdetail/581181468312888606/trinidad-and-tobago-economic-position-and-prospects.

21. Williams, *Convention Documents*, 16.

22. Williams, 16.

23. NAMOTI, *National Movement for the True Independence of Trinago* (Trinidad and Tobago: Central Committee of NAMOTI, 1975), 33.

24. Anselm London, "Unemployment: Why the PNM Failed Miserably," *Tapia* 3, no. 36 (1973): 6.

25. As Brian Meeks argues, Best understood his Tapia House Movement less as a grassroots organization with ambitions to seize political power than a "gadfly on the body politic, a permanent opposition and source of new ideas in the face of possible new bureaucratic clerisies." Meeks diagnoses the descent of Trinbagonian leftism into centralism and electoralism as a symptom of Best's refusal to cultivate the popular will at a decisive moment in the aftermath of February 1970 in Trinidad. See Meeks, *Critical Interventions in Caribbean Politics and Theory* (Jackson: University Press of Mississippi, 2014), quotation on 92.

26. Lloyd Best, *Independent Thought and Caribbean Freedom: Essays in Honour of Lloyd Best*, ed. S. Ryan (Mona, Jamaica: Sir Arthur Lewis Institute of Social and Economic Studies, 2003), 10.

27. Williams, *Convention Documents*, 8.

28. NAMOTI, *National Movement for True Independence*, 40.

29. See Andrew Apter, *The Pan-African Nation: Oil and the Spectacle of Culture in Nigeria* (Chicago: University of Chicago Press, 2005); and Fernando Coronil, *The Magical State: Nature, Money, and Modernity in Venezuela* (Chicago: University of Chicago Press, 1997).

30. This follows Timothy Mitchell's entreaty to understand the "interconnections between using fossil fuels and making democratic claims [by] tracing how these connections are built, the vulnerabilities and opportunities they create, and the narrow points of passage where control is particularly effective." Mitchell, *Carbon Democracy: Political Power in the Age of Oil* (London: Verso, 2011), 7.

31. Rogers, "Oil and Anthropology."

32. See Karl, *Paradox of Plenty*; and Ross, *Oil Curse*.

33. As Keston Perry observes in his critical survey of resource curse literature vis-à-vis the steel industry in Trinidad and Tobago, "Resource curse perspectives offer a limited view of how formerly colonized economies evolve over time, and why countries that have been endowed with natural resources do not achieve broader industrial transformation. They do not adequately account for the forces and contradictions unleashed by the global economy that are characterized by enduring colonial relations." Perry, "Continuity, Change and Contradictions in Late Steel-Based Industrialization: The 'Global Color Line' in Trinidad and Tobago's Postcolonial Economy," *Sociology Compass* 16, no. 12 (2022): 5.

34. Stuart Hall, *Selected Political Writings: The Great Moving Right Show and Other Essays* (Durham, NC: Duke University Press, 2017), 334.

35. Coronil, *The Magical State*.

36. See Limbert, *In the Time of Oil*.

37. As Cedric Robinson reasons, "[The political] is an ordering principle, distinguishing the lawful or authorized order of things while itself being the origin of the regulation.... We speak of the political both as an instrument for ordering society

and that order itself." Robinson, *The Terms of Order: Political Science and the Myth of Leadership* (Chapel Hill: University of North Carolina Press, 2016), 7.

38. In 1973, the member countries of OPEC included Algeria, Ecuador, Indonesia, Iran, Iraq, Kuwait, Libya, Nigeria, Qatar, Saudi Arabia, United Arab Emirates, and Venezuela.

39. Eric Eustace Williams, *Reorganisation of the Public Service: Three Speeches* (Port of Spain: P.N.M. Publishing, 1965), 83.

40. Williams, *Reorganisation of the Public Service*, 85.

41. People's National Movement, *Buy and Eat More Local* (Port of Spain: Charbol Commercial Printery, 1963).

42. Government of Trinidad and Tobago, *Third Five-Year Plan, 1969–1973* (Trinidad and Tobago: Government Printery, 1969), 211.

43. Government of Trinidad and Tobago, *Third Five-Year Plan*, 201.

44. Government of Trinidad and Tobago, 211.

45. Government of Trinidad and Tobago, *Report of the Commission of Enquiry into the Oil Industry in Trinidad and Tobago, 1963–1964* (Trinidad and Tobago: Government Printery, 1964).

46. Ray Kiely, *The Politics of Labour and Development in Trinidad* (Kingston, Jamaica: University of the West Indies Press, 1996), 102.

47. Government of Trinidad and Tobago, *Third Five-Year Plan*, 20.

48. See Oilfields Workers' Trade Union, *Oil in Turmoil and OWTU Memorandum on the Formation of a National Oil Co.* (San Fernando, Trinidad and Tobago: Vanguard Publishing, 1967).

49. Trevor M. A. Farrell, "'The Worship of the Golden Calf': An Oil Exporter's Industrial Strategy, Technology Policy and Project Planning during the Boom Years" (photocopy, Economics Department, U.W.I. St. Augustine, 1987).

50. See Williams, *Energy Crisis, 1973–1974*.

51. Williams, 7.

52. Lord Shorty, "Money Eh No Problem," Spotify, on *Soca Explosion*, Shorty Records, 1978. See also Mighty Bomber, "Oil Don't Spoil," cited in Graham E. L. Holton, "Oil, Race, and Calypso in Trinidad and Tobago, 1909–1990," in *Latin American Popular Culture Since Independence: An Introduction*, ed. W. Beezley and L. Curcio-Nagy (Plymouth, UK: Rowman & Littlefield, 2012), 201; and Chalkdust, "Money Ain't No Problem," on *Calypso vs. Soca*, Straker's Records, 1978.

53. The major industrial projects of this period included the ISCOTT iron and steel complex, the Tringen (Trinidad Nitrogen Company) and Fertrin (Fertilizers of Trinidad and Tobago) plants, and urea and methanol production facilities.

54. See F. S. J. Ledgister, *Class Alliances and the Liberal Authoritarian State: The Roots of Post-colonial Democracy in Jamaica, Trinidad and Tobago, and Surinam* (Trenton, NJ: Africa World Press, 1998).

55. Trinidad and Tobago Ministry of Petroleum and Mines, *Proceedings of the Conference on Best Use of Our Petroleum Resources* (Port of Spain: Trinidad and Tobago Ministry of Petroleum and Mines, 1975), 2.

56. T&T Ministry of Petroleum and Mines, *Proceedings on Best Use of Petroleum*, 3.

57. See Thackwray Driver, "The Genesis of the Point Lisas Industrial Estate," in *100 Years of Petroleum in Trinidad and Tobago* (London: First Strategic Insight, 2008), 116–20, accessed February 8, 2024, at FIRST Strategic Insight, https://firstforum.org/wp-content/uploads/2021/05/Publication_00011.pdf.

58. Farrell, "Worship of the Golden Calf," 86.

59. Eric Eustace Williams, *The Caribbean Man: Address of the Political Leader of the P.N.M., 21st Annual Convention—September 29, 1979* (Port of Spain: People's National Movement Publishing, 1979), 76.

60. Farrell, "Worship of the Golden Calf," 87.

61. Eric Eustace Williams, "The Problems of Industrialization," 1978, University of the West Indies, St. Augustine, Eric Williams Memorial Collection, 11.

62. Eric Eustace Williams, *Forged from the Love of Liberty: Selected Speeches of Dr. Eric Williams*, ed. P. Sutton (Port of Spain: Prentice Hall Press, 1981), 83.

63. Williams, "Problems of Industrialization," 49.

64. Cited in Farrell, "Worship of the Golden Calf," 111.

65. I employ the term *fix* deliberately, in the same fashion that the geographer David Harvey does in constructing his framework of the "spatial fix." In his estimation, "once the 'fix' is found or achieved then the problem is resolved and the desire evaporates. But, as in the case of the drug addict, it is implied that the resolution is temporary rather than permanent since the craving soon returns." Such is the case with the offshore sector in Trinidad and Tobago. D. Harvey, "Globalization and the 'Spatial Fix,'" *Geographische Revue* 2 (2001): 23.

66. Williams, *Caribbean Man*, 78.

67. Williams, 79–80.

68. Williams, 80.

69. Williams, 35.

70. Williams, 42. See also Black Stalin, "Caribbean Unity," on *To the Caribbean Man*, Wizards Records, 1978.

71. See Kaneesha Cherelle Parsard, "Barrack Yard Politics: From C. L. R. James's *The Case for West Indian Self-Government* to *Minty Alley*," *Small Axe* 22, no. 3 (2018): 13–27.

72. Williams, *Caribbean Man*, 83.

73. See Eric Eustace Williams, *The Negro in the Caribbean* (New York: A&B Books, 1994); and Michael Garfield Smith, *Plural Society in the British West Indies* (Berkeley: University of California Press, 1974).

74. Jafari S. Allen, *There's a Disco Ball between Us: A Theory of Black Gay Life* (Durham, NC: Duke University Press, 2022), 145.

75. Williams, *Caribbean Man*, 84.

76. Williams, 84.

77. See Jafari S. Allen, *¡Venceremos? The Erotics of Black Self-Making in Cuba* (Durham, NC: Duke University Press, 2011).

78. Personal interview with author, July 13, 2013.

79. On the question of ethnicity in Trinidad and Tobago, see Kevin Yelvington, ed., *Trinidad Ethnicity* (Knoxville: University of Tennessee Press, 1992); and J. Brent Crosson, "Own People: Race, 'Altered Solidarities,' and the Limits of Culture in Trinidad," *Small Axe* 18, no. 3 (2014): 18–34.

80. For more on Weekes, see Khafra Kambon, *For Bread, Justice, and Freedom: A Political Biography of George Weekes* (London: New Beacon, 1988).

81. Kiely, *Politics of Labour and Development*, 139.

82. NAMOTI, *National Movement for True Independence*, 39.

83. See Percy Hintzen, *The Costs of Regime Survival: Racial Mobilization, Elite Domination and the Control of the State in Guyana and Trinidad* (Cambridge: Cambridge University Press, 1989).

84. Mitchell, *Carbon Democracy*, 142.

85. Wendell Mottley, *Trinidad and Tobago Industrial Policy, 1959–2008: A Historical and Contemporary Analysis* (Kingston, Jamaica: Ian Randle Publishers, 2008), 28.

86. See Farrell, "Worship of the Golden Calf."

87. Andrew Barry, *Material Politics: Disputes along the Pipeline* (Malden, MA: Wiley, 2013), 110.

88. Farrell, "Worship of the Golden Calf."

89. Lord Relator, "Take a Rest," on *Relator the Real Master—1980 Calypso Monarch "Live"* (Makossa International Records, 1980).

90. Lord Relator, "Take a Rest."

91. Government of the Republic of Trinidad and Tobago, *Budget Speech* (Port of Spain: Government Printery, 1982), 31.

92. Government of the Republic of Trinidad and Tobago, *Budget Speech*, 31.

93. See Ramesh Ramsaran, "Aspects of Growth and Adjustment in Postindependence Trinidad and Tobago," *Social and Economic Studies* 48, nos. 1–2 (1999): 215–286.

94. See Michael Watts, "A Tale of Two Gulfs: Life, Death, and Dispossession along Two Oil Frontiers," *American Quarterly* 64, no. 3 (2012): 437–67.

95. David Scott, *Omens of Adversity: Tragedy, Time, Memory, Justice* (Durham, NC: Duke University Press, 2014), 4.

96. See Hall, *Selected Political Writings*; and Nicos Poulantzas, *State, Power, Socialism* (London: Verso, 2014).

97. Barry, *Material Politics*, 140.

Chapter Three

1. See J. Brent Crosson, "'The Earth is the Lord' or 'God is a Trini'? The Political Theology of Climate Change, Environmental Stewardship, and Petroleum Extraction," in *Climate Politics and the Power of Religion*, ed. E. Berry (Bloomington: Indiana University Press, 2022), 39–65.

2. See Rogers, "Oil and Anthropology."

3. See Apter, *Pan-African Nation*; and Coronil, *Magical State*.

4. Michael Watts, "Oil as Money: The Devil's Excrement and the Spectacle of Black Gold," in *Money, Power, and Space*, ed. R. Martin (Oxford: Blackwell, 1994), 418.

5. As Danilyn Rutherford concludes, every "assertion of sovereignty unfolds before the eyes of imagined others; every bid for power entails a confrontation with audiences of various sorts." Rutherford, *Laughing at Leviathan: Sovereignty and Audience in West Papua* (Chicago: University of Chicago Press, 2012), 4.

6. Kevin Ramnarine, "Address by the Minister of Energy and Energy Affairs, Trinidad and Tobago at the 12th Annual Energy Caribbean Conference," October 2, 2012, accessed February 10, 2024, 2, https://www.energy.gov.tt/wp-content/uploads/2013/11/12th%20Annual%20Energy%20Caribbean%20Conference.pdf.

7. See Veena Das and Deborah Poole, eds., *Anthropology in the Margins of the State* (Santa Fe, NM: School of American Research Press, 2004); David Graeber, *Lost People: Magic and the Legacy of Slavery in Madagascar* (Bloomington: Indiana University Press, 2007); Rivke Jaffe, "The Hybrid State: Crime and Citizenship in Urban Jamaica," *American Ethnologist* 40, no. 4 (2013): 734–48; A. R. Radcliffe-Brown, preface to *African Political Systems*, ed. M. Fortes and E. E. Evans-Pritchard (London: Oxford University Press, 1940), xi–xxiii; and Aradhana Sharma and Akhil Gupta, eds., *The Anthropology of the State: A Reader* (Malden, MA: Blackwell, 2006).

8. See Bonilla, *Non-sovereign Futures*; D. Scott, "Norms of Self-Determination"; Thomas, *Political Life in the Wake*; and Trouillot, *Haiti: State against Nation*.

9. Lauren Benton, *A Search for Sovereignty: Law and Geography in European Empires, 1400–1900* (Cambridge: Cambridge University Press, 2010), 10.

10. See Sahana Ghosh, "'Everything Must Match': Detection, Deception, and Migrant Illegality in the India–Bangladesh Borderland," *American Anthropologist* 121, no. 4 (2019): 870–83.

11. *Afro-Saxon* is a term coined by the Trinbagonian philosopher and economist Lloyd Best that derisively refers to people of African descent who uphold the ideals and commonsense beliefs of the displaced white colonial class.

12. See Shepherd and Ball, "Liquefied Natural Gas from Trinidad and Tobago."

13. Trevor Boopsingh, "The Last Decade—Liquefied Natural Gas and Its Impact," in *From Oil to Gas and Beyond: A Review of the Trinidad and Tobago Model and Analysis of Future Challenges*, ed. T. Boopsingh and G. McGuire (Lanham, MD: University Press of America, 2014), 63.

14. As Karen Ho reasons in her ethnography of Wall Street investment firms, the architecture of corporate buildings and the employment of private security are fashioned in order to police their quintessential borders. The sovereign effects of petro-states likewise are conjured in curated spaces inaccessible to wider publics. Ho, *Liquidated: An Ethnography of Wall Street* (Durham, NC: Duke University Press, 2009), 83.

15. The "investment profile" as a technology of postcolonial statecraft draws its conceptual foundation from Michael Ralph's elaboration of the diplomatic profile.

As he writes, "A country acquires its diplomatic profile through its history of interacting with other polities based on the consensus at which privileged countries have arrived. That diplomatic profile is in a sense a forensic profile: a composite history concerned with whether a country enjoys favorable standing.... That forensic profile is also a credit profile insofar as other countries use this criterion in deciding if a country is worthy of investment." M. Ralph, *Forensics of Capital* (Chicago: University of Chicago Press, 2015), 8.

16. As Kaushik Sunder Rajan reminds us, "vision" and "hype" operate as idealist prescriptions of economies of speculation, in which value is accrued principally through the production of hype as a "discursive terrain of promissory conjuration, where a vision of the future is sold to create the conditions of possibility of the present." Sunder Rajan, *Biocapital: The Constitution of Postgenomic Life* (Durham, NC: Duke University Press, 2006), 136.

17. Weszkalnys, "Geology, Potentiality, Speculation," 616.

18. Nicky White, Mark Thompson, and Tony Barwise, "Understanding the Thermal Evolution of Deep-Water Continental Margins," *Nature* 426 (2003): 334.

19. See Rajnauth and Boodoo, "Trinidad and Tobago's First Deepwater."

20. *Deepwater* is defined by the Trinidad and Tobago Ministry of Energy and Energy Affairs as ranging from depths of 600 to 3,500 meters (1,968 to 11,483 feet), but drilling ventures in excess of 400 meters (1,312 feet) are included as deepwater activities for the purposes of the revised tax code.

21. As Elizabeth Ferry and Mandana Limbert observe, the "projected depletion of resources often frames people's everyday experiences of their past, present, and future." The example of deepwater production in Trinidad, though, suggests that temporalities of depletion associated with peak oil, for instance, are subject to revision and renewal through the projected returns of newfangled technologies and extractive techniques. Ferry and Limbert, *Timely Assets*, 7.

22. Hannah Appel, Arthur Mason, and Michael Watts, eds., *Subterranean Estates: Life Worlds of Oil and Gas* (Ithaca, NY: Cornell University Press, 2015), 10.

23. Don Handelman, "Reflexivity in Festival and Other Cultural Events," in *Essays in the Sociology of Perception*, ed. M. Douglas (London: Routledge, 1982), 163.

24. Cozier, "Trinidad: Questions about Contemporary Histories," 349.

25. As Bateson observes in his writings on play and fantasy, the gambler qua artist engages in deceptive play through bluffs and misrepresentation not unlike the gestures characteristic of the petro-state masquerade during the protracted moment of deepwater play. Yet, as he concludes, in the domain of play, poker players "still insist, however, that the loser accept his loss as part of the game." The working people of Trinidad and Tobago, navigating long stretches of failed plays and industrial decline, are compelled to accept their losses as well. See Gregory Bateson, *Steps to an Ecology of Mind* (Chicago: University of Chicago Press, 2000), quotation on 183.

26. Yvonne Webb, "Rowley: Pray for Oil and Gas," *Trinidad and Tobago Guardian*, June 22, 2016, accessed February 7, 2023, https://www.guardian.co.tt/article-6.2.355346.204a92c45c.

27. Webb, "Rowley: Pray for Oil and Gas."

28. Webb.

29. "BHP Billiton Confirms Encouraging Results at LeClerc Well Offshore," TV6TNT.com, August 9, 2016, accessed February 7, 2023, https://www.tv6tnt.com/news/local/bhp-billiton-confirms-encouraging-results-at-leclerc-well-offshore/article_11676190-2aea-5410-9aec-02479adfcf2e.html.

30. Government of the Republic of Trinidad and Tobago, "Budget Statement 2019: 'Turnaround,'" October 1, 2018, accessed February 7, 2023, 23, https://www.finance.gov.tt/wp-content/uploads/2018/10/BUDGET-STATEMENT-2019-FINAL-WEB.pdf.

31. Government of the Republic of Trinidad and Tobago, "Budget Statement 2019," 21.

32. Ria Taitt, "HOT GAS: Imbert on Mid-year Budget Review," *Trinidad Express*, May 13, 2019, accessed February 10, 2024, https://trinidadexpress.com/news/local/hot-gas/article_1fa935e2-75e6-11e9-ab74-27ad24c7af0b.html.

33. Government of the Republic of Trinidad and Tobago, "Budget Statement 2020: Stability | Strength | Growth," October 7, 2019, accessed February 7, 2023, 18, https://www.finance.gov.tt/wp-content/uploads/2019/10/Budget-Statement-2020-Amended-web.pdf.

34. Office of the Prime Minister, Republic of Trinidad and Tobago, "Announcement of the Drilling of the BHP Broadside Well," September 15, 2020, accessed February 10, 2024, https://www.opm.gov.tt/announcement-of-drilling-of-bhp-broadside-well/. Transcriptions for the press conference via Zoom by the author, September 15, 2020.

35. The fragility of the compact between the government of Trinidad and Tobago and BHP parallels Stuart Kirsch's ethnography of BHP mining interests in Papua New Guinea and their manifold legal challenges in Australian courts. As Kirsch observes, "There was always a question whether the second phase of the mine would be economically viable, although the state made its contract with the mining company contingent on the continuation of the project after the gold cap was exhausted. Over the history of the mine, BHP threatened to walk away from the project several times, exercising its political leverage over the state, which had become economically dependent on the taxes and other economic benefits provided by the mine. Papua New Guinea also had a strong interest in demonstrating to the international community that it was a desirable location for investment capital. BHP finally left the project in 2001, because the Ok Tedi mine's ongoing environmental impacts posed significant economic liabilities and reputational costs." See Stuart Kirsch, *Mining Capitalism: The Relationship between Corporations and Their Critics* (Oakland: University of California Press, 2014), quotation on 20.

36. As Darryl Li makes clear in his historical ethnography of mujahideen veterans of the Bosnian War (1992–1995), while the state claims a monopoly on the miracle, its political theology is taken up as a grammar of insurgent devotion and solidarity: "The sovereign state tries to bring the power of the miraculous to earth and harness it as a weapon, forever unstable; in contrast, the jihad lets the miraculous be, treating it as a potentiality that can suddenly condense the atmosphere like the flying horsemen of Vozuća, disrupting the order of things as a sign of God's favor." We might follow Li's lead in our appraisal of the miracle of the Trinbagonian petro-state. Here, the sovereign state endeavors to lift the miracle of hydrocarbons out of the earth to preserve its monopoly on legitimate violence and displace other visions of miraculous transcendence guided by mass politics and direct democracy. Li, *The Universal Enemy: Jihad, Empire, and the Challenge of Solidarity* (Stanford, CA: Stanford University Press, 2019), 87.

37. Carl Schmitt, *Political Theology: Four Chapters on the Concept of Sovereignty*, trans. G. Schwab (Chicago: University of Chicago Press, 2005), 36.

38. Schmitt, *Political Theology*, 5.

39. Graeber and Sahlins, *On Kings*, 23.

40. Hobbes, *Leviathan*, 287.

41. Hannah Appel, "Offshore Work: Oil, Modularity, and the How of Capitalism in Equatorial Guinea," *American Ethnologist* 39, no. 4: 692–709.

42. Hobbes, *Leviathan*, 291.

43. Carl Schmitt, *The Leviathan in the State Theory of Thomas Hobbes: Meaning and Failure of a Political Symbol*, trans. G. Schwab (Chicago: University of Chicago Press, 2008), 53.

44. See Michael-Rolph Trouillot, *Silencing the Past: Power and the Production of History* (Boston: Beacon, 1995).

45. Bonilla, "Ordinary Sovereignty," 156.

46. On Hobbes's investments in colonial enterprises in North America and the Caribbean, see Noel Malcolm, *Aspects of Hobbes* (Oxford: Oxford University Press, 2004).

47. Graeber and Sahlins, *On Kings*, 22.

48. Hughes, *Energy without Conscience*, 147.

49. Deborah A. Thomas, *Exceptional Violence: Embodied Citizenship in Transnational Jamaica* (Durham, NC: Duke University Press, 2011).

50. See Dylan Kerrigan, "Transnational Anti-Black Racism and State Violence in Trinidad," *Cultural Anthropology Online* (2015); and Leniqueca Welcome, "To Be Black Is to . . . : The Production of Blackness in and beyond Trinidad," *Small Axe* 26, no. 2 (2022): 108–18.

51. Make It Hapn, "Mus Eat Ah Food," Bandcamp, on *I vs. Me*, 2010.

52. Make It Hapn.

53. Abrams, "Difficulty of Studying the State," 82.

54. As Yarimar Bonilla reasons in her ethnography of organized labor in the French overseas department of Guadeloupe: "The problem/project of postcolonial

sovereignty has similarly entailed the advancement of a particular set of aspirations, attachments, ideals, and desires.... It also became associated with a restrictive ideology that suggests that national borders can and should serve as containers for homogeneous content." Bonilla, *Non-sovereign Futures*, 13.

55. See Trouillot, *Haiti: State against Nation*, 31.

Chapter Four

1. In a classic essay on "liming" in Trinidad as "the art of doing nothing," Thomas Eriksen maps the contours of these informal gatherings as charged with social and political significance. Humor, as Eriksen puts it, "pervades the central literary tradition of Trinidad (and the Caribbean); namely, the calypso. It may take the form of political satire, dirty jokes or witty puns; a good calypso nearly always contains a humourous element. During liming, too, the ability to make people laugh is highly esteemed." Eriksen, "Liming in Trinidad: The Art of Doing Nothing," *Folk* 32 (1990): 34. On "liming" and "ole talk," see Carmen L. McClish, "Good Liming in Trinidad: The Art of Doing Something," *Liminalities: A Journal of Performance Studies* 12, no. 4 (2016); and Camille Nakhid, Josh Mosca, and Shani Nakhid-Schuster, "Liming as Research Methodology, Ole Talk as Research Method—a Caribbean Methodology," *Journal of Education and Development in the Caribbean* 18, no. 2 (2020): 1–18.

2. Jacques Lacan, *The Seminar of Jacques Lacan: The Other Side of Psychoanalysis, Book XVII*, trans. R. Grigg (New York: Norton, 2007), 72; emphasis mine.

3. Here, I call up Sue Gal's expansive critical oeuvre on language ideology and the construction of publics. As she writes in a critical departure from the logics of an a priori Habermasian public sphere: "Publics are created through the circulation of discourses as people hear, see or read a message and then engage it in some way: by shows of interest, including imitation, commentary, borrowing, quotation, citation, and of course translation. At each step there can be acceptance, parody, ridicule, opposition or even rejection. In this process, participants take messages out of one context and insert or recontextualise them in another space and time. A self-aware public emerges as a mutual watching or listening. The recontextualisation of each [other's] commentary engenders further commentary that is repeated in turn, and thus circulates and invites yet more commentary. In short, publics can be understood as a form of 'interdiscursivity,' an idea derived from Bakhtin, who wrote about the 'complex event of encountering and interacting with another's word.' Those encounters and interactions are the very means through which publics coalesce." Gal, "Contradictions of Standard Language in Europe: Implications for the Study of Practices and Publics," *Social Anthropology* 14, no. 2 (2006): 173.

4. Here, we might look to William Mazzarella for insights into Manning's postcolonial jouissance: "It gets confusing in part because there's something about pleasure that is both economical and beyond economy. The utilitarians and the

rational choice economists would have us believe that we are constantly trying to maximize our pleasure and minimize our pain. Clearly this is not the case. Everywhere we look we can see people pursuing pleasures that tear them apart. Because at some level the terrible pleasure of being true to yourself is deeper than the pleasure of self-interest. Aaron Schuster calls that the *trouble with pleasure*. Lauren Berlant calls it *cruel optimism*. Jacques Lacan says that enjoyment—that heedless and reckless enjoyment that he calls *jouissance—begins with a tickle and ends up in a blaze of petrol*." Mazzarella reminds us to look to cognate formations, such as Berlant's cruel optimism, to capture the elemental drive of the petro-state masquerade. Here, we might ask if Lacan's blaze of petrol refers to the fires of insurgent workers' sabotage or a quiet gas flare that burns off industrial excess. Perhaps when the state's masquerade is successful, it presents as the latter, and when its semiotic vehicles breakdown unceremoniously, it presents as the former. In all, the petro-state constitutes a psychoanalytic form and semiotic vehicle as much as it does an ideal political or economic type. Mazzarella, "Pleasure and Its Bystanders: A Ludibrium," *Portable Gray* 5, no. 2 (2022): 254.

5. Michael Silverstein, "The 'Message' in the (Political) Battle," *Language & Communication* 31, no. 3 (2011): 204.

6. Verdel Bishop, "IMAX 3D Comes to TT," *Trinidad and Tobago Newsday*, April 9, 2011, accessed February 7, 2023, http://archives.newsday.co.tt/2011/04/09/imax-3d-comes-to-tt/.

7. Constantine V. Nakassis, *Onscreen/Offscreen* (Toronto: University of Toronto Press, 2023), 19.

8. Afra Raymond, *Property Matters: A Compilation from the "Business Guardian" Column* (Port of Spain: Raymond & Pierre, 2005), 70.

9. Bruce Paddington and Keith Q. Warner, "The Emergence of Caribbean Feature Films," *Black Camera* 1, no. 1 (2009): 94.

10. Adrienne Brown, *The Black Skyscraper: Architecture and the Perception of Race* (Baltimore: Johns Hopkins University Press, 2017), 3.

11. A. Brown, *The Black Skyscraper*, 4.

12. Manning's effort to appropriate the tropical modernism of Miami took place at the expense of a more careful inquiry into the racial histories and geographies of south Florida that trace the "spatial and temporal edges of Black Miami's mid-twentieth century hemispheric creolization process as a Southern U.S. town, a Caribbean city and a numerically- and linguistically-dominant Latin American metropolis." Donette Francis and Allison Harris, "Introduction: Looking for Black Miami," *Anthurium* 16, no. 1 (2020): 10.

13. Silverstein, "'Message' in the (Political) Battle," 209.

14. Patrick Markey, "Obama Cool Meets Chavez Mania at Americas Summit," Reuters, April 20, 2009, accessed February 7, 2023, https://www.reuters.com/article/us-summit-obama-chavez/obama-cool-meets-chavez-mania-at-americas-summit-idUSTRE53J3MW20090420.

NOTES TO PAGES 125–131

15. Jada Loutoo, "Activist Takes to the Streets," *Trinidad and Tobago Newsday*, April 16, 2009, accessed February 7, 2023, http://archives.newsday.co.tt/2009/04/16/activist-takes-to-the-streets/.

16. Venus Honore-Gopie, "Vagrant Removal Still Ongoing," *Trinidad and Tobago Newsday*, April 16, 2009, accessed February 7, 2023, http://archives.newsday.co.tt/2009/04/16/vagrant-removal-still-ongoing/.

17. Andre Bagoo, "PoS Red Zone," *Trinidad and Tobago Newsday*, March 5, 2009, accessed February 7, 2023, http://archives.newsday.co.tt/2009/03/05/pos-red-zone/.

18. "Wall Built for Americas Summit Seen as Symbol of Wealth Disparity in Trinidad," *Guardian* (UK), April 16, 2009, accessed February 7, 2023, https://www.theguardian.com/world/2009/apr/16/trinidad-tobago-americas-summit.

19. Organization of American States, "An Address by the Honourable Patrick Manning, Prime Minister of the Republic of Trinidad and Tobago at the Opening Ceremony of the Fifth Summit of the Americas," April 17, 2009, accessed February 7, 2023, http://www.summit-americas.org/V_Summit/remarks_tto_en.pdf.

20. Organization of American States, "Official Remarks of United States President Barack Obama at the Opening Ceremony of the Fifth Summit of the Americas," April 17, 2009, accessed February 7, 2023, http://www.summit-americas.org/V_Summit/remarks_usa_en.pdf.

21. Hansard, House of Representatives, Trinidad and Tobago: Parliament of the Republic of Trinidad and Tobago, May 23, 2008, accessed February 8, 2024, https://www.ttparliament.org/wp-content/uploads/2022/01/hh20080523.pdf.

22. "Some Cup Venues Still Not Ready," *Jamaica Gleaner*, March 11, 2007.

23. Hansard, May 23, 2008.

24. Government of the Republic of Trinidad and Tobago, *Report of the Commission of Enquiry into the Construction Sector*, March 29, 2010, accessed February 7, 2023, xxxv, https://www.ttparliament.org/wpcontent/uploads/2022/01/20100406-CommEnqConstSect.pdf.

25. Government of the Republic of Trinidad and Tobago, *Report into the Construction Sector*, 132.

26. Hansard, May 23, 2008; emphasis mine.

27. Prior Beharry, "'Hart Real PM in T&T,'" *Trinidad and Tobago Guardian*, August 15, 2009, accessed February 7, 2023, https://www.guardian.co.tt/article-6.2.319836.2b6adcb67f.

28. Laughlin mused in his blog entry after Hart fled the country: "Last night the news broke that Hart, formerly protected by Manning, was forced to resign from Udecott and his positions at other state agencies, and has fled the country with his family. This morning everybody asking how many blue notes this cobo managed to pack in his luggage." Laughlin, "The Flight of the Cobo," March 7, 2010, http://nicholaslaughlin.blogspot.com/2010/03/flight-of-cobo-my-carnival-monday.html.

29. Andre Bagoo, "Hart Resigns," *Trinidad and Tobago Newsday*, March 8, 2010, accessed February 7, 2023, http://archives.newsday.co.tt/2010/03/08/hart-resigns/.

30. Government of the Republic of Trinidad and Tobago, *Report into the Construction Sector*, 54.

31. Government of the Republic of Trinidad and Tobago, 57.

32. ACTT (Artists' Coalition of Trinidad and Tobago), "The Tragedy and Hidden History of NAPA" (2010), 2, accessed February 7, 2023, https://artistscoalition.files.wordpress.com/2012/09/the-tragedy-and-hidden-history-of-napa.pdf.

33. ACTT, "Tragedy and Hidden History," 20.

34. ACTT, 26.

35. Jean Baudrillard apprehends the politics of the simulation astutely when he posits the simulacrum as that which is "no longer measured against some ideal or negative instance." Again, for Manning, his efforts to emulate Miami or the spectacle-image of development did not aspire to the real contours of Miami as much as its visual outline as perceived from a comfortable offshore distance. The trouble with Manning is less his failure to make good on his promise of developed country status than the undefined character of this designation in the first instance. Baudrillard, *Simulations* (Cambridge, MA: Semiotext(e), 1983), 3.

36. Shaliza Hassanali, "UWI $500M Debe Campus Still Unoccupied," CNC3, June 4, 2023, accessed October 31, 2023, https://www.cnc3.co.tt/uwi-500m-debe-campus-still-unoccupied/.

Chapter Five

1. Machel Montano, "Ministry of Road (M.O.R.)," video, 4:44, February 21, 2014, accessed February 2, 2023, at YouTube, https://www.youtube.com/watch?v=zUxfgSdYNN4.

2. In Trinbagonian English, *mas* refers to the Carnival masquerade typically held on the Tuesday immediately preceding Ash Wednesday in the Lenten calendar. Often it is discussed in terms of *playing mas*, in which masqueraders don costumes associated with particular Carnival bands.

3. See Roberto Da Matta, "An Interpretation of *Carnaval*," *SubStance* 12, no. 1 (1983): 162–70.

4. "Kamla: They Can't Stop Us from Building Highway," *Trinidad Express*, May 24, 2012.

5. See, for example, Dimitris Dalakoglou and Penelope Harvey, eds., *Roads and Anthropology: Ethnography, Infrastructures, (Im)mobility* (New York: Routledge, 2015); and Penny Harvey and Hannah Knox, *Roads: An Anthropology of Infrastructure and Expertise* (Ithaca, NY: Cornell University Press, 2015).

6. See David Graeber, *The Utopia of Rules: on Technology, Stupidity, and the Secret Joys of Bureaucracy* (Brooklyn: Melville House, 2015); Akhil Gupta, *Red Tape: Bureaucracy, Structural Violence, and Poverty in India* (Durham, NC: Duke University Press, 2012); James Ferguson and Akhil Gupta, "Spatializing States:

Toward and Ethnography of Neoliberal Governmentality," *American Ethnologist* 29, no. 4 (2002): 981–1002; Michael Herzfeld, *The Social Production of Indifference* (Chicago: University of Chicago Press, 1992); and Matthew Hull, *Government of Paper: The Materiality of Bureaucracy in Urban Pakistan* (Berkeley: University of California Press, 2012).

7. See Abrams, "Difficulty of Studying the State"; Apter, *Pan-African Nation*; Coronil, *Magical State*; and Michael Taussig, *The Magic of the State* (New York: Routledge, 1997).

8. Bronislaw Malinowski, *Magic, Science and Religion, and Other Essays* (New York: Doubleday, 1954), 90.

9. As Julie Chu writes on the "workings of disrepair" in urban China, "[Disrepair] offers a vantage point to engage infrastructure as a sociotechnical ensemble of contingently allied forces, each of which can fray and break out from its embedded functioning as part of an otherwise neglected backdrop. In the throes of redevelopment, disrepair can invert or blur the distinctions between background and foreground. Even as its unfolding remains hidden and illegible, it can lead to a redistribution of the sensible across the political landscape." Chu, "When Infrastructures Attack: The Workings of Disrepair in China," *American Ethnologist* 41, no. 2 (2014): 353.

10. On faulty or unfinished infrastructures as indexes of state power and neglect, see Nikhil Anand, "Leaky States: Water Audits, Ignorance, and the Politics of Infrastructure," *Public Culture* 27, no. 2 (2015): 305–30; Nikhil Anand, "Pressure: The PoliTechnics of Water Supply in Mumbai," *Cultural Anthropology* 26, no. 4 (2012): 542–64; and Nikhil Anand, Akhil Gupta, and Hannah Appel, eds., *The Promise of Infrastructure* (Durham, NC: Duke University Press, 2018).

11. Royal Commonwealth Society, *Proceedings of the Royal Colonial Institute, Vol. 38* (London: Royal Colonial Institute, 1907), 235.

12. L. A. A. De Verteuil, *Trinidad: Its Geography, Natural Resources, Administration, Present Condition, and Prospects* (London: Cassell, 1884), 212.

13. Bridget Brereton, *Race Relations in Colonial Trinidad, 1870–1900* (Cambridge: Cambridge University Press, 2002), 15.

14. Michael Mann, "The Autonomous Power of the State: Its Origins, Mechanisms and Results," *European Journal of Sociology / Archives Européennes de Sociologie / Europäisches Archiv für Soziologie* 25, no. 2 (1984): 189.

15. As Brian Larkin memorably observes, "Infrastructures also exist as forms separate from their purely technical functioning, and they need to be analyzed as concrete semiotic and aesthetic vehicles oriented to addressees." Larkin, "The Politics and Poetics of Infrastructure," *Annual Review of Anthropology* 42, no. 1 (2013): 329.

16. Government of the Republic of Trinidad and Tobago, *Budget Speech*, 14.

17. For critical scholarship on the coup, see Selwyn D. Ryan, *The Muslimeen Grab for Power: Race, Religion, and Revolution in Trinidad and Tobago* (Port of Spain: Inprint Caribbean, 1991).

18. "Manning Promises Better Roads," *Trinidad and Tobago Newsday*, September 3, 2003.

19. "Eight Years of Victories for Kublalsingh," *Trinidad Express*, November 21, 2012, accessed February 7, 2023, https://trinidadexpress.com/news/local/eight-years-of-victories-for-kublalsingh/article_6b19b09c-be8e-5902-8ea6-fb94bccfc757.html.

20. See Selwyn R. Cudjoe, ed., *Indian Time Ah Come in Trinidad and Tobago* (Wellesley, MA: Calaloux Publications, 2010).

21. Janine Mendes-Franco, "Trinidad & Tobago: No Simple Highway," Global Voices, November 28, 2012, accessed March 3, 2014, https://globalvoices.org/2012/11/28/trinidad-tobago-no-simple-highway/.

22. Sianne Ngai, *Theory of the Gimmick: Aesthetic Judgment and Capitalist Form* (Cambridge, MA: Harvard University Press, 2020), 96.

23. *Report of the Independent Review Committee of the Debe to Mon Desir Segment of the San Fernando to Point Fortin Highway*, March 3, 2013, accessed February 8, 2023, 138, https://jcctt.org/wp-content/uploads/2020/11/highway-report3-march_compressed.pdf.

24. Joel Julien, "Kamla Takes a Break from HRM," *Trinidad Express*, October 30, 2014.

25. Author's transcription of a recording of the public event in Nelson Mandela Park, Port of Spain, October 12, 2014.

26. On the concept of state simplification, see James C. Scott, *Seeing like a State: How Certain Schemes to Improve the Human Condition Have Failed* (New Haven, CT: Yale University Press, 1998).

27. Poulantzas, *State, Power, Socialism*, 69. See also Michel-Rolph Trouillot, "The Anthropology of the State in the Age of Globalization: Close Encounters of the Deceptive Kind," *Current Anthropology* 42, no. 1 (2001): 125–38.

28. See Ernesto Laclau and Chantal Mouffe, *Hegemony and Socialist Strategy: Towards a Radical Democratic Politics* (London: Verso, 2014).

29. Antonio Gramsci, *Selections from the Prison Notebooks of Antonio Gramsci*, trans. Q. Hoare and G. Nowell-Smith (New York: International Publishers, 1971), 244.

30. Walter Rodney, "Contemporary Political Trends in the English-Speaking Caribbean," in *Caribbean Political Thought: Theories of the Post-Colonial State*, ed. A. Kamugisha (Kingston, Jamaica: Ian Randle, 2013), 3.

31. Dylan Kerrigan, "Bobol as a Transhistorical Cultural Logic: The Coloniality of Corruption in Trinidad," *Caribbean Quarterly* 66, no. 2 (2020): 210.

32. See Macdonald Stainsby, *Tar Sands in T&T? A Look at the World's Dirtiest Oil, from Canada to Trinidad and Tobago* (Montreal: Katasoho, 2013).

33. As Akhil Gupta notes in an insightful commentary, infrastructures are often governed by a modernist telos in which "it is assumed that projects, once started, will be completed. Thus, infrastructure that is not yet in place is deemed

incomplete, on its way to completion." Gupta, "Suspension," *Cultural Anthropology Online*, September 24, 2015, https://culanth.org/fieldsights/suspension.

34. See Gupta, *Red Tape*; and Daniel Jordan Smith, *A Culture of Corruption: Everyday Deception and Popular Discontent in Nigeria* (Princeton, NJ: Princeton University Press, 2008).

35. See Sharma and Gupta, *Anthropology of the State*.

36. See Dimitris Dalakoglou, "The Road: An Ethnography of the Albanian–Greek Cross-Border Motorway," *American Ethnologist* 37, no. 1 (2010): 132–49.

37. See James Holston, *Insurgent Citizenship: Disjunctions of Democracy and Modernity in Brazil* (Princeton, NJ: Princeton University Press, 2008).

38. Organisation for National Reconstruction, *Why Nothing Works in Trinidad and Tobago* (Port of Spain: Organisation for National Reconstruction, 1981), 20.

39. Invisible Committee, *To Our Friends* (Cambridge, MA: MIT Press, 2015), 75.

40. Government of the Republic of Trinidad and Tobago, "PM Persad-Bissessar's Address on the State of the Economy," January 9, 2015, accessed February 8, 2023, http://www.news.gov.tt/content/pm-persad-bissessars-address-state-economy#.Y-OesS_MLe8.

41. Karl Marx, *Grundrisse: Foundations of the Critique of Political Economy* (London: Penguin, 2005), 524.

42. Marx, *Grundrisse*, 530.

43. Guy Debord, *Society of the Spectacle* (Detroit: Black & Red, 1983), 13.

44. See, for example, Erik Harms, *Saigon's Edge: On the Margins of Ho Chi Minh City* (Minneapolis: University of Minnesota Press, 2011).

45. Gramsci, *Selections from the Prison Notebooks*, 422. Elsewhere, Kate Crehan meticulously clarifies the Gramscian concepts of "common sense" and "good sense" from an anthropological perspective in her recent monograph, *Gramsci's Common Sense* (Durham, NC: Duke University Press, 2016).

46. Gramsci, *Selections from the Prison Notebooks*, 328.

47. Gramsci, 331.

48. Gramsci, 12. See also Slavoj Žižek, Ernesto Laclau, and Judith Butler, *Contingency, Hegemony, Universality: Contemporary Dialogues on the Left* (London: Verso, 2011).

49. Kathryn Takabvirwa, "Citizens in Uniform: Roadblocks and the Policing of Everyday Life in Zimbabwe," *American Ethnologist* 50, no. 2 (2023): 244.

50. On the concept of the postcolony, see Achille Mbembe, *On the Postcolony* (Berkeley: University of California Press, 2001).

51. Michel Foucault, *Discipline and Punish: The Birth of the Prison*, trans. A. Sheridan (New York: Random House, 1975), 201.

52. Trouillot, *Haiti: State against Nation*, 23.

53. See Thomas, *Exceptional Violence*.

54. Rivke Jaffe, "Toward an Anthropology of the Caribbean State," *Small Axe* 18, no. 1 (2014): 176.

55. See Das and Poole, *Anthropology in the Margins*.

56. On this point, the treatment of Caribbean state formations as deficient neatly parallels the gendered discourses of pathological family units that depart from a Western, heteropatriarchal model. As Lynn Bolles has put it, "Where family organizations fall outside the ideal, they are, from the perspective of the [structural-functionalist] theory, socially pathological. The result for the Caribbean was a foregone conclusion. Working class/peasant/black Caribbean domestic organizations were labelled deviant and disorganized." The repertoires of gendered survival exhibited by Jamaican working-class women in Bolles's study—of "making do"—are therefore the grounds on which a new political order might be drawn outside the normative domain of the state and the bourgeois family. Bolles, *Sister Jamaica: A Study of Women, Work and Households in Kingston* (Lanham, MD: University Press of America, 1996), 6.

57. Max Horkheimer and Theodor W. Adorno, *Dialectic of Enlightenment*, trans. G. Noeri (Stanford, CA: Stanford University Press, 2002), 191.

58. Herbert Marcuse, *The Aesthetic Dimension: Toward a Critique of Marxist Aesthetics* (Boston: Beacon Press, 1979), 73.

Coda

1. On James as a "paradoxical Pan-Africanist," see Paul Buhle, "C. L. R. James: Paradoxical Pan-Africanist," in *Imagining Home: Class, Culture, and Nationalism in the African Diaspora*, ed. S. Lemelle and R. Kelley (London: Verso, 1994): 158–66.

2. For Lamming's eulogy of James as an "evangelist," see "C. L. R. James Funeral Celebration of a Life," tape 3, Banyan Archive, 1989, available at Alexander Street (password required), https://video.alexanderstreet.com/watch/c-l-r-james-funeral-celebration-of-a-life-tape-3.

3. Kaneesha Parsard reminds us, in her contribution on the early fiction and political writings of James, that his earliest contributions reflected an expansive definition of politics extending beyond the executive seat of Downing Street or the legislative theaters of Westminster or the Red House. Instead, as she argues with reference to James's only novel, *Minty Alley* (1936), "a barrack yard politics depends not on the modern, bourgeois political actor but rather on the women and men of the informal sector. . . . This reading sheds new light on approaches to politics in Caribbean studies, in which understandings of the political in the late colonial period have largely focused on the formation of party politics among Africans and Indians and on the labor rebellions of the 1930s." From the barrack yards may many more masquerades bloom! Parsard, "Barrack Yard Politics," 26.

4. C. L. R. James, *Party Politics in the West Indies* (San Juan, Trinidad: Vedic Enterprises, 1962), 28.

5. On the role of direct democracy in the political thought of C. L. R. James, see Matthew Quest, "Direct Democracy and the Search for Identity for Colonized People: The Contemporary Meanings of C. L. R. James's Classical Athens," *Classical Receptions Journal* 9, no. 2 (2017): 237–67.

6. C. L. R. James, *Beyond a Boundary* (New York: Pantheon, 1983), 249.

7. James, *Party Politics*, 4.

8. Christian Høgsbjerg tenders an exception to this "curiously neglected" thread of James's political writings in his own inquiry into the Carnivalesque and the Caribbean direct democratic tradition. See Høgsbjerg, "'The Independence, Energy and Creative Talent of Carnival Can Do Other Wonders': C. L. R. James on Carnival," *Caribbean Quarterly* 65, no. 4 (2019): 513.

9. James, *Beyond a Boundary*, 197.

10. C. L. R. James, "Lincoln, Carnival, George Padmore: Writings from the *Nation*," in *The C. L. R. James Reader*, ed. A. Grimshaw (Oxford: Blackwell, 1992), 287.

11. As George Lamming put it in his treatise on the role of the intellectual in the Caribbean, this manifests as a tension between Caribbean studies as a vocation and the political necessity of intellectual work that proceeds beyond the insular domain of the postcolonial state and the academy: "This engagement of the intellectual worker with labor and mass organization is very fundamental because we do not quite often regard knowledge as a form of property, which it is. In the old Caribbean, the white planter class ruled by virtue of what they *owned*. In the new Caribbean, the political directorate and the professional classes rule by virtue of what they *know*. They don't *own*, they *know*. And there is a sense in which there is a similarity between the two. Just as the old owning class was very reluctant to distribute that wealth, the new knowing class is very reluctant to distribute this property of knowledge. And I do not think that there can be any hope for liberation of the territory from the legacy of colonialism unless there is the widest possible distribution of this property of knowledge." Lamming, "The Role of the Intellectual in the Caribbean," *Cimarrón* 1, no. 1 (1985): 21.

12. James, "Lincoln, Carnival, George Padmore," 288.

13. James, 288; emphasis mine.

14. Roy Augier, "Something to Discuss: C. L. R. James, *Party Politics in the West Indies*," *New World Quarterly* 2, no. 1 (1965): 87; emphasis mine.

15. F. Harvey, *Rise and Fall of Party Politics*, 55.

16. Williams, *Convention Documents*, 13.

17. Crosson, *Experiments with Power*.

18. Crosson, 231.

19. Crosson, 98.

20. See Hughes, *Energy without Conscience*.

21. Bahaw, "Rowley: Trinidad and Tobago Holding On."

22. Wynter, "Novel and History," 102. Furthermore, Kaneesha Parsard stages a quarrel with Wynter's essay to trouble the provision ground as a privileged site of

insurgent potential. Surveying the landscape of the twenty-first-century Caribbean as a region beholden to structural adjustment policies and climate crisis, Parsard observes that this "moment is not the 'clash' that Wynter anticipates. Instead, it calls for siphoning, as the descendants of the enslaved and indentured are cast out from the plantation to uphold the international division of labor in new markets. In the place of *homo oeconomicus*, siphoning creates another subject or protagonist, the hustler or scammer—the architect of informal and illicit economies in the Caribbean and throughout the global South." Parsard, "Siphon, or What Was the Plot? Revisiting Sylvia Wynter's 'Novel and History, Plot and Plantation,'" *Representations* 162, no. 1 (2023): 60.

23. Ligon, *True and Exact History*, 65.

24. C. L. R. James, "The Making of the Caribbean People," in *Spheres of Existence: Selected Writings* (Westport, CT: Lawrence Hill, 1980), 176.

25. "Annual Conference of Delegates," *Vanguard*, November 26, 1982, 4.

26. Lloyd Best, "Race, Class and Ethnicity: A Caribbean Interpretation" (CERLAC Colloquia Paper, York University, April 2004), accessed February 8, 2023, 16, https://www.yorku.ca/cerlac/wp-content/uploads/sites/259/2021/01/Best.pdf.

27. Constance Rita Sutton, "The Scene of the Action: A Wildcat Strike in Barbados" (PhD diss., Columbia University, 1969), 156.

28. My evangelism of the people's masquerade resembles what Dominic Boyer elsewhere has christened "revellion" in a neologism that merges the French verbs *reveler* (to be disorderly, to make merry) and *rebeller* (to revolt). Boyer's clarion call for post-carbon futures is a celebration of "a mode of insurgency that is playful—in both the experimental and ludic senses of play—a riot that is riotous." I, perhaps, go a step further in my insistence that the masquerade not only prefigure alternative futures but also be taken up as an end in and of itself. Here, the time "at play" enjoyed by deepwater hydrocarbon firms is inverted by the mass politics of road work. Boyer, "Revolution and *Revellion*: Toward a Solarity Worth Living," *South Atlantic Quarterly* 120, no. 1 (2021): 34.

29. C. L. R. James, *Notes on Dialectics* (Westport, CT: Lawrence Hill, 1981), 117.

30. As Kimathi Mohammed—a student of James in Detroit's League of Revolutionary Black Workers—concludes: "The relationship between spontaneity and organization is very tricky and complex. . . . But with the accumulation of new universal-historical facts one thing is certain: the essential condition for a revolutionary reconstitution of society is the self-movement and creative political activity of the masses. In other words, spontaneity must be King." Mohammed, *Organization & Spontaneity* (Atlanta: On Our Own Authority!, 2013), 49.

31. Mical Teja and Freetown Collective, "Mas," Spotify, on *Mas—Single*, System Thirty Two Music, 2022.

32. D. Scott, *Omens of Adversity*, 6.

33. C. L. R. James and John Fitzpatrick, "You Never Know When It's Going to Explode," *Living Marxism*, April 1989.

34. See Francis Fukuyama, "The End of History?," *National Interest*, no. 16 (1989): 3–18.

35. James, "Seizure of Power," 3.

36. Where David Scott understands James's *The Black Jacobins* (1938; and dominant readings of *The Black Jacobins* by contemporary critics) as beholden to a "longing for total revolution, and the longing in particular for an anticolonial revolution," we might look to James's later writings on the postcolonial state in Trinidad and Ghana and post-Stalin social uprisings in Hungary and Poland as representative of a tendency unmoored from the desire for total revolution (and to that I would add the total sovereignty of the state masquerade) in favor of the unending multiplication of workers' revolts against the value form. For James, the dialectic of spontaneity and organization does not reach an end with the Haitian Constitution of 1804 or the formation of a Bolshevik government. The masquerade of working-class power can and must go on. D. Scott, *Conscripts of Modernity: The Tragedy of Colonial Enlightenment* (Durham, NC: Duke University Press, 2004), 92.

37. Leniqueca Welcome, "Getting Away with Murder: Reflection on Policing in the Trinidadian City," *City & Society* 33, no. 1 (2021): 2.

38. Welcome, "Getting Away with Murder," 5.

39. Walter Rodney, "The Struggle Goes On" (public address, Georgetown, Guyana, September 1979), accessed October 16, 2023, at History Is a Weapon, https://www.historyisaweapon.com/defcon1/rodnstrugoe.html.

40. James and Fitzpatrick, "You Never Know When."

Bibliography

Abrams, Philip. "Notes on the Difficulty of Studying the State." *Journal of Historical Sociology* 1, no. 1 (1988): 58–89.

Aching, Gerard. *Masking and Power: Carnival and Popular Culture in the Caribbean*. Minneapolis: University of Minnesota Press, 2002.

ACTT (Artists' Coalition of Trinidad and Tobago). "The Tragedy and Hidden History of NAPA" (2010). Accessed February 7, 2023. https://artistscoalition.files.wordpress.com/2012/09/the-tragedy-and-hidden-history-of-napa.pdf.

Adunbi, Omolade. *Oil Wealth and Insurgency in Nigeria*. Bloomington: Indiana University Press, 2015.

Agard-Jones, Vanessa. "Bodies in the System." *Small Axe* 42 (2013): 182–92.

Allen, Jafari S. *There's a Disco Ball between Us: A Theory of Black Gay Life*. Durham, NC: Duke University Press, 2022.

———. *¡Venceremos? The Erotics of Black Self-Making in Cuba*. Durham, NC: Duke University Press, 2011.

Anand, Nikhil. "Leaky States: Water Audits, Ignorance, and the Politics of Infrastructure." *Public Culture* 27, no. 2 (2015): 305–30.

———. "Pressure: The PoliTechnics of Water Supply in Mumbai." *Cultural Anthropology* 26, no. 4 (2012): 542–64.

Anand, Nikhil, Akhil Gupta, and Hannah Appel, eds. *The Promise of Infrastructure*. Durham, NC: Duke University Press, 2018.

Appel, Hannah. *The Licit Life of Capitalism: US Oil in Equatorial Guinea*. Durham, NC: Duke University Press, 2019.

———. "Offshore Work: Oil, Modularity, and the How of Capitalism in Equatorial Guinea." *American Ethnologist* 39, no. 4: 692–709.

Appel, Hannah, Arthur Mason, and Michael Watts, eds. *Subterranean Estates: Life Worlds of Oil and Gas*. Ithaca, NY: Cornell University Press, 2015.

Apter, Andrew. *The Pan-African Nation: Oil and the Spectacle of Culture in Nigeria*. Chicago: University of Chicago Press, 2005.

Atilla the Hun. "Commission's Report." Spotify. On *Treasury Scandal*. Caribya Music, 1950.

Augier, Roy. "Something to Discuss: C. L. R. James, *Party Politics in the West Indies.*" *New World Quarterly* 2, no. 1 (1965): 84–91.

Bacon, Peter R. *Flora and Fauna of the Caribbean: An Introduction to the Ecology of the West Indies.* Port of Spain, Trinidad: Key Caribbean Publications, 1978.

Bagoo, Andre. "Hart Resigns." *Trinidad and Tobago Newsday*, March 8, 2010. Accessed February 7, 2023. http://archives.newsday.co.tt/2010/03/08/hart-resigns/.

———. "PoS Red Zone," *Trinidad and Tobago Newsday*, March 5, 2009. Accessed February 7, 2023. http://archives.newsday.co.tt/2009/03/05/pos-red-zone/.

Bahaw, Darren. "Rowley: Trinidad and Tobago Holding On to Hydrocarbon Market," *Trinidad and Tobago Newsday*, November 7, 2021.

Baker, Jessica Swanston. "Small Islands, Large Radio: Archipelagic Listening in the Caribbean." In *Contemporary Archipelagic Thinking: Toward New Comparative Methodologies and Disciplinary Formations*, ed. M. Stephens and Y. Martínez-San Miguel. Lanham, MD: Rowman & Littlefield, 2020, 383–402.

Barry, Andrew. *Material Politics: Disputes along the Pipeline.* Malden, MA: Wiley, 2013.

Basdeo, Sahadeo. *Labour Organisation and Labour Reform in Trinidad, 1919–1939.* St. Augustine, Trinidad: Institute of Social and Economic Research, University of the West Indies, 1983.

Bateson, Gregory. *Steps to an Ecology of Mind.* Chicago: University of Chicago Press, 2000.

Baudrillard, Jean. *Simulations.* Cambridge, MA: Semiotext(e), 1983.

Beeby-Thompson, Arthur. *Oil Pioneer: Selected Experience and Incidents Associated with Sixty Years of World-Wide Petroleum Exploration and Oilfield Development.* London: Sidgwick and Jackson, 1961.

Beharry, Prior. "'Hart Real PM in T&T.'" *Trinidad and Tobago Guardian*, August 15, 2009. Accessed February 7, 2023. https://www.guardian.co.tt/article-6.2.319836.2b6adcb67f.

Benton, Lauren. *A Search for Sovereignty: Law and Geography in European Empires, 1400–1900.* Cambridge: Cambridge University Press, 2010.

Best, Lloyd. *Independent Thought and Caribbean Freedom: Essays in Honour of Lloyd Best.* Edited by S. Ryan. Mona, Jamaica: Sir Arthur Lewis Institute of Social and Economic Studies, 2003.

———. "Race, Class and Ethnicity: A Caribbean Interpretation." CERLAC Colloquia Paper, York University, April 2004. Accessed February 8, 2023. https://www.yorku.ca/cerlac/wp-content/uploads/sites/259/2021/01/Best.pdf.

Bishop, Verdel. "IMAX 3D Comes to TT." *Trinidad and Tobago Newsday*, April 9, 2011. Accessed February 7, 2023. http://archives.newsday.co.tt/2011/04/09/imax-3d-comes-to-tt/.

Black Stalin. "Caribbean Unity." On *To the Caribbean Man.* Wizards Records, 1978.

Bolles, A. Lynn. *Sister Jamaica: A Study of Women, Work and Households in Kingston.* Lanham, MD: University Press of America, 1996.

Bonilla, Yarimar. *Non-sovereign Futures: French Caribbean Politics in the Wake of Disenchantment*. Chicago: University of Chicago Press, 2015.

———. "Ordinary Sovereignty." *Small Axe* 17, no 3 (2013): 152–65.

———. "Postdisaster Futures: Hopeful Pessimism, Imperial Ruination, and *La futura cuir*." *Small Axe* 24, no. 2 (2020): 147–62.

Boopsingh, Trevor. "The Last Decade—Liquefied Natural Gas and Its Impact." In *From Oil to Gas and Beyond: A Review of the Trinidad and Tobago Model and Analysis of Future Challenges*, edited by T. Boopsingh and G. McGuire, 41–65. Lanham, MD: University Press of America, 2014.

Boyer, Dominic. *No More Fossils*. Minneapolis: University of Minnesota Press, 2023.

———. "Revolution and *Revellion*: Toward a Solarity Worth Living." *South Atlantic Quarterly* 120, no. 1 (2021): 25–37.

Brereton, Bridget. *A History of Modern Trinidad, 1783–1962*. Kingston, Jamaica: Heinemann, 1981.

———. *Race Relations in Colonial Trinidad, 1870–1900*. Cambridge: Cambridge University Press, 2002.

Brown, Adrienne. *The Black Skyscraper: Architecture and the Perception of Race*. Baltimore: Johns Hopkins University Press, 2017.

Brown, Deryck. "The Failed Coup: The Jamesian Connection." In *The Black Power Revolution, 1970: A Retrospective*, edited by S. Ryan and T. Stewart, 543–78. St. Augustine, Trinidad and Tobago: I.S.E.R., 1995.

Browne, Kevin Adonis. *High Mas: Carnival and the Poetics of Caribbean Culture*. Jackson: University Press of Mississippi, 2018.

Buhle, Paul. "C. L. R. James: Paradoxical Pan-Africanist." In *Imagining Home: Class, Culture, and Nationalism in the African Diaspora*, edited by S. Lemelle and R. Kelley, 158–66. London: Verso, 1994.

Bunce, Robin, and Paul Field. *Darcus Howe: A Political Biography*. London: Bloomsbury, 2014.

Burton, Richard D. E. *Afro-Creole: Power, Opposition, and Play in the Caribbean*. Ithaca, NY: Cornell University Press, 1997.

Cabatingan, Lee. *A Region among States: Law and Non-sovereignty in the Caribbean*. Chicago: University of Chicago Press, 2023.

Carter, Martin. "A Free Community of Valid Persons." *Kyk-Over-Al* 44 (1993): 30–32.

Casimir, Jean. *The Haitians: A Decolonial History*. Chapel Hill: University of North Carolina Press, 2020.

Chalkdust. "Money Ain't No Problem." On *Calypso vs. Soca*. Straker's Records, 1978.

Chu, Julie Y. "When Infrastructures Attack: The Workings of Disrepair in China." *American Ethnologist* 41, no. 2 (2014): 351–67.

Coronil, Fernando. *The Magical State: Nature, Money, and Modernity in Venezuela*. Chicago: University of Chicago Press, 1997.

Cozier, Chris. "Trinidad: Questions about Contemporary Histories." In *Caribe insular: Exclusión, fragmentación y paraíso*, 348–49. Badajoz, Spain: Museo Extremeño e Iberoamericano de Arte Contemporáneo, 1998.

Crehan, Kate. *Gramsci's Common Sense*. Durham, NC: Duke University Press, 2016.

Crosson, J. Brent. "'The Earth is the Lord' or 'God is a Trini'? The Political Theology of Climate Change, Environmental Stewardship, and Petroleum Extraction." In *Climate Politics and the Power of Religion*, edited by E. Berry, 39–65. Bloomington: Indiana University Press, 2022.

———. *Experiments with Power: Obeah and the Remaking of Religion in Trinidad*. Chicago: University of Chicago Press, 2020.

———. "Own People: Race, 'Altered Solidarities,' and the Limits of Culture in Trinidad." *Small Axe* 18, no. 3 (2014): 18–34.

Cudjoe, Selwyn R., ed. *Indian Time Ah Come in Trinidad and Tobago*. Wellesley, MA: Calaloux Publications, 2010.

Dalakoglou, Dimitris. "The Road: An Ethnography of the Albanian–Greek Cross-Border Motorway." *American Ethnologist* 37, no. 1 (2010): 132–49.

Dalakoglou, Dimitris, and Penelope Harvey, eds. *Roads and Anthropology: Ethnography, Infrastructures, (Im)mobility*. New York: Routledge, 2015.

Da Matta, Roberto. "An Interpretation of *Carnaval*." *SubStance* 12, no. 1 (1983): 162–70.

Das, Veena, and Deborah Poole, eds. *Anthropology in the Margins of the State*. Santa Fe, NM: School of American Research Press, 2004.

Debord, Guy. *Society of the Spectacle*. Detroit: Black & Red, 1983.

de-Landè, Shayne. "Unveiling Revolutionary Threads: A Thematic Analysis of the Jab Molassie as a Lens into the 1979 Grenadian Revolution." Master's thesis, University of West London, 2023.

De Verteuil, L. A. A. *Trinidad: Its Geography, Natural Resources, Administration, Present Condition, and Prospects*. London: Cassell, 1884.

Driver, Thackwray. "The Genesis of the Point Lisas Industrial Estate." In *100 Years of Petroleum in Trinidad and Tobago*, 116–20. London: First Strategic Insight, 2008. Accessed February 9, 2024, at FIRST Strategic Insight. https://firstforum.org/wp-content/uploads/2021/05/Publication_00011.pdf.

Edwards, Joseph [a.k.a. Fundi]. *Workers' Self-Management in the Caribbean* (Atlanta: On Our Own Authority!, 2014).

Edwards, Zophia. "Resistance and Reforms: The Role of Subaltern Agency in Colonial State Development." In *Rethinking the Colonial State*, edited by S. Rud and S. Ivarsson, 175–202. Bingley, UK: Emerald.

Eriksen, Thomas Hylland. "Liming in Trinidad: The Art of Doing Nothing." *Folk* 32 (1990): 23–43.

Farrell, Trevor M. A. "'The Worship of the Golden Calf': An Oil Exporter's Industrial Strategy, Technology Policy and Project Planning during the Boom Years." Photocopy, Economics Department, U.W.I. St. Augustine, 1987.

Ferguson, James. *Expectations of Modernity: Myths and Meaning of Urban Life on the Zambian Copperbelt*. Berkeley: University of California Press, 1999.

Ferguson, James, and Akhil Gupta. "Spatializing States: Toward and Ethnography of Neoliberal Governmentality." *American Ethnologist* 29, no. 4 (2002): 981–1002.

Ferry, Elizabeth Emma, and Mandana E. Limbert, eds. *Timely Assets: The Politics of Resources and Their Temporalities*. Santa Fe, NM: School for Advanced Research, 2008.

Fleming, Julius B. Jr. *Black Patience: Performance, Civil Rights, and the Unfinished Project of Emancipation*. New York: New York University Press, 2022.

Forster, John. *Trinidad and Tobago Disturbances, 1937: Report of Commission*. London: H. M. Stationery Office, 1938.

Foucault, Michel. *Discipline and Punish: The Birth of the Prison*. Translated by A. Sheridan. (New York: Random House, 1975).

Francis, Donette, and Allison Harris. "Introduction: Looking for Black Miami." *Anthurium* 16, no. 1 (2020): 1–17.

Fukuyama, Francis. "The End of History?" *National Interest*, no. 16 (1989): 3–18.

Gal, Susan. "Contradictions of Standard Language in Europe: Implications for the Study of Practices and Publics," *Social Anthropology* 14, no. 2 (2006): 163–81.

Ghosh, Sahana. "'Everything Must Match': Detection, Deception, and Migrant Illegality in the India–Bangladesh Borderland." *American Anthropologist* 121, no. 4 (2019): 870–83.

Gill, Lyndon Kamaal. "Transfiguring Trinidad and Tobago: Queer Cultural Production, Erotic Subjectivity and the Praxis of Black Queer Anthropology," PhD diss., Harvard University, 2010.

Girvan, Norman. *Corporate Imperialism: Conflict and Expropriation, Transnational Corporations and Economic Nationalism in the Third World*. White Plains, NY: M. E. Sharpe, 1976.

———. "50 Years of In-dependence in Jamaica: Reflections." SALISES 50-50 Conference, University of the West Indies—Mona, Kingston, Jamaica, August 22, 2012. Accessed February 9, 2024, at Yumpu. https://www.yumpu.com/en/document/view/51388635/reflections-on-fifty-years-of-in-dependence-norman-girvan.

Gonzales, Adriana Gabrielle. "Sowing Solidary Futures: Migration, Land, and Collective Survival in an Ordinary Caribbean Community." Bachelor's thesis, University of Chicago, 2021.

Government of the Republic of Trinidad and Tobago. *Budget Speech*. Port of Spain: Government Printery, 1982.

———. "Budget Statement 2019: 'Turnaround.'" October 1, 2018. Accessed February 7, 2023. https://www.finance.gov.tt/wp-content/uploads/2018/10/BUDGET-STATEMENT-2019-FINAL-WEB.pdf.

———. "Budget Statement 2020: Stability | Strength | Growth." October 7, 2019. Accessed February 7, 2023. https://www.finance.gov.tt/wp-content/uploads/2019/10/Budget-Statement-2020-Amended-web.pdf.

———. "PM Persad-Bissessar's Address on the State of the Economy." January 9, 2015. Accessed February 8, 2023. http://www.news.gov.tt/content/pm-persad-bissessars-address-state-economy#.Y-OesS_MLe8.

———. *Report of the Commission of Enquiry into the Construction Sector*. March 29, 2010. Accessed February 7, 2023. https://www.ttparliament.org/wpcontent/uploads/2022/01/20100406-CommEnqConstSect.pdf.

Government of Trinidad and Tobago. *Report of the Commission of Enquiry into the Oil Industry in Trinidad and Tobago, 1963–1964*. Trinidad and Tobago: Government Printery, 1964.

———. *Third Five-Year Plan, 1969–1973*. Trinidad and Tobago: Government Printery, 1969.

Graeber, David. *Lost People: Magic and the Legacy of Slavery in Madagascar*. Bloomington: Indiana University Press, 2007.

———. *The Utopia of Rules: on Technology, Stupidity, and the Secret Joys of Bureaucracy*. Brooklyn: Melville House, 2015.

Graeber, David, and Marshall Sahlins. *On Kings*. Chicago: HAU Books, 2017.

Gramsci, Antonio. *Selections from the Prison Notebooks of Antonio Gramsci*. Translated by Q. Hoare and G. Nowell-Smith. New York: International Publishers, 1971.

Gupta, Akhil. *Red Tape: Bureaucracy, Structural Violence, and Poverty in India*. Durham, NC: Duke University Press, 2012.

———. "Suspension." *Cultural Anthropology Online*. September 24, 2015. https://culanth.org/fieldsights/suspension.

Hall, Stuart. *Selected Political Writings: The Great Moving Right Show and Other Essays*. Durham, NC: Duke University Press, 2017.

Handelman, Don. "Reflexivity in Festival and Other Cultural Events." In *Essays in the Sociology of Perception*, edited by M. Douglas, 162–90. London: Routledge, 1982.

Hansen, Thomas Blom, and Finn Stepputat. "Sovereignty Revisited." *Annual Review of Anthropology* 35, no. 1 (2006): 295–315.

Harms, Erik. *Saigon's Edge: On the Margins of Ho Chi Minh City*. Minneapolis: University of Minnesota Press, 2011.

Harrison, Michelle. *King Sugar: Jamaica, the Caribbean and the World Sugar Industry*. New York: New York University Press, 2001.

Harvey, David. "Globalization and the 'Spatial Fix.'" *Geographische Revue* 2 (2001): 23.

Harvey, Franklyn. *Rise and Fall of Party Politics in Trinidad and Tobago*. Toronto: New Beginning Movement, 1974.

Harvey, Penny, and Hannah Knox. *Roads: An Anthropology of Infrastructure and Expertise*. Ithaca, NY: Cornell University Press, 2015.

Hassanali, Shaliza. "UWI $500M Debe Campus Still Unoccupied." CNC3, June 4, 2023. Accessed October 31, 2023. https://www.cnc3.co.tt/uwi-500m-debe-campus-still-unoccupied/.

Henry, J. D. *Oil Fields of the Empire*. London: Bradbury, Agnew, 1910.

Herzfeld, Michael. *The Social Production of Indifference*. Chicago: University of Chicago Press, 1992.

Hill, Errol. *The Trinidad Carnival: Mandate for a National Theatre*. Austin: University of Texas Press, 1972.

Hintzen, Percy. *The Costs of Regime Survival: Racial Mobilization, Elite Domination and the Control of the State in Guyana and Trinidad*. Cambridge: Cambridge University Press, 1989.

Ho, Karen. *Liquidated: An Ethnography of Wall Street*. Durham, NC: Duke University Press, 2009.

Hobbes, Thomas. *Leviathan*. New York: Penguin Classics, 2017.

Høgsbjerg, Christian. "'The Independence, Energy and Creative Talent of Carnival Can Do Other Wonders': C. L. R. James on Carnival." *Caribbean Quarterly* 65, no. 4 (2019): 513–33.

Holston, James. *Insurgent Citizenship: Disjunctions of Democracy and Modernity in Brazil*. Princeton, NJ: Princeton University Press, 2008.

Holton, Graham E. L. "Oil, Race, and Calypso in Trinidad and Tobago, 1909–1990." In *Latin American Popular Culture Since Independence: An Introduction*, edited by W. Beezley and L. Curcio-Nagy, 193–204. Plymouth, UK: Rowman & Littlefield, 2012.

Honore-Gopie, Venus. "Vagrant Removal Still Ongoing." *Trinidad and Tobago Newsday*, April 16, 2009. Accessed February 7, 2023. http://archives.newsday.co.tt/2009/04/16/vagrant-removal-still-ongoing/.

Horkheimer, Max, and Theodor W. Adorno. *Dialectic of Enlightenment*. Translated by G. Noeri. Stanford, CA: Stanford University Press, 2002.

Howe, Cymene, Jessica Lockrem, Hannah Appel, Edward Hackett, Dominic Boyer, Randal Hall, Matthew Schneider-Mayerson, et al. "Paradoxical Infrastructures: Ruins, Retrofit, and Risk." *Science, Technology & Human Values* 41, no. 3 (2016): 547–65.

Hu, Cameron. "Knowing Destroying: The Geopolitics of Fracking and the Metaphysics of Imperialism." PhD diss., University of Chicago, 2021.

Hudson, Peter James. "Imperial Designs: The Royal Bank of Canada in the Caribbean." *Race & Class* 52, no. 1 (2010): 33–48.

Hughes, David McDermott. *Energy without Conscience: Oil, Climate Change, and Complicity*. Durham, NC: Duke University Press, 2017.

Hull, Matthew. *Government of Paper: The Materiality of Bureaucracy in Urban Pakistan*. Berkeley: University of California Press, 2012.

Invisible Committee. *To Our Friends*. Cambridge, MA: MIT Press, 2015.

Jaffe, Rivke. "The Hybrid State: Crime and Citizenship in Urban Jamaica." *American Ethnologist* 40, no. 4 (2013): 734–48.

———. "Toward an Anthropology of the Caribbean State." *Small Axe* 18, no. 1 (2014): 173–80.

James, C. L. R. *Beyond a Boundary*. New York: Pantheon, 1983.
———. *Every Cook Can Govern: A Study of Democracy in Ancient Greece*. Detroit: Correspondence Publishing, 1956.
———. "George Padmore: Black Marxist Revolutionary—a Memoir [1976]." In *At the Rendezvous of Victory: Selected Writings*, 251–263. London: Allison and Busby, 1984.
———. "Interviews with Kenneth Ramchand." September 5, 1980. Accessed October 1, 2023, at Marxists Internet Archive. https://www.marxists.org/archive/james-clr/works/1980/09/banyan.htm.
———. *The Life of Captain Cipriani*. Durham, NC: Duke University Press, 2014.
———. "Lincoln, Carnival, George Padmore: Writings from the *Nation*." In *The C. L. R. James Reader*, edited by A. Grimshaw, 281–95. Oxford: Blackwell, 1992.
———. "The Making of the Caribbean People." In *Spheres of Existence: Selected Writings*, 173–90. Westport, CT: Lawrence Hill, 1980.
———. *Notes on Dialectics*. Westport, CT: Lawrence Hill, 1981.
———. *Party Politics in the West Indies*. San Juan, Trinidad: Vedic Enterprises, 1962.
———. "The Seizure of Power." 1975. Columbia University, Rare Book and Manuscript Library, C. L. R. James Papers, box 11, folder 4.
———. "Walter Rodney and the Question of Power." January 30, 1981, accessed February 8, 2024. Available at Marxists Internet Archive, https://www.marxists.org/archive/james-clr/works/1981/01/rodney.htm.
James, C. L. R., and John Fitzpatrick. "You Never Know When It's Going to Explode." *Living Marxism*, April 1989.
Jobson, Ryan Cecil. "Facing the Flames: The Herskovitses, Trinidad, and the Anthropological Imagination." *American Ethnologist* 50, no. 3 (2023): 368–74.
———. "Road Work: Highways and Hegemony in Trinidad and Tobago." *Journal of Latin American and Caribbean Anthropology* 23, no. 3 (2018): 457–77.
———. "States of Crisis, Flags of Convenience: An Introduction." *Small Axe* 24, no. 2 (2020): 67–77.
Johnson, W. Chris. "Guerrilla Ganja Gun Girls: Policing Black Revolutionaries from Notting Hill to Laventille." *Gender & History* 26, no. 3 (2015): 661–87.
Julien, Joel. "Kamla Takes a Break from HRM." *Trinidad Express*, October 30, 2014.
Kadalie, Modibo. *Pan-African Social Ecology*. Atlanta: On Our Own Authority!, 2019.
Kambon, Khafra. *For Bread, Justice, and Freedom*. London: New Beacon, 1988.
Kamugisha, Aaron. *Beyond Coloniality: Citizenship and Freedom in the Caribbean Intellectual Tradition*. Bloomington: Indiana University Press, 2019.
Kapila, Kriti. *Nullius: The Anthropology of Ownership, Sovereignty, and the Law in India*. Chicago: HAU Books, 2022.
Karl, Terry Lynn. *The Paradox of Plenty*. Berkeley: University of California Press, 1997.

Kerrigan, Dylan. "Bobol as a Transhistorical Cultural Logic: The Coloniality of Corruption in Trinidad." *Caribbean Quarterly* 66, no. 2 (2020): 195–216.

———. "Transnational Anti-Black Racism and State Violence in Trinidad." *Cultural Anthropology Online* (2015). https://culanth.org/fieldsights/transnational-anti-black-racism-and-state-violence-in-trinidad.

Kerr-Ritchie, J. R. *Rites of August First: Emancipation Day in the Black Atlantic World*. Baton Rouge: Louisiana State University Press, 2007.

Kes. "Savannah Grass." Spotify. On *Savannah Grass—Single*. Ineffable Records, 2019.

Kiely, Ray. *The Politics of Labour and Development in Trinidad*. Kingston, Jamaica: University of the West Indies Press, 1996.

Kincaid, Jamaica. *A Small Place*. New York: Farrar, Straus and Giroux, 1998.

Kirsch, Stuart. *Mining Capitalism: The Relationship between Corporations and Their Critics*. Oakland: University of California Press, 2014.

Lacan, Jacques. *The Seminar of Jacques Lacan: The Other Side of Psychoanalysis, Book XVII*. Translated by R. Grigg. New York: Norton, 2007.

Laclau, Ernesto, and Chantal Mouffe. *Hegemony and Socialist Strategy: Towards a Radical Democratic Politics*. London: Verso, 2014.

Lamming, George. "The Role of the Intellectual in the Caribbean." *Cimarrón* 1, no. 1 (1985): 21.

Larkin, Brian. "The Politics and Poetics of Infrastructure." *Annual Review of Anthropology* 42, no. 1 (2013): 327–43.

Laughlin, Nicholas. "The Flight of the Cobo." March 7, 2010. http://nicholaslaughlin.blogspot.com/2010/03/flight-of-cobo-my-carnival-monday.html.

Le Bon, Gustave. *The Crowd: A Study of the Popular Mind*. London: T. F. Unwin, 1903.

Ledgister, F. S. J. *Class Alliances and the Liberal Authoritarian State: The Roots of Post-colonial Democracy in Jamaica, Trinidad and Tobago, and Surinam*. Trenton, NJ: Africa World Press, 1998.

Li, Darryl. *The Universal Enemy: Jihad, Empire, and the Challenge of Solidarity*. Stanford, CA: Stanford University Press, 2019.

Ligon, Richard. *A True and Exact History of the Island of Barbados*. Indianapolis: Hackett, 2011.

Limbert, Mandana. *In the Time of Oil: Piety, Memory, and Social Life in an Omani Town*. Stanford, CA: Stanford University Press, 2010.

Lord Relator. "Take a Rest." On *Relator the Real Master—1980 Calypso Monarch "Live."* Makossa International Records, 1980.

Lord Shorty. "Money Eh No Problem." Spotify. On *Soca Explosion*. Shorty Records, 1978.

Loubon, Michelle. "Tributes Flow for 'Brinz': Prof Brinsley Samaroo—April 14, 1940 to July 9, 2023." *Trinidad Express*, July 15, 2023.

Loutoo, Jada. "Activist Takes to the Streets." *Trinidad and Tobago Newsday*, April 16, 2009. Accessed February 7, 2023. http://archives.newsday.co.tt/2009/04/16/activist-takes-to-the-streets/.

MacDonald, Scott. *Trinidad and Tobago: Democracy and Development in the Caribbean*. New York: Praeger, 1986.
Mahabir, Kumar. "The Impact of Hindi on Trinidad English." *Caribbean Quarterly* 45, no. 4 (1999): 13–34.
Make It Hapn. "Mus Eat Ah Food." Bandcamp. On *I vs. Me*. 2010.
Malcolm, Noel. *Aspects of Hobbes*. Oxford: Oxford University Press, 2004.
Malinowski, Bronislaw. *Magic, Science and Religion, and Other Essays*. New York: Doubleday, 1954.
Mann, Michael. "The Autonomous Power of the State: Its Origins, Mechanisms and Results." *European Journal of Sociology / Archives Européennes de Sociologie / Europäisches Archiv für Soziologie* 25, no. 2 (1984): 185–213.
Marcuse, Herbert. *The Aesthetic Dimension: Toward a Critique of Marxist Aesthetics*. Boston: Beacon Press, 1979.
Markey, Patrick. "Obama Cool Meets Chavez Mania at Americas Summit." Reuters, April 20, 2009. Accessed February 7, 2023. https://www.reuters.com/article/us-summit-obama-chavez/obama-cool-meets-chavez-mania-at-americas-summit-idUSTRE53J3MW20090420.
Marx, Karl. *Grundrisse: Foundations of the Critique of Political Economy*. London: Penguin, 2005.
Mazzarella, William. "The Myth of the Multitude, or, Who's Afraid of the Crowd?" *Critical Inquiry* 36, no. 4 (2010): 697–727.
———. "Pleasure and Its Bystanders: A Ludibrium." *Portable Gray* 5, no. 2 (2022): 254.
Mbembe, Achille. *On the Postcolony*. Berkeley: University of California Press, 2001.
McClish, Carmen L. "Good Liming in Trinidad: The Art of Doing Something." *Liminalities: A Journal of Performance Studies* 12, no. 4 (2016).
McDowell, Robin. "'There Are Lives Here': The African and African American Cemeteries of the Bonnet Carré Spillway." *Radical History Review* 147 (2023): 35–54.
McGovern, Mike. *Unmasking the State: Making Guinea Modern*. Chicago: University of Chicago Press, 2013.
Meeks, Brian. *Critical Interventions in Caribbean Politics and Theory*. Jackson: University Press of Mississippi, 2014.
———. "NUFF at the Cusp of an Idea: Grassroots Guerrillas and the Politics of the 1970s in Trinidad and Tobago." *Social Identities* 5, no. 4 (1999): 415–39.
Mendes-Franco, Janine. "Trinidad & Tobago: No Simple Highway." Global Voices, November 28, 2012. Accessed March 3, 2014. https://globalvoices.org/2012/11/28/trinidad-tobago-no-simple-highway/.
Millette, James. "Toward the Black Power Revolt of 1970." In *The Black Power Revolution, 1970: A Retrospective*, edited by S. Ryan and T. Stewart, 59–96. St. Augustine, Trinidad and Tobago: I.S.E.R., 1995.
Mintz, Sidney W. *Caribbean Transformations*. Chicago: Aldine, 1974.

———. *Sweetness and Power: The Place of Sugar in Modern History*. New York: Penguin, 1985.

Mitchell, Timothy. *Carbon Democracy: Political Power in the Age of Oil*. London: Verso, 2011.

Mohabir, Nalini, and Ronald Cummings, eds. *The Fire That Time: Transnational Black Radicalism and the Sir George Williams Occupation*. Montreal: Black Rose Books, 2022.

Mohammed, Kimathi. *Organization and Spontaneity*. Atlanta: On Our Own Authority!, 2013.

Mottley, Wendell. *Trinidad and Tobago Industrial Policy, 1959–2008: A Historical and Contemporary Analysis*. Kingston, Jamaica: Ian Randle, 2008.

Naipaul, V. S. *The Middle Passage*. New York: Random House, 2010. First published 1962.

———. "Power to the Caribbean People." *New York Review of Books*, September 3, 1970.

Nakassis, Constantine V. *Onscreen/Offscreen*. Toronto: University of Toronto Press, 2023.

Nakhid, Camille, Josh Mosca, and Shani Nakhid-Schuster. "Liming as Research Methodology, Ole Talk as Research Method—a Caribbean Methodology." *Journal of Education and Development in the Caribbean* 18, no. 2 (2020): 1–18.

NAMOTI. *National Movement for the True Independence of Trinago*. Trinidad and Tobago: Central Committee of NAMOTI, 1975.

Neptune, Harvey R. *Caliban and the Yankees: Trinidad and the United States Occupation*. Chapel Hill: University of North Carolina Press, 2007.

Ngai, Sianne. *Theory of the Gimmick: Aesthetic Judgment and Capitalist Form*. Cambridge, MA: Harvard University Press, 2020.

Obika, Nyahuma. *An Introduction to the Life and Times of Tubal Uriah Buzz Butler*. Maracas, Trinidad and Tobago: College Press, 1983.

O'Connor, P. E. T. *Some Trinidad Yesterdays*. Port of Spain: Inprint Caribbean, 1978.

Office of the Prime Minister, Republic of Trinidad and Tobago. "Announcement of the Drilling of the BHP Broadside Well." September 15, 2020. Accessed February 10, 2024. https://www.opm.gov.tt/announcement-of-drilling-of-bhp-broadside-well/.

Oilfields Workers' Trade Union. *Oil in Turmoil and OWTU Memorandum on the Formation of a National Oil Co.* San Fernando, Trinidad and Tobago: Vanguard Publishing, 1967.

Organisation for National Reconstruction. *Why Nothing Works in Trinidad and Tobago*. Port of Spain: Organisation for National Reconstruction, 1981.

Organization of American States. "An Address by the Honourable Patrick Manning, Prime Minister of the Republic of Trinidad and Tobago at the Opening Ceremony of the Fifth Summit of the Americas." April 17, 2009. Accessed February 7, 2023. http://www.summit-americas.org/V_Summit/remarks_tto_en.pdf.

———. "Official Remarks of United States President Barack Obama at the Opening Ceremony of the Fifth Summit of the Americas." April 17, 2009. Accessed February 7, 2023. http://www.summit-americas.org/V_Summit/remarks_usa_en.pdf.

Owusu, Darcus. "The Long March to Caroni." *Vanguard*, March 21, 1970.

Oxaal, Ivar. *Black Intellectuals Come to Power: The Rise of Creole Nationalism in Trinidad and Tobago*. Cambridge, MA: Schenkman Publishing, 1968.

Paddington, Bruce, and Keith Q. Warner. "The Emergence of Caribbean Feature Films." *Black Camera* 1, no. 1 (Winter 2009): 91–108.

Padmore, George. "Imperialism in the West Indies." *International Negro Workers' Review* 1, no. 1 (January 1931): 16–20.

Parsard, Kaneesha Cherelle. "Barrack Yard Politics: From C. L. R. James's *The Case for West Indian Self-Government* to *Minty Alley*." *Small Axe* 22, no. 3 (2018): 13–27.

———. "Siphon, or What Was the Plot? Revisiting Sylvia Wynter's 'Novel and History, Plot and Plantation.'" *Representations* 162, no. 1 (2023): 56–64.

Partap, Harry. "CLR James: Williams Was No Genius . . . the Oil Saved Him." *Trinidad Express*, April 7, 1981.

People's National Movement. *Buy and Eat More Local*. Port-of-Spain: Charbol Commercial Printery, 1963.

Perry, Keston K. "Continuity, Change and Contradictions in Late Steel-Based Industrialization: The 'Global Color Line' in Trinidad and Tobago's Postcolonial Economy." *Sociology Compass* 16, no. 12 (2022): 1–17.

Poulantzas, Nicos. *State, Power, Socialism*. London: Verso, 2014.

Quest, Matthew. "Direct Democracy and the Search for Identity for Colonized People: The Contemporary Meanings of C. L. R. James's Classical Athens." *Classical Receptions Journal* 9, no. 2 (2017): 237–67.

———. "'Every Cook Can Govern': Direct Democracy, Workers' Self Management and the Creative Foundations of C. L. R. James' Political Thought." *CLR James Journal* 19, nos. 1–2 (2013): 374–91.

Radcliffe-Brown, A. R. Preface to *African Political Systems*, xi–xxiii. Edited by M. Fortes and E. E. Evans-Pritchard. London: Oxford University Press, 1940.

Rajnauth, Jerome, and Craig Boodoo. "Trinidad and Tobago's First Deepwater Drilling Campaign." *West Indian Journal of Engineering* 36, no. 2 (2013): 4–14.

Ralph, Laurence. *Renegade Dreams: Living through Injury in Gangland Chicago*. Chicago: University of Chicago Press, 2014.

Ralph, Michael. *Forensics of Capital*. Chicago: University of Chicago Press, 2015.

———. "Killing Time." *Social Text* 26, no. 4 (2008): 1–29.

Ramnarine, Kevin. "Address by the Minister of Energy and Energy Affairs, Trinidad and Tobago at the 12th Annual Energy Caribbean Conference." October 2, 2012. https://www.energy.gov.tt/wp-content/uploads/2013/11/12th%20Annual%20Energy%20Caribbean%20Conference.pdf.

———. "Statement to Parliament on Energy Policy." Port of Spain, Trinidad and Tobago, April 24, 2015. http://www.news.gov.tt/sites/default/files/Statement%20to%20Parliament%20on%20Energy%20Policy_final%20%2024.4.2015.pdf.

Ramsaran, Ramesh. "Aspects of Growth and Adjustment in Post-independence Trinidad and Tobago." *Social and Economic Studies* 48, nos. 1–2 (1999): 215–286.

Raymond, Afra. *Property Matters: A Compilation from the "Business Guardian" Column*. Port of Spain: Raymond & Pierre, 2005.

Reddock, Rhoda. *Women, Labour and Politics in Trinidad and Tobago: A History*. London: Zed Books, 1994.

Rennie, A. Bukka. *The History of the Working-Class in Trinidad and Tobago in the 20th Century (1919–1956)*. Port of Spain: New Beginning Movement, 1974.

Robinson, Cedric. *The Terms of Order: Political Science and the Myth of Leadership*. Chapel Hill: University of North Carolina Press, 2016.

Rodney, Walter. "Contemporary Political Trends in the English-Speaking Caribbean." In *Caribbean Political Thought: Theories of the Post-colonial State*, edited by A. Kamugisha, 1–8. Kingston, Jamaica: Ian Randle, 2013.

———. "The Struggle Goes On." Speech, Georgetown, Guyana, September 1979. Accessed October 16, 2023, at History Is a Weapon. https://www.historyisaweapon.com/defcon1/rodnstrugoe.html.

Rogers, Douglas. "Oil and Anthropology." *Annual Review of Anthropology* 44, no. 1 (2015): 365–80.

Ross, Michael L. *The Oil Curse: How Petroleum Wealth Shapes the Development of Nations*. Princeton, NJ: Princeton University Press, 2001.

Rouse, Irving. *The Tainos: Rise and Decline of the People Who Greeted Columbus*. New Haven, CT: Yale University Press, 1992.

Rowley, Keith. "Prime Minister Rowley's Statement at World Leaders Summit—COP26." Office of the Prime Minister, Republic of Trinidad and Tobago, November 2, 2021. https://www.opm.gov.tt/prime-minister-rowleys-statement-at-world-leaders-summit-cop26/.

Royal Commonwealth Society. *Proceedings of the Royal Colonial Institute*. London: Royal Colonial Institute, 1907.

Rutherford, Danilyn. *Laughing at Leviathan: Sovereignty and Audience in West Papua*. Chicago: University of Chicago Press, 2012.

Ryan, Selwyn D. *Eric Williams: The Myth and the Man*. Kingston, Jamaica: University Press of the West Indies, 2009.

———. *The Muslimeen Grab for Power: Race, Religion, and Revolution in Trinidad and Tobago*. Port of Spain: Inprint Caribbean, 1991.

———. *Race and Nationalism in Trinidad and Tobago: A Study of Decolonization in a Multiracial Society*. Toronto: University of Toronto Press, 1972.

Samaroo, Brinsley. "The Trinidad Workingmen's Association and the Origins of Popular Protest in a Crown Colony." *Social and Economic Studies* 21, no. 2 (1972) 205–22.

Schmitt, Carl. *The Leviathan in the State Theory of Thomas Hobbes: Meaning and Failure of a Political Symbol*. Translated by G. Schwab. Chicago: University of Chicago Press, 2008.

———. *Political Theology: Four Chapters on the Concept of Sovereignty*. Translated by G. Schwab. Chicago: University of Chicago Press, 2005.

Schneider-Meyerson, Matthew. *Peak Oil: Apocalyptic Environmentalism and Libertarian Political Culture*. Chicago: University of Chicago Press, 2015.

Scott, David. *Conscripts of Modernity: The Tragedy of Colonial Enlightenment*. Durham, NC: Duke University Press, 2004.

———. "Norms of Self-Determination: Thinking Sovereignty Through." *Middle East Law and Governance* 4, nos. 2–3 (2012): 195–224.

———. *Omens of Adversity: Tragedy, Time, Memory, Justice*. Durham, NC: Duke University Press, 2014.

Scott, James C. *Seeing like a State: How Certain Schemes to Improve the Human Condition Have Failed*. New Haven, CT: Yale University Press, 1998.

Seow, Victor. *Carbon Technocracy: Energy Regimes in Modern East Asia*. Chicago: University of Chicago Press, 2022.

Shah, Raffique. "Reflections on the Mutiny and Trial." In *The Black Power Revolution, 1970: A Retrospective*, edited by S. Ryan and T. Stewart, 509–22. St. Augustine, Trinidad and Tobago: I.S.E.R., 1995.

Sharma, Aradhana, and Akhil Gupta, eds. *The Anthropology of the State: A Reader*. Malden, MA: Blackwell, 2006.

Shepherd, Rob, and James Ball. "Liquefied Natural Gas from Trinidad and Tobago: The Atlantic LNG Project." In *Natural Gas and Geopolitics: From 1970 to 2040*, edited by D. Victor, A. Jaffe, and M. Hayes, 268–318. Cambridge: Cambridge University Press, 2006.

Silverstein, Michael. "The 'Message' in the (Political) Battle." *Language & Communication* 31, no. 3 (2011): 203–16.

Simms, Rachel, and Errol Simms. "The Building Blocks of Successful Regional Integration: Lessons for CSME from Other Integration Schemes." *Social and Economic Studies* 56, no. 4 (2007): 255–85.

Smith, Daniel Jordan. *A Culture of Corruption: Everyday Deception and Popular Discontent in Nigeria*. Princeton, NJ: Princeton University Press, 2008.

Smith, Michael Garfield. *Plural Society in the British West Indies*. Berkeley: University of California Press, 1974.

Stainsby, Macdonald. *Tar Sands in T&T? A Look at the World's Dirtiest Oil, from Canada to Trinidad and Tobago*. Montreal: Katasoho, 2013.

Stephens, Michelle. "What Is an Island? Caribbean Studies and the Contemporary Visual Artist." *Small Axe* 17, no. 2 (2013): 8–26.

Sunder Rajan, Kaushik. *Biocapital: The Constitution of Postgenomic Life*. Durham, NC: Duke University Press, 2006.

Sutton, Constance Rita. "The Scene of the Action: A Wildcat Strike in Barbados." PhD diss., Columbia University, 1969.

Taitt, Ria. "HOT GAS: Imbert on Mid-year Budget Review." *Trinidad Express*, May 13, 2019. Accessed February 10, 2024. https://trinidadexpress.com/news/lo cal/hot-gas/article_1fa935e2-75e6-11e9-ab74-27ad24c7af0b.html.

Takabvirwa, Kathryn. "Citizens in Uniform: Roadblocks and the Policing of Everyday Life in Zimbabwe." *American Ethnologist* 50, no. 2 (2023): 236–46.

Taussig, Michael. *The Magic of the State*. New York: Routledge, 1997.

Teelucksingh, Jerome. *Ideology, Politics, and Radicalism of the Afro-Caribbean*. New York: Palgrave, 2016.

Teja, Mical, and Freetown Collective. "Mas." Spotify. On *Mas—Single*. System Thirty Two Music, 2022.

Thomas, Deborah A. *Exceptional Violence: Embodied Citizenship in Transnational Jamaica*. Durham, NC: Duke University Press, 2011.

———. *Political Life in the Wake of the Plantation: Sovereignty, Witnessing, Repair*. Durham, NC: Duke University Press, 2019.

Tillerson, Rex. "Energy Leading the Way: From Investment and Innovation to 21st Century Economic Transformation." In *Business in a Changing Society*, edited by A. Koopmann, 29–36. Zurich: Neue Zürcher Zeitung, 2014.

Trinidad and Tobago Ministry of Petroleum and Mines. *Proceedings of the Conference on Best Use of Our Petroleum Resources*. Port of Spain: Trinidad and Tobago Ministry of Petroleum and Mines, 1975.

Trouillot, Michel-Rolph. "The Anthropology of the State in the Age of Globalization: Close Encounters of the Deceptive Kind." *Current Anthropology* 42, no. 1 (2001): 125–38.

———. *Haiti: State against Nation*. New York: Monthly Review Press, 1990.

———. *Peasants and Capital: Dominica in the World Economy*. Baltimore: Johns Hopkins University Press, 1988.

———. *Silencing the Past: Power and the Production of History*. Boston: Beacon, 1995.

Warner-Lewis, Maureen. *Trinidad Yoruba: From Mother Tongue to Memory*. Kingston, Jamaica: University of the West Indies Press, 1997.

Watts, Michael. "Oil as Money: The Devil's Excrement and the Spectacle of Black Gold." In *Money, Power, and Space*, edited by R. Martin, 406–45. Oxford: Blackwell, 1994.

———. "Resource Curse? Governmentality, Oil and Power in the Niger Delta, Nigeria." *Geopolitics* 9, no. 1 (2004): 50–80.

———. "A Tale of Two Gulfs: Life, Death, and Dispossession along Two Oil Frontiers." *American Quarterly* 64, no. 3 (2012): 437–67.

Webb, Yvonne. "Rowley: Pray for Oil and Gas." *Trinidad and Tobago Guardian*, June 22, 2016. Accessed February 7, 2023. https://www.guardian.co.tt/arti cle-6.2.355346.204a92c45c.

Weber, Max. "Politics as a Vocation." In *From Max Weber: Essays in Sociology*, edited by H. Gerth and C. Mills, 77–128. New York: Oxford University Press, 1946.

Welcome, Leniqueca. "Getting Away with Murder: Reflection on Policing in the Trinidadian City." *City & Society* 33, no. 1 (2021): 1–7.

———. "To Be Black Is to . . . : The Production of Blackness in and beyond Trinidad." *Small Axe* 26, no. 2 (2022): 108–18.
Weszkalnys, Gisa. "Geology, Potentiality, Speculation: On the Indeterminacy of First Oil." *Cultural Anthropology* 30, no. 4 (2015): 611–39.
Wethe, David. "Mothballing the World's Fanciest Oil Rigs Is a Massive Gamble." Bloomberg.com, September 9, 2016. Accessed February 8, 2024. https://www.bloomberg.com/news/articles/2016-09-19/at-500-million-a-pop-it-s-an-oil-gamble-that-has-no-precedent.
White, Nicky, Mark Thompson, and Tony Barwise. "Understanding the Thermal Evolution of Deep-Water Continental Margins." *Nature* 426 (2003): 334–43.
Williams, Eric Eustace. *Capitalism and Slavery*. Chapel Hill: University of North Carolina Press, 1994.
———. *The Caribbean Man: Address of the Political Leader of the P.N.M., 21st Annual Convention—September 29, 1979*. Port of Spain: People's National Movement Publishing, 1979.
———. *Convention Documents*. Port of Spain: People's National Movement, 1973.
———. *The Energy Crisis, 1973–1974: Three Addresses by Dr. Eric Williams*. Port of Spain: Public Relations Division, Office of the Prime Minister, 1974.
———. *Forged from the Love of Liberty: Selected Speeches of Dr. Eric Williams*. Edited by P. Sutton. Port of Spain: Prentice Hall, 1981.
———. "Massa Day Done (Public Lecture at Woodford Square, 22 March 1961)." *Callaloo* 20, no. 4 (1997): 724–30.
———. *The Negro in the Caribbean*. New York: A&B Books, 1994.
———. "The Problems of Industrialization." 1978. University of the West Indies, St. Augustine, Eric Williams Memorial Collection.
———. *Reorganisation of the Public Service: Three Speeches*. Port of Spain: P. N. M. Publishing, 1965.
World Bank. "Trinidad and Tobago—Economic Position and Prospects." July 31, 1974. Accessed February 9, 2024. https://documents.worldbank.org/en/publication/documents-reports/documentdetail/581181468312888606/trinidad-and-tobago-economic-position-and-prospects.
———. "The World Bank in Trinidad and Tobago: Overview." n.d. Accessed February 5, 2023, https://www.worldbank.org/en/country/trinidadandtobago/overview#1.
Wynter, Sylvia. "Novel and History, Plot and Plantation." *Savacou* 5 (1971): 95–102.
Yelvington, Kevin, ed. *Trinidad Ethnicity*. Knoxville: University of Tennessee Press, 1992.
Žižek, Slavoj, Ernesto Laclau, and Judith Butler. *Contingency, Hegemony, Universality: Contemporary Dialogues on the Left*. London: Verso, 2011.

Index

Page numbers in italics refer to figures.

Abrams, Philip, 19–20
Aching, Gerard, 25
Achong, Tito, 58–59
Adunbi, Omolade, 181n9
Afro-Saxon political hegemony, 28, 94, 136, 203n11
agriculture: counter-plantation system, 48, 49, 59; decline of sugar production, 34, 36, 39, 41, 45, 70–71; and drought of 1970s, 65; and infrastructure concentrated around ports and sugar estates, 35, 144; labor shortages, 36–37; program of development and import substitution, 70–72; transition from plantation agriculture to carbon fuels, 3, 5, 6, 12–13, 35–37, 39, 181n9
Akosombo Dam, Ghana, 74
Alice Yard collaborative art space, 130
Allen, Kurt, "Too Bright," composition for Carnival 2010, 135–37, 139
All Trinidad Sugar Estates and Factory Workers' Trade Union, 81
Amalgamated Workers Union, 157
Amoco, offshore discovery of oil and gas, 75, 96
anthropology of the Caribbean, 6–7, 15, 163, 183n21
Antigua, 2, 5
Apex Oilfields: Fyzabad oilfield, 44; profits and projected production in 1936, 44; strike of 1935, 40, 50; strike of 1937, 54
Appel, Hannah, ethnography of offshore oil in Equatorial Guinea, 15–16

Arab–Israeli War, 69
ArcelorMittal, closure of Point Lisas steel plant, 105
Arima, Trinidad, 4
Armstrong, James, Armstrong report on disputed highway segment, 150–51
Arouca, Trinidad, 4
Artists' Coalition of Trinidad and Tobago (ACTT), *The Tragedy and Hidden History of NAPA*, 133–34
Aswan Dam, 74
Atilla the Hun, "Commission's Report," 59
Atlantic LNG project, Point Fortin, 5, 96–97; shortfall of gas supply, 29, 106
Augier, Roy, 167

Baker, Arthur, 22–23, 24, 156
Baker, Jessica Swanston, "Small Islands, Large Radio," 186n36
Bakhtin, Mikhail, 207n3
Barataria, Trinidad, 4
Barbados: plantation economy, 2–3; uprising of enslaved Africans in, 169–70
Barry, Andrew, 84
Bateson, Gregory, 104, 204n25
Baudrillard, Jean, 210n35
Beeby-Thompson, Arthur, 35
Belmont, Trinidad, 3
Berlant, Lauren, 207n4
Berlin Wall, fall of, 171
Best, Lloyd, 66–67, 170, 199n25, 203n11
BG, offshore drilling campaigns, 96

BHP Billiton: Broadside well, 106–7, *107*, 109–10; deepwater-exploration blocks, T&T, 15, 104–10, 205n35; LeClerc well, 105; offshore drilling campaigns, 96
Black Power Revolution of 1970, 28, 63–65, 81; and Caroni march, 64, 198n13; and high unemployment and strained relations between organized labor and government, 63, 71, 72; and mutiny of Trinbagonian soldiers, 64; and politics of mas, 170; Williams and, 65, 66, 86, 94, 168, 173–74
Black Stalin: "The Caribbean Man," 78, 79; "piece of the action," 81
Black workers: barred from choice positions in oilfields and in local constabulary forces, 41; preference for oilfield work over plantation labor, 36–37, 48; work stoppages against oil companies and hunger marches, 40
"Bloody Tuesday," 81
bobol (corruption), 154
Bois Caïman, and Haitian Revolution, 170
Bolles, Lynn, 214n56
Bomber, 74
Bonilla, Yarimar, 32–33, 206n54
Booz Allen Hamilton, 84
Boyer, Dominic, 216n28
Brechin Castle, Trinidad, 5
Brereton, Bridget, 2
Brian Lara Cricket Stadium, Tarouba, 128–29, 155
British Empire Workers and Citizens Home Rule Party (BEW & CHP), 40–41, 47–49, 51, 55, 58
British Navy, conversion of fleet from coal to oil power, 35
British Petroleum (BP): joint venture in T&T with Tesoro Petroleum Company to purchase assets, 72, 73; offshore drilling campaigns, 96
British West Indies, emancipation of, and Carnival masquerade, 21
Browne, Adrienne, 123
Browne, Avery, 126
Browne, Kevin, *High Mas*, 24
Burton, Richard, 23
Bush, George W., 125
Butler, Uriah "Buzz," 8; appeal to workers to seize power from colonial administration, 56; arrest and imprisonment in 1939, 57; attempts of authorities to arrest, during strike of 1937, 52, 54; and British Empire Workers and Citizens Home Rule Party (BEW & CHP), or Butler Party, 40–41, 47–49, 51, 55, 58; call for general sit-down strike on June 22, 1937, 51; call for seizure of private land for food cultivation, 48–49; call for working-class unity across racial lines, 51, 56; establishment of British Empire Workers, Peasants, and Rate Payers Union, 57; evangelical oratory, 47, 48, 56, 194n83; hunger march from Fyzabad to Port of Spain, 40; and Jab Molassie, 188n59; sedition trial, *The King v. Uriah Butler*, 55, 195n84; support for wildcat strike and expulsion from OWTU, 57

Cabatingan, Lee, 187n38
Cadman, John, 45
calypso and calypsonians: Kurt Allen, 135–37, 139; Atilla the Hun, 59; Black Stalin, 78, 79, 81; Bomber, 74; Chalkdust, 74; focus on corruption, 154; and fusion genres, 112; and humor, 207n1; Lord Invader, 26; Lord Relator, 86; Lord Shorty, 74; Mighty Sparrow, 170; protest repertoire of, 112–13
Calypso Monarch (formerly Calypso King), 30, 59, 86, 135
Cambridge Analytica consulting firm, 137–38
Canadian tar sand extractions, 9
Caribbean Community (CARICOM), 13
Caribbean states: anti-Black state violence in, 172–74; and "barrack yard politics," 214n3; as big small places, 6–7, 186n36; and climate change, 168–69; history of settler dispossession, plantation slavery, and monocrop economies, 1, 2, 111; and informal and illicit economies, 215n22; multinational corporations as obstacles to postcolonial sovereignty, 62, 67; neoliberal consensus, 171; peasants of, 6; reliance on production of miracles, 114, 206n36; role of intellectual in, 167, 215n11; states as "overexpressed" through performances and displays, 21, 187n38; treatment of as deficient,

INDEX

214n56; uprisings of 1930s, 42. *See also* postcolonial state sovereignty, Caribbean
Carmichael, Stokely, 63
Carnival masquerade, T&T: Allen's "Too Bright," composition for Carnival 2010, 135–37, 139; Carnival work as preparation for independence, 166–68; confrontation with authorities in form of, 25, 42, 53, 130–31; Kambule rebellion of 1881, 22–23, 25, 170; as *mas*, 188n55; post-emancipation Carnival masquerade as parody of state military parades, 21–22; as "ritual inversion" of societal norms and hierarchies, 141. *See also* policing, T&T; road work, as insurgent political practice
Caroni sugar estate, 5; and march of 1934, 37–39, 42; and march of 1970, 64, 198n13; and myth of racialized geography, 80, 142
Carter, Martin, 27
Casimir, Jean, 59, 197n146
Chalkdust, 74
Chambers, George (prime minister of T&T), 86–87, 145
Chavez, Hugo, and Fifth Summit of the Americas, 124, 125
Chu, Julie, 211n9
Churchill, Winston, 35
Churchill-Roosevelt Highway, Trinidad, 4, 144
Cipriani, Arthur, 58, 173; and Fabian socialist movement, 38–39; post in colonial legislature, 41; and Trinidad Labour Party (TLP), 39, 49–50, 54
Citizens Home Rule Party. *See* British Empire Workers and Citizens Home Rule Party (BEW & CHP)
Cleaver, Eldridge, 63
climate change, 168–69
Clinton, Israel Moses, murder of, 172
cocoa markets, negative shocks of late 1920s, 41
cold stacking of deepwater drillships, 11–12, 13–14, 17, 184n6
colonial era, T&T: British takeover from Spanish in 1797 and institution of plantation slave society, 2–3; *Cédula de población*, 1783, 2; colonial settlement by Spanish with limited plantation economy, 1–2; post-emancipation conscription of indentured labor from East Asia, 3, 34; Slavery Abolition Act, 1833, 3, 21; termination of indenture system in 1917, 34; transition from plantation agriculture to carbon fuels, 3, 5, 6, 12–13, 35–37, 39, 181n9; violence against people as natural order, 42
Coronil, Fernando, 69
counter-plantation system, 59, 197n146
Couva, Trinidad, 5
Couva Children's Hospital and Training Center, 139, 157
COVID-19, and shocks to T&T oil and gas industry, 106
Cozier, Christopher, and Carnival tradition as "roadworks," 25
Crawford, Hasely, gold-medal victory at Montreal Olympics, 73
Crehan, Kate, 213n45
Crosson, Brent, 23, 91, 168; *Experiments with Power*, 168; and obeah in Trinidad, 192n46; "rural cosmopolitanism," 182n17
Cuba, 5

Debe–Mon Desir segment of Point Fortin Highway, 146–57; award of highway construction contract as design-build agreement, 150; construction of at Gandhi Village, 160, *160*; Debe–San Francique Action Committee, 146; Highway Re-route Movement, 31, 142, 146, 147–50, 151–54; masquerade of as entire Point Fortin Highway, 161; potential displacement of established communities, 146, 157–58; proposed site of Mon Desir interchange, 157–58, *158*. *See also* Kublalsingh, Wayne
Deepwater Champion Transocean drillship, 8–10, *9*; cold stacking in Gulf of Paria, 11–12, 13–14; and Vanuatu flag, 33
Deepwater Invictus drillship, 105, 106–7, 109
deepwater oil and gas production, 8–10; and "Atlantic Mirror" theory, 100; cold stacking of deepwater drillships, 11–12, 13–14, 17, 184n6; defined by T&T Ministry of Energy and Energy Affairs, 204n20; in emerging and frontier areas, 99–100; "Golden Triangle," 99; moratorium on

deepwater oil and gas production (*cont.*)
  in US territorial waters, 10; prohibitive costs and low probability of success of, 29, 92, 101, 102. *See also* petro-state, T&T, and deepwater production
Defoe, Daniel, *Robinson Crusoe*, 32
de-Landè, Shayne, 188n59
design-build contracts: allocation of all phases of construction projects to a single entity, 131–34; and contract for Point Fortin Highway, 150, 159; Manning and, 132, 150; Persad-Bissessar and, 138–39, 150; UDeCOTT and Calder Hart and proliferation of, 131–32, 134–35; and Uff Commission, 131–32, 150
Diamond, Noel, murder of, 172
dougla persons, 80
Duvalier, François, 23

Eastern Venezuela Basin, 98
eat ah food, as reference to corruption practices, 112
Eriksen, Thomas, 207n1
ExxonMobil, deepwater expansion, 8, 9

Fabian socialist movement, 38
Ferry, Elizabeth, 184n6, 204n21
Fertilizer Company of Trinidad and Tobago (Fertrin), Point Lisas Industrial Estate, 76, 200n53
Fifth Summit of the Americas, first Caribbean meeting of OAS (April 2009): and Barack Obama, 30, 124–25, 126–27; and barrier concealing low-income Beetham Gardens, 126; and cleaning streets of unhoused "vagrants," 125–26; Manning's mas, 117, *118*, 120–27; restricted Red Zone and Yellow and Blue Zones, 126
Fleming, Julius, 191n31
Fletcher, Murchison, colonial governor, 53–54
Floyd, George, murder of, 172
Flying Squad secret-police force, 66
Forest Reserve, Trinidad, 5
Forster, John, 59
fracking. *See* shale extractions (hydraulic fracturing)
Francois, Elma, 41
Freeling, Sanford, colonial governor, 22
Freetown Collective, 170

Fundi (Joseph Edwards), 20–21, 33
Fushun, Manchuria, and claims of inexhaustible coal, 193n58
Fyzabad, Trinidad, 5, 12; Apex Oilfields, 44, 46–47, 49; and strike of 1937, 51, 52, 54, 58
Fyzabad Declaration (April 2010), 146, 147

Gairy, Eric, 23
Gal, Sue, 207n3
Galeano, Eduardo, *Las venas abiertas de América Latina*, 125
Garlin, Bunji, 135
general strike of 1937, 50–57, 170, 183n21; Butler and, 51, 52, 54–55, 56, 57; Carnivalesque masquerading of strikers, 53; extension of strikes to entire oil belt and other industries, 51–52, 53; and formation of Oilfields Workers' Trade Union (OWTU), 55; and government call-up of British marines, 54; James on, 8, 23, 26, 27; sit-down strike on June 19 at Leaseholders' Forest Reserve field, 51; spread of protests throughout British West Indies, 8, 27; violent clashes with police and killing of policemen and strikers, 51, 52, 53; and workers' call for living wages and land for subsistence agriculture, 41–42; work stoppage at Pointe-a-Pierre refinery, 53; work stoppages leading up to, 50–51
George, Iwer, 135
Gill, Lyndon, 3
Girvan, Norman, 188n59
Gonzales, Adriana, 197n146
Gordon, Arthur, colonial governor of Trinidad, 144
Graeber, David, 110, 111, 187n43
Gramsci, Antonio, 153, 155, 162, 213n45
Granger, Geddes, 65
Greater Antilles, 5
Greaves, Ornella, 172, 173
Grenada, 5; Jab Molassie in Carnival, 188n59; revolution of 1983, 171
Grenada Union of Returned Soldiers, 40
Griffith, Gary, 173
Guayaguayare, Trinidad, 5
Guinea, state socialism, 186n31
Gulf of Paria, 11–12, 13–14, 117
Gupta, Akhil, 212n33

INDEX

Guyana, first major offshore oil discovery in, 9

Haitian emancipation, 6, 217n36
Hart, Calder "Cobo," 127–31, 132, 133, 134, 150, 209n28
Harvey, David, 201n65
Harvey, Franklyn, 168
Headley, Jim, 39, 41
Henry, Vivian, 54
Herskovits, Melville and Frances, 183n21
Hickling, Horace, 46
Highway Re-route Movement (HRM), 31, 142, 146; disruption of Persad-Bissessar's highway masquerade, 148–49; and Project 40 youth organization, 148; protest camp in Port of Spain, 147–48; tour of route of disputed highway segment, 157–61. *See also* Debe–Mon Desir segment of Point Fortin Highway
Hill, Errol, 21
Hispaniola, 5
Ho, Karen, 203n14
Hobbes, Thomas: doctrine of state sovereignty, 18, 19, 33, 92–93, 111, 168; investor in Virginia and Somers Isles (Bermuda) Companies, 111; *Leviathan*, 32, 111; and miracles, 110–11
Høgsbjerg, Christian, 215n8
Hosay riots of 1884, 134, 170
Howe, Darius, 64
Hu, Cameron, 183n4
Hudson-Phillips, Karl, 156
Hughes, David, 169
Hyatt Regency, Port of Spain, 30, 117–18, *118*, 121, *122*, 123

Imbert, Colm, 106, 129, 131
Independence Constitution of 1962, Trinidad, 65
Industrial Stabilisation Act of 1965 (ISA), 71–72
inexhaustibility, language of, and masquerade, 27–28, 44–46, 193n58
International Monetary Fund (IMF), 87, 145
International Waterfront Centre, Port of Spain, 30, 117–18, *118*, 121
International Workers' Day, 49
Iron and Steel Company of Trinidad and Tobago (ISCOTT), Point Lisas Industrial Estate, 76, 77, 78, 200n53; massive losses between 1983 and 1986, 85; sponge iron production, 83; technical difficulties, 83–85
Island-Wide Cane Farmers Trade Union, 81

Jab Molassie, 188n59
Jacob, Joel, murder of, 172
Jamaat al Muslimeen coup of 1990, 145
Jamaica, 5; gendered survival of working-class women, 214n56; plantation economy, 2–3; and spread of Trinidad's general strike of 1937, 27
James, C. L. R., 7; address to Oilfield Workers' Trade Union in 1982, 170; autonomist Marxism, 66; "The Birth of a Nation," 34; *The Black Jacobins*, 217n36; "Carnival," 140; and Carnival as preparation for independence, 166–67, 170, 172, 215n8, 217n36; early life, 5–6; as editor of PNM *Nation*, 165–66; as evangelist of direct democracy, 165–66, 189n76; expansive definition of politics, 214n3; "George Padmore," 1; and impending confrontation between government and people, 23, 26, 42, 165, 170, 171–72, 188n52; "The Making of the Caribbean People," 169; on oil boom of 1973, 63; *Party Politics in the West Indies*, 90, 115, 167; on peasants of Trinidad, 6; *P.N.M. Go Forward*, 167; on "scrap of an island," 5; "The Seizure of Power," 8; on strike of 1937, 27; and transformation of south Trinidad, 6; *Trinidad Express*, 61

Kadalie, Modibo, 20
Kambon, Khafra, 198n13
Kambule, as procession and practice in general, 187n44
Kambule rebellion of 1881, 22–23, 25, 170
Kamugisha, Aaron, 188n52
Kapila, Kriti, 186n29
Khan, Franklin, 106–8
Kiely, Ray, 82
Kincaid, Jamaica, *A Small Place*, 5, 6, 186n36
King, Charlie, 52
Kirsch, Stuart, 205n35
Kublalsingh, Wayne: as adviser to Highway Re-route Movement, 146; halting of proposed industrial smelter plants

Kublalsingh, Wayne (*cont.*)
from 2005 to 2010, 146; hunger strike of November 15, 2012, 148–50; mediation session between government and Joint Consultative Council, 150; protest camps, marches, and hunger strikes against Debe–Mon Desir segment, 147–50, 151–54; second hunger strike of 2014, 151–52, 154

labor conditions, oil industry: and industry as opportunity for future, 59; low wages, racial abuse and discrimination, poor worker accommodations, and disease, 41–42, 46–47, 49; reduction in labor force and austerity measures of 1960s, 71–72
labor in Trinidad: artificial racialized distinction between Indian rural workers and Black urban labor, 38; Black workers' rejection of plantation labor, 36–37; Indian laborers, new generation of, 39–40; retrenchment of workers in sugar estates, 34, 36, 39, 41; and tension between emancipatory program of land and technocratic fantasy of permanent oil resources, 59–60. *See also* general strike of 1937
labor organizations: All Trinidad Sugar Estates and Factory Workers' Trade Union, 81; Amalgamated Workers Union, 157; Island-Wide Cane Farmers Trade Union, 81; Oilfields Workers' Trade Union (OWTU), 55–57, 63–64, 72, 80–81; Steel Workers Union of T&T, 157; Transport and Industrial Workers Union, 81
La Brea, Trinidad, 5
Lacan, Jacques, 119, 207n4
Lamming, George, 215n11
Larkin, Brian, 211n15
Las Alturas Towers project, condemned and demolished due to poor construction, 134–35, 137, 139, 155
Lassalle, Rex, 65
Laughlin, Nicolas: and Cat in Bag Productions' "Cobo Town," 130–31, *130*, 135; "The Flight of the Cobo," 209n28
Laventille, Trinidad, 3
Le Bon, Gustave, 192n40
Li, Darryl, 206n36

Ligon, Richard, *A True and Exact History of the Island of Barbados*, 32, 33, 169–70
Limbert, Mandana, 184n6, 204n21
"liming" as "art of doing nothing," 123, 207n1
Lockerbie, Don, 128
Lopinot, Trinidad, 4
Lord Invader, 26
Lord Relator: "Food Prices," 86; "Take Ah Rest Mr. Prime Minister," 86
Lord Shorty, "Money Eh No Problem," 74
Louisiana's "Cancer Alley," 181n9
Louverture, Toussaint, 23
Lum, Edward Lee, 35

Maharaj, Ramesh, 127–30, 131
Maharaj, Stephen, 56
Make It Hapn, "Mus Eat Ah Food," 112–13
Malcolm X, 63
Manning, Patrick (prime minister of T&T), 17; and allegations of corruption of procurement processes, 127–31; call for snap election and defeat, 137–38; construction of skyscrapers on Port of Spain coastline, 117–20; extension of design-build contracts, 132, 150; "Miami mas" directed at multinational companies and foreign political leaders, 117, *118*, 120–27, 208n12; mocked as "mimic man," 117; privileging exterior features of buildings over functionality, 134, 210n35; promises of expanded road transportation, 145; unequal distributions of oil and gas windfalls, 30, 117; *Vision 2020 Draft National Strategic Plan*, 120, 134. *See also* Fifth Summit of the Americas, first Caribbean meeting of OAS (April 2009)
Manzanilla–Mayaro Road, Trinidad, 159
Marx, Karl: *Das Kapital*, 32; *Grundrisse*, 161
mas, 134, 188n55, 210n2. See also play a mas
"MAS" (Mical Teja x Freetown Collective), 170
Mayaro, Trinidad, 5, 117
Mazzarella, William, 192n40, 207n4
McDonald, Marlene, 133
McDowell, Robin, 181n9
McGovern, Mike, *Unmasking the State*, 186n31
Meeks, Brian, 199n25

INDEX

Merrimac Oil Company, and first oil well drilling in T&T, 12
Mighty Sparrow, 170
Ministry of Legal Affairs Building, Port of Spain, 128
Minshall, Peter, 148
Mitchell, Timothy, 199n30
Mohammed, Kimathi, 216n30
Montano, Bobby, 75
Montano, Machel, 135; "M.O.R.," 140–41
Morant Bay Rebellion (Jamaica, 1865), 24, 170
More, Thomas, 31
Morvant, Trinidad: founded by formerly enslaved Africans, 3; protests against police killings, 172
Moses, McDonald, 56
Mostofi, Baghair, and commission inquiring into oil industry, 71–72
Movement for Social Justice, 146
Mugabe, Robert, Zimbabwe reign, 162–63

Naipaul, V. S., 2, 5, 117
Nasser, Gamal, 74, 77, 85, 115
National Academy for the Performing Arts (NAPA): building as masquerade of success, 133, 134; design and construction errors, 133–34, 155; design-build contract with Shanghai Construction group, 133, 134; mimicking of Sydney Opera House, 117, 132–33, 133; *The Tragedy and Hidden History of NAPA*, 133–34
National Alliance for Reconstruction (NAR): cuts to petroleum tax to encourage investment, 87; and Jamaat al Muslimeen coup of 1990, 145; structural adjustment in accordance with IMF directives, 87, 145
National Infrastructure Development Company (NIDCO), 157–58
National Joint Action Committee, 65, 146
National Movement for the True Independence of Trinidad and Tobago (NAMOTI), 67–68, 81, 82
National Unemployed Movement (NUM), 40; hunger march on Emancipation Day in 1935, 41
National Union of Freedom Fighters (NUFF), call for revolutionary democracy, 65, 82

natural gas development, in T&T: as combustion fuel for petrochemical production, 94; downstream demand for gas and turn to deepwater production, 97; gas liquefaction facility (Atlantic LNG) in Point Fortin, 5, 29, 96–97, 106; negative price shocks and international competition, 95–96; offshore drilling campaigns by BP, BG, and BHP Billiton, 96; T&T model of natural resource management, 94–95, 95
Neal & Massy, 81
Negro Welfare, Social, and Cultural Association (NWSCA), 47, 49, 53
Nehru, Jawaharlal, 74, 85, 115
Neptune, Harvey, 41
New Beginning Movement, 81
New Jewel Movement, Grenada, 21, 88
Ngai, Sianne, 149
Niger Delta: deepwater basin, 98; slavery and oil extraction, 181n9
Nigeria, #EndSARS protest against Special Anti-robbery Squad, 172
Nkrumah, Kwame, 74, 115

OAS. *See* Organization of American States
Obama, Barack: at Fifth Summit of the Americas (2009), 30, 124–25, 126–27; moratorium on deepwater drilling in US territorial waters, 10; presidential run of 2008, 137
obeah, in Trinidad, 23, 168, 192n46
oil extraction innovations: Canadian tar sand extractions, 9; deepwater production, 9, 92, 184n13; and era of fossil fuel abundance, 9–10; shale extractions (hydraulic fracturing), 9, 10, 14, 184n13
Oilfields Workers' Trade Union (OWTU), 157; call to nationalize oil industry, 72; and estrangement of working people from state bureaucrats in 1970, 63–64; expulsion of Butler from union, 56–57; first registered trade union in British West Indies, 55; radical faction, 80–81; and retrenched workers with Petrotrin closure, 105–6
oil prices: and COVID-19 pandemic in North America, 16; 1965 to 1973 decline, 62, 65; 1973 boom, 63, 69–70, 76, 82, 144; 1990s decline, 145; 2000s boom, 146; 2014 decline, 157

One Woodbrook Place, Port of Spain, 121, 122
On Kings (Sahlins and Graeber), 111
Orange Grove sugar estate, 4; and strike of 1937, 53
O'Reilly, Lennox, 45
Organisation for National Reconstruction (ONR), *Why Nothing Works in Trinidad and Tobago*, 156
Organization of American States (OAS), first Caribbean meeting of, 120
Organization of the Petroleum Exporting Countries (OPEC): controlled production cuts, 10; member countries in 1973, 200n38; raise in oil prices and embargo due to Arab–Israeli War, 69
Ormsby-Gore, William, 54

Papua New Guinea, and BHP mining interests, 205n35
Paris Commune, 23
Parsard, Kaneesha, 214n3, 215n22
Pastor, Steve, 105
Paul, Cecil, 80
peasants, landless: anti-systemic, decolonial acts, 197n146; cultivation of crops in unsanctioned plots, 48, 49, 59; rejection of plantation labor, 37, 48, 59
People (working-class publication), 38, 44–45
People's National Movement (PNM), 28, 79, 90; and elections of 1976, 82; industrialization program and infrastructure development, 94–97, 144; loss of support, 17, 87; program supporting local food production in 1963, 70; return to power in 2015, 17, 104; as vanguard of West Indian self-government, 61–62
People's Partnership (PP): and "Debe–Mon Desir segment," 142; dissolution and reports of corruption, 104; fiscal reforms, 103; Fyzabad Declaration, 146, 147; multiracial cross-regional coalition, 90, 137, 146–47; Persad-Bissessar and, 91
Percival, Bertie, 40
Pereira, Vincent, 107
Perry, Keston, 199n33
Persad-Bissessar, Kamla (prime minister of T&T), 13; awarding of design-build contracts, 138–39, 150; award of design-build contract for Point Fortin Highway construction, 150; and Debe–Mon Desir segment of Point Fortin Highway, 142, 146, 147, 152–53; election victory of 2010, 137–38; masquerade of permanence through highways, hospitals, and university campuses, 147, 157; People's Partnership government, 90–91, 103, 104, 137; performance of deepwater oil discovery, 15, 90–93, 101–2; ties to predominantly Hindu communities in south Trinidad, 147, 152; and United National Congress, 146; and University of the West Indies, Debe campus, 138, 139
Persian Gulf War, 145
Petit Morne public housing project, 157–58
petro-state, T&T, and deepwater production: acceptance of deepwater-exploration blocks from bpTT, BHP Billiton, and BG, 103; deepwater as miracle divorced from realities of road, 90, 111–12, 114, 206n36; "de-risking" of deepwater ventures through stories of success, 14–15, 90–92, 98–99, 100–104; and discouragement of alternatives to carbon-fuel industrialization, 112; Energy Conference, "Gearing Up for the Deepwater Challenge," 99–100; failure of deepwater wells drilled between 1999 and 2003, 14, 29, 92, 97, 101; failure of LeClerc well to yield oil, 105; investment profile, 99, 203n15; map of T&T offshore and deepwater acreage, 106, 107; and masquerade of permanence, 88–89, 90–92, 97, 103–4, 204n25; multinational investors pursuit of more lucrative frontiers, 97, 98; oil discovery in Southwest Soldado maritime field, 90–91; Persad-Bissessar performance of deepwater oil discovery, 15, 90–93, 101–2; prohibitive costs and low probability of success, 29, 92, 101, 102–3; Rowley's staging of deepwater masquerade based on professional expertise as geologist, 106–10; and special provisions to decrease Petroleum Profits Tax, 101–2. *See also* deepwater oil and gas production
petro-state, T&T, "industrialization by invitation" model, 63, 72; boom in oil prices in 1973, 69–70, 76, 82; declining

INDEX 243

production levels of oil and natural gas in 2020–21, 14; dependence on extractive infrastructures and multinational companies, 13, 28–29, 62, 67, 92, 116; increased production between 1965 and 1968, 71; Mostofi Commission and establishment of Ministry of Petroleum and Mines in 1963, 71, 72; postcolonial political future linked to oil and gas, 12, 26, 44, 62; Shell and Texaco abandonment of Trinidad for frontier regions, 28, 30, 63, 72, 109; single largest supplier of oil in British Empire in 1937, 44, 50, 72

petro-state, T&T, infrastructure investments in high-modernist schemes: allegations of corruption and Uff Commission report, 127–31; faulty and unfinished infrastructures, 143, 155, 211n9, 212n33; Hyatt Regency, 30, 117–18, *118*, 121, *122*, *123*; infrastructure as semiotic vehicles, 144, 211n15; International Waterfront Centre, 30, 117–18, *118*, 121, 123–24; Las Alturas Towers project, 134–35, 137, 139, 155; Manning's "Miami mas" directed at multinational companies and foreign political leaders, 30, 117, *118*, 120–24; National Academy for the Performing Arts (NAPA), 117, 132–33, *133*, 155; One Woodbrook Place, 121, *122*; Persad-Bissessar design-build schemes, 138–39; privileging of exterior features of buildings over functionality, 132–34; reinvention of Port of Spain from urban space for residents to outward-facing "shock architecture," 121, *122*, 123–24; University of the West Indies, Debe campus, design-build project, 138; viewed by many Trinbagonians as waste of public funds, 118–20

petro-state, T&T, masquerade of permanence, 43–50, 58; alliance in support of imperial oil preference in 1936, 43–44; annual oil company gala of 1936, 45–46; assurance of permanent oil production and political order, 68, 83, 114; and attempts to frame protest and police retaliation as crime prevention, 172–74; and "black patience," 191n31; debates about oil resources as limited or inexhaustible, 27–28, 44–45; distance between material uncertainty and its representation, 184n13; Manning's "Miami mas" directed at multinational companies and foreign political leaders, 117, *118*, 120–27, 208n12; masquerade threatened by external market shocks and grassroots insurgencies, 26–31; and perpetual projects of renewal, 68–69, 155, 201n65, 204n21; Persad-Bissessar performance of deepwater oil discovery, 15, 90–93, 101–2; public performances to demonstrate legitimacy to citizens and multinational corporations, 16–17, 26–27, 30–31, 185n22; and "resource curse," 68, 199n33; Williams' masquerade of permanence based upon petrochemicals and heavy metals, 73–75, 76–79, 88. *See also* petro-state, T&T, infrastructure investments in high-modernist schemes; petro-state, T&T, state-led industrial development

petro-state, T&T, state-led industrial development: and assumption of permanency, 88; COVID-19, and shocks to oil and gas industry, 106; financing of oil, gas, and petrochemical facilities, 13, 28–29, 30, 94–97; markets for natural gas derivatives, 13, 14, 74; nationalization of oil industry, 72–73; petrochemical and steel production facilities at Point Lisas, 5, 73, 74–75, 76–77, 96, 105, 200n53; Trinidad and Tobago Oil Company (TRINTOC), 73; Williams' masquerade of permanence based upon petrochemicals and heavy metals, 73–75, 76–79, 88. *See also* natural gas development, in T&T

petro-states: governance issues ("Dutch Disease" and "resource curse"), 15; masquerade of permanence to generate corporate interest and capital investment, 20–21, 93, 100–101; optimistic view of petrodollars and their social and political effects, 15; power of based on oil prices and funding for civic works and social programs, 91–92; as psychoanalytic form and semiotic vehicle, 207n4. *See also* postcolonial state sovereignty, Caribbean

Petrotrin oil refinery: closure of, 105; state-owned, 102

Phase II steelpan yard, 121
play a mas: costuming associated with particular Carnival bands, 210n2; Nicolas Laughlin and Cat in Bag Productions' "Cobo Town," *130*, 130–31; participation of citizens in annual Carnival masquerade, 31; performance of a masquerade on the road, 31, 103–4
Pointe-a-Pierre oil refinery, 44; closure of, 5, 12
Point Fortin: Atlantic LNG gas liquefaction facility, 5, 29, 96–97, 106; contemporary conditions, 117; former Shell refinery, 73
Point Fortin Highway. *See* San Fernando to Point Fortin Highway
Point Lisas Industrial Estate, Trinidad: ArcelorMittal closure of steel plant, 105; Fertilizer Company of Trinidad and Tobago (Fertrin), 76, 200n53; fiscal downturn and divestment of downstream assets, 96; Iron and Steel Company of Trinidad and Tobago (ISCOTT), 76, 77, 78, 83–85, 200n53; natural gas-powered steel mills and petrochemical plants, 5, 73, 74–75, 76–77; state representation as transition from colonial economy to postcolonial modernity, 76–77; Tringen ammonia production facility, 76, 200n53; urea and methanol production facilities, 76, 200n53
policing, T&T: attempts to masquerade protest suppression as crime prevention, 112, 172–73; Kambule rebellion of 1881 and subsequent years, and police repression and violence, 22–25, 156, 170; origin of modern police in figures of clowns, 187n43; state police violence targeting "crime hotspots," 172–74
Port of Spain, Trinidad: Brian Lara Promenade, 125; capital city and former seat of colonial governments, 3; map of major landmarks and developments in downtown and Woodbrook, *122*; Nazi U-boat attack on, 57; Phase II steelpan yard, 121. *See also* National Academy for the Performing Arts (NAPA); petro-state, T&T, infrastructure investments in high-modernist schemes
Port of Spain Gazette, 21–22

postcolonial state sovereignty, Caribbean: adherence to bureaucratic procedure, 163; and creation of illusions, 19, 186n29; and economies of speculation, 100–101, 204n16; hegemony based on dominance and consent of citizens, 153; hindered by dependence on multinational capital, 62, 67; masquerade of power inherited from colonial models, 169–70; and myth of inevitability of hydrocarbon reservoirs, 112, 114, 168, 169; and popular discourses of corruption, 154–55; and pursuit of certainty, 92–93; state claim to monopoly on legitimate violence, 172–74; and state of *in-dependence*, 189n71; suspension between colonial governance and unfulfilled promise, 163–64; sustained by masquerades of permanent power, 93, 104, 110–11, 114, 164; tension between absolute and aspirational, 18–19, 31–33, 93; unsustainability, 112. *See also* petro-state, T&T, masquerade of permanence
Project 40 youth organization, 148
publics, as "interdiscursivity," 207n3

Quest, Matthew, 189n76

railways, colonial era, 68, 144, 199n33
Ralph, Laurence, on trope of "socially isolated" ghetto, 182n19
Ralph, Michael, 184n6, 203n15
Ramleela, 134
Ramnarine, Kevin, 15, 92
Ramnath, Kelvin, 129
Rampersad, Indira, 152
Ramsingh, Shireen, 148, 152–53, 158
Raymond, Afra, 132, 138, 150
Rennie, Bukka, 47
Repsol, 96, 116
"resource curse," 68, 199n33
revolution, inevitability of, and Marxist–Leninist formations, 88
Rienzi, Adrian Cola, 54–55, 56, 57, 58
road, as route of transit and commerce, 141; Churchill–Roosevelt Highway, 144; colonial era alternatives to vehicular roadways, 143–44; common view of road work as expansion of state's power through construction, 161;

INDEX 245

Manzanilla–Mayaro Road, 159; masquerade of state promises of road extensions, 144–45; postcolonial infrastructure expansion varying with swings in oil and gas prices, 145; road work as marker of social progress regardless of utility, 161–62; Sir Solomon Hochoy Highway extension, 139; visible, unfinished objects, 155–56. *See also* road work, as insurgent political practice; San Fernando to Point Fortin Highway

road-march anthems, 135

road work, as insurgent political practice, 26–31; hunger marches of colonial workers from oilfields and agricultural estates in 1930s, 27, 37–43; Black Power uprising of 1970, 27, 63–65, 71, 72, 170, 198n13; Carnival revelers of February 15, 2010, and scandal of Calder Hart, 130–31, *130*; challenge to petro-state masquerade, 26, 30–31, 42–43, 141, 143, 155, 156, 162, 163–64; as end rather than means, 170, 216n28, 216n30; Highway Re-route Movement (HRM), 31, 142, 146, 147–50, 151–54; interruption and occupation of public infrastructures with marches and blockades, 25, 26, 31; masquerade potential to erupt into genuine uprising, 156–57; National Movement for the True Independence of Trinidad and Tobago (NAMOTI), 67–68; as productive of emancipatory politics, 193n40; "Trinidad not a real country," 116–17. *See also* general strike of 1937; policing, T&T

Roberts, Patrice, 135

Robinson, A. N. R. (prime minister of T&T), 87

Robinson, Cedric, 199n37

Rodney, Walter, 154, 173

Rogers, Doug, 15

Roget, Ancel, OWTU President, 160–61

Roodal, Timothy, 49–50, 54

Rowley, Keith (prime minister of T&T): objection to Manning's procurement process for construction projects, 127, 131; participation in petro-state masquerade of permanence, 17–18, 169; staging of deepwater masquerade based on professional expertise as geologist, 104–10

Royal Commission of Enquiry on labor disturbances, 55, 59

Rust, Randolph, 35

Rutherford, Danilyn, 203n5

Sahlins, Marshall, 110, 111

Saint Kitts, 2

Samaroo, Brinsley, 198n13

Sammy, Junior, 129, 141

San Domingue, Haiti, plantation economy, 2

San Fernando, Trinidad, 5, 80

San Fernando to Point Fortin Highway: design-build contract, 150; Manning's plan for, 146; Persad-Bissessar and, 142, 146, 147, 152–53; Williams's promise of, 144–45, 159. *See also* Debe–Mon Desir segment of Point Fortin Highway

San Juan, Trinidad, 4

São Tomé and Príncipe, 16, 185n22

Schmitt, Carl, 110, 111

Schuster, Aaron, 207n4

Scott, David, 88, 171, 217n36

Seow, Victor, 193n58

Serpent's Mouth, 2

Shah, Raffique, 65

shale extractions (hydraulic fracturing), 9, 10, 14; short-cycle investment, 183n4

"shock architecture," 123–24

Silverstein, Michael, 120

Siparia–Erin District Agricultural Society, 36

Sir Solomon Hochoy Highway extension, 139

Smith, M. G., plural society thesis, 78

soca, 112, 135, 140

Soldado maritime field oil discoveries, 62, 91

South Trinidad Chamber of Industry and Commerce, 75

sovereignty. *See* postcolonial state sovereignty, Caribbean

Stainsby, Macdonald, 155

Stanley, MacDonald, 55, 194n83

Steel Workers Union of T&T, 157

St. Rose Greaves, Verna, protest at Fifth Summit of the Americas, 125

St. Vincent and the Grenadines, 5

sugar, West Indies: government run estates, 81; innovation of beet sugar and decline of sugar industry, 34, 45, 71; retrenchment

sugar, West Indies (*cont.*)
  of workers due to negative price shocks, 34, 36, 39, 41
sugar and steel, juxtaposition of in Williams' masquerade of permanence, 76–77
sugar production, 34, 36, 39, 41, 45, 71
Sunder Rajan, Kaushik, economies of speculation, 204n16
Sutton, Connie, 170

Takabvirwa, Kathryn, 162–63
Tapia, 66–67
Tapia House Movement, 66–67, 199n25
"Tattoo Gangs" in oil regions, 35
Taylor, Breonna, murder of, 172
Teelucksingh, Jerome, 42
Teja, Mical, 170
Tesoro Petroleum Company, 72
Texaco: abandonment of Trinidad for frontier regions, 28, 72, 109; labor negotiations with ULF, 81; onshore drilling and offshore production in 1965 and 1968, 71
Thomas, Deborah, 112
Tillerson, Rex, 9
Tobago Organization of the People, 146
Toco, Trinidad, 4
Transocean, cold stacking of drillships in Gulf of Paria, 11–12, 13–14, 17
Transport and Industrial Workers Union, 81
Tringen ammonia production facility, Point Lisas Industrial Estate, 76, 200n53
Trinidad: as big small place, 6, 7, 186n36; Independence Constitution of 1962, 65; independence from British (August 31, 1962), 28, 62, 65; map of, 4; racial geography, imagined and actual, 80–81; separation from South American mainland, 1–2
Trinidad and Tobago (T&T). *See* Carnival masquerade, T&T; colonial era, T&T; policing, T&T; *and* petro-state, T&T, entries
Trinidad and Tobago Deepwater Atlantic Area, 106, *107*
Trinidad and Tobago Oil Company (TRINTOC), 73
Trinidad Guardian, 44
Trinidad Labour Party (TLP), 38, 39; Fyzabad branch, 40; labor aristocracy, 49–50
Trinidad Leaseholders, 44, 51, 53
Trinidad Ministry of Petroleum and Mines: "Best Use of Our Petroleum Resources" summit of 1975, 75; establishment of, 71
Trouillot, Michel-Rolph, 6, 7, 114, 163
Trump, Donald J., 10
Tunapuna, Trinidad, 4, 6
Túpac Amaru rebellion of 1780, 78

Uff, John, 128–29
Uff Commission: distrust of design-build contracts, 131–32, 150; exposé of preferential construction contracts and kickbacks for politicians, 128–30
UN Climate Change Conference (COP26), 17–18
"Unemployment: Why the PNM Failed Miserably," *Tapia*, 66–67
United Labour Front (ULF): "Bloody Tuesday" (March 1975), 81; formalization as political party, 81–82
United National Congress, 17, 146, 147
United National Independence Party, 81
University of the West Indies, Debe campus, 138, 139
Urban Development Corporation of Trinidad and Tobago (UDeCOTT): Calder Hart and Uff Commission findings of corruption, 127–31; design-build contracts, 131–32; Las Alturas Towers project, condemned and demolished due to construction errors, 134–35, 137, 139, 155; and National Academy for the Performing Arts, 134
Usine Ste. Madeleine sugar factory, and strike of 1937, 53

Victor, Rubadiri, 134
vodou, 23

wajang, 127
Warner, Jack, 137, 147
Weber, Max, 24–25
Weekes, George (president general of OWTU), 81, 118
Welcome, Leniqueca, 173
West Indies Federation, 62, 67
Weszkalnys, Gisa, 16, 100, 185n22
Williams, Eric (first prime minister of T&T): announcement of retirement in 1973, 61–62, 65–66; *Capitalism and Slavery*, 77;

"The Caribbean Man" speech, 78–79, 88; death in office in 1981, 86; "doctor politics," 17, 23, 136, 168; founder of PNM, 17; industrialization program, 28–29, 117, 144; juxtaposition of sugar and steel in masquerade of permanence, 76–77; march to US military base at Chaguaramas in 1960, 28, 61, 71, 167; masquerade of permanence, 73–75, 76–79, 83, 85, 88, 94, 167; "Massa Day Done" address to citizens in 1961, 61–62, 135; *The Negro in the Caribbean*, 78–79; and People's National Movement party, 28; promise to build San Fernando–Point Fortin Highway, 144–45, 159; pursuit of agricultural development in 1963, 70–71; reelection run in response to 1973 rise in oil prices, 69; representation of ULF, 82; response to Black Power revolt in 1970, 65, 66, 173–74

Woodford, Ralph, colonial governor, appeal for influx of enslaved to Trinidad, 3

World War II, and T&T: Nazi U-boat attack on Port of Spain, 57; occupation by US forces until independence in 1961, 57

Wynter, Sylvia, and inevitability of confrontation between government and people, 23–24, 169, 188n52, 215n22

Yoruba Town, Trinidad, 4